SELECTED WRITINGS ON JUDAISM, THE TALMUD AND JEWISH MYSTICISM

ISRAEL ABRAHAMS   ARSÈNE DARMESTETER
JOSHUA ABELSON

FV Éditions

CONTENTS

JUDAISM
By Israel Abrahams

Foreword	3
1. The Legacy From The Past	5
2. Religion As Law	11
3. Articles Of Faith	16
4. Some Concepts Of Judaism	25
5. Some Observances Of Judaism	32
6. Jewish Mysticism	40
7. Eschatology	46
8. The Survival Of Judaism	53

THE TALMUD
By Arsène Darmesteter

PREFATORY NOTE	65
THE TALMUD	67

PART FIRST: ANALYTIC SKETCH OF THE TALMUD

1. GENERAL CHARACTERISTICS	73
2. THE HALACHA	79
3. THE HAGGADA	88

PART SECOND: THE FORMATION OF THE TALMUD—THE SPIRIT OF ITS FORMATION

4. THE HALACHA ACCORDING TO THE SYNAGOGUE	109
5. HISTORY OF THE EORMATION OF THE HALACHA	113
6. INFLUENCE OF EVENTS ON THE DEVELOPMENT OF THE HALACHA	122
7. SPIRIT OF THE HALACHIC DEVELOPMENT	126
8. THE TALMUD IN THE MIDDLE AGES AND MODERN TIMES	130

JEWISH MYSTICISM
By Joshua Abelson

Preface	139
Introduction	141
1. Some Early Elements: Essenism	151
2. The Merkabah (Chariot) Mysticism	161
3. Philo: Metatron: Wisdom	172
4. Kingdom Of Heaven: Fellowship: Shechinah	188
5. The Book 'Yetsirah'	199
6. Some General Features Of The 'Zohar' Mysticism	210
7. The Ten Sefirot	221
8. The Soul	232
Concluding Note	243

JUDAISM

By Israel Abrahams

Israel Abrahams (1858-1925) was reader in rabbinics and Talmudic literature at the University of Cambridge. He became one of the most distinguished Jewish scholars of his time and wrote several classic works on Judaism.

FOREWORD

The writer has attempted in this volume to take up a few of the most characteristic points in Jewish doctrine and practice, and to explain some of the various phases through which they have passed, since the first centuries of the Christian era.

The presentation is probably much less detached than is the case with other volumes in this series. But the difference was scarcely avoidable. The writer was not expounding a religious system which has no relation to his own life. On the contrary, the writer is himself a Jew, and thus is deeply concerned personally in the matters discussed in the book.

The reader must be warned to keep this fact in mind throughout. On the one hand, the book must suffer a loss of objectivity; but, on the other hand, there may be some compensating gain of intensity. The author trusts, at all events, that, though he has not written with indifference, he has escaped the pitfall of undue partiality.

I. A.

THE LEGACY FROM THE PAST

The aim of this little book is to present in brief outline some of the leading conceptions of the religion familiar since the Christian Era under the name Judaism.

The word 'Judaism' occurs for the first time at about 100 B.C., in the Graeco-Jewish literature. In the second book of the Maccabees (ii. 21, viii. 1), 'Judaism' signifies the religion of the Jews as contrasted with Hellenism, the religion of the Greeks. In the New Testament (Gal. i. 13) the same word seems to denote the Pharisaic system as an antithesis to the Gentile Christianity. In Hebrew the corresponding noun never occurs in the Bible, and it is rare even in the Rabbinic books. When it does meet us, *Jahaduth* implies the monotheism of the Jews as opposed to the polytheism of the heathen.

Thus the term 'Judaism' did not pass through quite the same transitions as did the name 'Jew.' Judaism appears from the first as a religion transcending tribal bounds. The 'Jew,' on the other hand, was originally a Judaean, a member of the Southern Confederacy called in the Bible Judah, and by the Greeks and Romans Judaea. Soon, however, 'Jew' came to include what had earlier been the Northern Confederacy of Israel as well, so that in the post-exilic period *Jehudi* or 'Jew' means an adherent of Judaism without regard to local nationality.

Judaism, then, is here taken to represent that later development of the Religion of Israel which began with the reorganisation after the Babylonian Exile (444 B.C.), and was crystallised by the Roman Exile (during the first centuries of the Christian Era). The exact period which will be here seized as a starting-point is the moment when the people of Israel were losing, never so far to regain, their territorial association with Palestine, and were becoming (what they have ever since been) a community as distinct from a nation. They remained, it is true, a distinct race, and this is still in a sense true. Yet at various periods a number of proselytes have been admitted, and in other ways the purity of the race has been affected. At all events territorial nationality ceased from a date which may be roughly fixed at 135 A.D., when the last desperate revolt under Bar-Cochba failed, and Hadrian drew his Roman plough over the city of Jerusalem and the Temple area. A new city with a new name arose on the ruins. The ruins afterwards reasserted themselves, and Aelia Capitolina as a designation of Jerusalem is familiar only to archaeologists.

But though the name of Hadrian's new city has faded, the effect of its foundation remained. Aelia Capitolina, with its market-places and theatre, replaced the olden narrow-streeted town; a House of Venus reared its stately form in the north, and a Sanctuary to Jupiter covered, in the east, the site of the former Temple. Heathen colonists were introduced, and the Jew, who was to become in future centuries an alien everywhere, was made by Hadrian an alien in his fatherland. For the Roman Emperor denied to Jews the right of entry into Jerusalem. Thus Hadrian completed the work of Titus, and Judaism was divorced from its local habitation. More unreservedly than during the Babylonian Exile, Judaism in the Roman Exile perforce became the religion of a community and not of a state; and Israel for the first time constituted a Church. But it was a Church with no visible home. Christianity for several centuries was to have a centre at Rome, Islam at Mecca. But Judaism had and has no centre at all.

It will be obvious that the aim of the present book makes it both superfluous and inappropriate to discuss the vexed problems connected with the origins of the Religion of Israel, its aspects in primitive times, its passage through a national to an ethical monotheism, its expansion into the universalism of the second Isaiah. What concerns us here is merely the legacy which the Religion of Israel bequeathed to

Judaism as we have defined it. This legacy and the manner in which it was treasured, enlarged, and administered will occupy us in the rest of this book.

But this much must be premised. If the Religion of Israel passed through the stages of totemism, animism, and polydemonism; if it was indebted to Canaanite, Kenite, Babylonian, Persian, Greek, and other foreign influences; if it experienced a stage of monolatry or henotheism (in which Israel recognised one God, but did not think of that God as the only God of all men) before ethical monotheism of the universalistic type was reached; if, further, all these stages and the moral and religious ideas connected with each left a more or less clear mark in the sacred literature of Israel; then the legacy which Judaism received from its past was a syncretism of the whole of the religious experiences of Israel as interpreted in the light of Israel's latest, highest, most approved standards. Like the Bourbon, the Jew forgets nothing; but unlike the Bourbon, the Jew is always learning. The domestic stories of the Patriarchs were not rejected as unprofitable when Israel became deeply impregnated with the monogamous teachings of writers like the author of the last chapter of Proverbs; the character of David was idealised by the spiritual associations of the Psalter, parts of which tradition ascribed to him; the earthly life was etherialised and much of the sacred literature reinterpreted in the light of an added belief in immortality; God, in the early literature a tribal non-moral deity, was in the later literature a righteous ruler who with Amos and Hosea loved and demanded righteousness in man. Judaism took over as one indivisible body of sacred teachings both the early and the later literature in which these varying conceptions of God were enshrined; the Law was accepted as the guiding rule of life, the ritual of ceremony and sacrifice was treasured as a holy memory, and as a memory not contradictory of the prophetic exaltation of inward religion but as consistent with that exaltation, as interpreting it, as but another aspect of Micah's enunciation of the demands of God: 'What doth the Lord require of thee but to do justly, to love mercy, and to walk humbly with thy God?'

Judaism, in short, included for the Jew all that had gone before. But for St. Paul's attitude of hostility to the Law, but for the deep-seated conviction that the Pauline Christianity was a denial of the Jewish monotheism, the Jew might have accepted much of the teaching of Jesus as an integral part of Judaism. In the realm of ideas which he conceived as belonging to his tradition the Jew was not logical; he did not pick and choose; he absorbed the whole. In the Jewish theology of all ages we find the most obvious contradictions. There was no attempt at reconciliation of such contradictions; they were juxtaposed in a mechanical mixture, there was no chemical compound. The Jew was always a man of moods, and his religion responded to those varying phases of feeling and belief and action. Hence such varying judgments have been formed of him and his religion. If, after the mediaeval philosophy had attempted to systematise Judaism, the religion remained unsystematic, it is easy to understand that in the earlier centuries of the Christian Era contradictions between past and present, between different strata of religious thought, caused no trouble to the Jew so long as those contradictions could be fitted into his general scheme of life. Though he was the product of development, development was an idea foreign to his conception of the ways of God with man. And to this extent he was right. For though men's ideas of God change, God Himself is changeless. The Jew transferred the changelessness of God to men's changing ideas about him. With childlike naivete he accepted all, he adopted all, and he syncretised it all as best he could into the loose system on which Pharisaism grafted itself. The legacy of the past thus was the past.

One element in the legacy was negative. The Temple and the Sacrificial system were gone for ever. That this must have powerfully affected Judaism goes without saying. Synagogue replaced Temple, prayer assumed the function of sacrifice, penitence and not the blood of bulls supplied the ritual of atonement. Events had prepared the way for this change and had prevented it attaining the character of an upheaval. For synagogues had grown up all over the land soon after the fifth century B.C.; regular services of prayer with instruction in the Scriptures had been established long before the Christian Era; the inward atonement had been preferred to, or at least associated with, the outward rite before the outward rite was torn away. It may be that, as Professor Burkitt has suggested, the awful experiences of the fall of Jerusalem and the destruction of the Temple produced within Pharisaism a moral reformation which drove the Jew within and thus spiritualised Judaism. For undoubtedly the Pharisee of the Gospels is by no means the Pharisee as we meet him in the Jewish books. There was always a latent power and tendency in Judaism towards inward religion; and it may be that this power was intensified, this tendency encouraged, by the loss of Temple and its Sacrificial rites.

But though the Temple had gone the Covenant remained. Not so much in name as in essence. We do not hear much of the Covenant in the Rabbinic books, but its spirit pervades Judaism. Of all the legacy of the past the Covenant was the most inspiring element. Beginning with Abraham, the Covenant established a special relation between God and Abraham's seed. 'I have known him, that he may command his children and his household after him, that they may keep the way of the Lord to do righteousness and judgment' (Gen. xviii. 19). Of this Covenant, the outward sign was the rite of circumcision. Renewed with Moses, and followed in traditional opinion by the Ten Commandments, the Sinaitic Covenant was a further link in the bond between God and His people. Of this Mosaic Covenant the outward sign was the Sabbath. It is of no moment for our present argument whether Abraham and Moses were historical persons or figments of tradition. A Gamaliel would have as little doubted their reality as would a St. Paul. And whatever Criticism may be doing with Abraham, it is coming more and more to see that behind the eighth-century prophets there must have towered the figure of a, if not of the traditional, Moses; behind the prophets a, if not the, Law. Be that as it may, to the Jew of the Christian Era, Abraham and Moses were real and the Covenant unalterable. By the syncretism which has been already described Jeremiah's New Covenant was not regarded as new. Nor was it new; it represented a change of stress, not of contents. When he said (Jer. xxxi. 33), 'This is the covenant which I will make with the house of Israel, after those days, saith the Lord; I will put my law in their inward parts, and in their heart will I write it,' Jeremiah, it has been held, was making Christianity possible. But he was also making Judaism possible. Here and nowhere else is to be found the principle which enabled Judaism to survive the loss of Temple and nationality. And the New Covenant was in no sense inconsistent with the Old. For not only does Jeremiah proceed to add in the self-same verse, 'I will be their God, and they will be my people,' but the New Covenant is specifically made with the house of Judah and of Israel, and it is associated with the permanence of the seed of Israel as a separate people and with the Divine rebuilding of Jerusalem. The Jew had no thought of analysing these verses into the words of the true Jeremiah and those of his editors. The point is that over and above, in complementary explanation of, the Abrahamic and Mosaic Covenants with their external signs, over and above the Call of the Patriarch and the Theophany of Sinai, was the Jeremian Covenant written in Israel's heart.

The Covenant conferred a distinction and imposed a duty. It was a bond between a gracious God and a grateful Israel. It dignified history, for it interpreted history in terms of providence and purpose; it transfigured virtue by making virtue service; it was the salt of life, for how could present degradation demoralise, seeing that God was in it, to fulfil His part of the bond, to hold Israel as His jewel, though Rome might despise? The Covenant made the Jew self-confident and arrogant, but these very faults were needed to save him. It was his only defence against the world's scorn. He forgot that the correlative of the Covenant was Isaiah's 'Covenant-People'—missionary to the Gentiles and the World. He relegated his world-mission (which Christianity and Islam in part gloriously fulfilled) to a dim Messianic future, and was content if in his own present he remained faithful to his mission to himself.

Above all, the legacy from the past came to Judaism hallowed and humanised by all the experience of redemption and suffering which had marked Israel's course in ages past, and was to mark his course in ages to come. The Exodus, the Exile, the Maccabean heroism, the Roman catastrophe; Prophet, Wise Man, Priest and Scribe,—all had left their trace. Judaism was a religion based on a book and on a tradition; but it was also a religion based on a unique experience. The book might be misread, the tradition encumbered, but the experience was eternally clear and inspiring. It shone through the Roman Diaspora as it afterwards illuminated the Roman Ghetto, making the present tolerable by the memory of the past and the hope of the future.

RELIGION AS LAW

The feature of Judaism which first attracts an outsider's attention, and which claims a front place in this survey, is its 'Nomism' or 'Legalism.' Life was placed under the control of Law. Not only morality, but religion also, was codified. 'Nomism,' it has been truly said, 'has always formed a fundamental trait of Judaism, one of whose chief aims has ever been to mould life in all its varying relations according to the Law, and to make obedience to the commandments a necessity and a custom' (Lauterbach, *Jewish Encyclopedia*, ix. 326). Only the latest development of Judaism is away from this direction. Individualism is nowadays replacing the olden solidarity. Thus, at the Central Conference of American Rabbis, held in July 1906 at Indianapolis, a project to formulate a system of laws for modern use was promptly rejected. The chief modern problem in Jewish life is just this: To what extent, and in what manner, can Judaism still place itself under the reign of Law?

But for many centuries, certainly up to the French Revolution, Religion as Law was the dominant conception in Judaism. Before examining the validity of this conception a word is necessary as to the mode in which it expressed itself. Conduct, social and individual, moral and ritual, was regulated in the minutest details. As the Dayan M. Hyamson has said, the maxim *De minimis non curat lex* was not applicable to the Jewish Law. This Law was a system of opinion and of practice and of feeling in which the great principles of morality, the deepest concerns of spiritual religion, the genuinely essential requirements of ritual, all found a prominent place. To assert that Pharisaism included the small and excluded the great, that it enforced rules and forgot principles, that it exalted the letter and neglected the spirit, is a palpable libel. Pharisaism was founded on God. On this foundation was erected a structure which embraced the eternal principles of religion. But the system, it must be added, went far beyond this. It held that there was a right and a wrong way of doing things in themselves trivial. Prescription ruled in a stupendous array of matters which other systems deliberately left to the fancy, the judgment, the conscience of the individual. Law seized upon the whole life, both in its inward experiences and outward manifestations. Harnack characterises the system harshly enough. Christianity did not add to Judaism, it subtracted. Expanding a famous epigram of Wellhausen's, Harnack admits that everything taught in the Gospels 'was also to be found in the Prophets, and even in the Jewish tradition of their time. The Pharisees themselves were in possession of it; but, unfortunately, they were in possession of much else besides. With them it was weighted, darkened, distorted, rendered ineffective and deprived of its force by a thousand things which they also held to be religious, and every whit as important as mercy and judgment. They reduced everything into one fabric; the good and holy was only one woof in a broad earthly warp' (*What is Christianity?* p. 47). It is necessary to qualify this judgment, but it does bring out the all-pervadingness of Law in Judaism. 'And thou shalt speak of them when thou sittest in thine house, when thou walkest by the way, when thou liest down and when thou risest up' (Deut. vi. 7). The Word of God was to occupy the Jew's thoughts constantly; in his daily employment and during his manifold activities; when at work and when at rest. And as a correlative, the Law must direct this complex life, the Code must authorise action or forbid it, must turn the thoughts and emotions in one direction and divert them from another.

Nothing in the history of religions can be cited as a complete parallel to this. But incomplete parallels abound. A very large portion of all men's lives is regulated from without: by the Bible and other sacred books; by the institutions and rites of religion; by the law of the land; by the imposed rules of accepted guides, poets, philosophers, physicians; and above all by social conventions, current fashions, and popular maxims. Only in the rarest case is an exceptional man the monstrosity which, we are told, every Israelite was in the epoch of the Judges—a law unto himself.

But in Judaism, until the period of modern reform, this fact of human life was not merely an unconscious truism, it was consciously admitted. And it was realised in a Code.

Or rather in a series of Codes. First came the *Mishnah*, a Code compiled at about the year 200 A.D., but the result of a Pharisaic activity extending over more than two centuries. While Christianity was producing the Gospels and the rest of the New Testament—the work in large part of Jews, or of men born in the circle of Judaism—Judaism in its other manifestation was working at the Code known as the *Mishnah*. This word means 'repetition,' or 'teaching by repetition'; it was an oral tradition reduced to writing long after much of its contents had been sifted in the discussions of the schools. In part earlier and in part later than the *Mishnah* was the *Midrash* ('inquiry,' 'interpretation'), not a Code, but a two-fold exposition of Scripture; homiletic with copious use of parable, and legalistic with an eye to the regulation of conduct. Then came the *Talmud* in two recensions, the Palestinian and the Babylonian, the latter completed about 500 A.D. For some centuries afterwards the Geonim (heads of the Rabbinical Universities in Persia) continued to analyse and define the legal prescriptions and ritual of Judaism, adding and changing in accord with the needs of the day; for Tradition was a living, fluid thing. Then in the eleventh century Isaac of Fez (Alfasi) formulated a guide to Talmudic Law, and about a hundred years later (1180) Maimonides produced his *Strong Hand*, a Code of law and custom which influenced Jewish life ever after. Other codifications were made; but finally, in the sixteenth century, Joseph Caro (mystic and legalist) compiled the *Table Prepared* (*Shulchan Aruch*), which, with masterly skill, collected the whole of the traditional law, arranged it under convenient heads in chapters and paragraphs, and carried down to our own day the Rabbinic conception of life. Under this Code, with more or less relaxation, the great bulk of Jews still live. But the revolt against it, or emancipation from it, is progressing every year, for the olden Jewish conception of religion and the old Jewish theory of life are, as hinted above, becoming seriously undermined.

Now in what precedes there has been some intentional ambiguity in the use of the word Law. Much of the misunderstanding of Judaism has arisen from this ambiguity. 'Law' is in no adequate sense what the Jews themselves understood by the nomism of their religion. In modern times Law and Religion tend more and more to separate, and to speak of Judaism as Law *eo ipso* implies a divorce of Judaism from Religion. The old antithesis between letter and spirit is but a phase of the same criticism. Law must specify, and the lawyer interprets Acts of Parliament by their letter; he refuses to be guided by the motives of the Act, he is concerned with what the Act distinctly formulates in set terms. In this sense Judaism never was a Legal Religion. It did most assiduously seek to get to the underlying motives of the written laws, and all the expansions of the Law were based on a desire more fully to realise the meaning and intention of the written Code. In other words, the Law was looked upon as the expression of the Will of God. Man was to yield to that Will for two reasons. First, because God is the perfect ideal of goodness. That ideal was for man to revere, and, so far as in him lay, to imitate. 'As I am merciful, be thou merciful; because I am gracious, be thou gracious.' The 'Imitation of God' is a notion which constantly meets us in Rabbinic literature. It is based on the Scriptural text: 'Be ye holy, for I the Lord am holy.' 'God, the ideal of all morality, is the founder of man's moral nature.' This is Professor Lazarus' modern way of putting it. But in substance it is the Jewish conception through all the ages. And there is a second reason. The Jew would not have understood the possibility of any other expression of the Divine Will than the expression which Judaism enshrined. For though he held that the Law was something imposed from without, he identified this imposed Law with the law which his own moral nature posited. The Rabbis tell us that certain things in the written Law could have been reached by man without the Law. The Law was in large part a correspondence to man's moral nature. This Rabbinic idea Lazarus sums up in the epigram: 'Moral laws, then, are not laws because they are written; they are written because they are laws.' The moral principle is autonomous, but its archetype is God. The ultimate reason, like the highest aim of morality, should be in itself. The threat of punishment and the promise of reward are the psychologic means to secure the fulfilment of laws, never the reasons for the laws, nor the motives to action. It is easy and necessary sometimes to praise and justify eudemonism, but, as Lazarus adds, 'Not a state to be reached, not a good to be won, not an evil to be warded off, is the impelling force of morality, but itself furnishes the creative impulse, the supreme commanding authority' (*Ethics of Judaism*, I. chap, ii.). And so the Rabbi of the third century B.C., Antigonos of Socho, put it in the memorable saying: 'Be not like servants who minister to their master upon the condition of receiving a reward; but be like servants who minister to their master without the condition of receiving a reward; and let the Fear of heaven be upon you' (Aboth, i. 3).

Clearly the multiplication of rules obscures principles. The object of codification, to get at the full meaning of principles, is defeated by its own success. For it is always easier to follow rules than to apply principles. Virtues are more attainable than virtue, characteristics than character. And while it is false to assert that Judaism attached more importance to ritual than to religion, yet, the two being placed on one and the same plane, it is possible to find in co-existence ritual piety and moral baseness. Such a combination is ugly, and people do not stop to think whether the baseness would be more or less if the ritual piety were absent instead of present. But it is the fact that on the whole the Jewish codification of religion did not produce the evil results possible or even likely to accrue. The Jew was always distinguished for his domestic virtues, his purity of life, his sobriety, his charity, his devotion. These were the immediate consequence of his Law-abiding disposition and theory. Perhaps there was some lack of enthusiasm, something too much of the temperate. But the facts of life always brought their corrective. Martyrdom was the means by which the Jewish consciousness was kept at a glowing heat. And as the Jew was constantly called upon to die for his religion, the religion ennobled the life which was willingly surrendered for the religion. The Messianic Hope was vitalised by persecution. The Jew, devotee of practical ideals, became also a dreamer. His visions of God were ever present to remind him that the law which he codified was to him the Law of God.

ARTICLES OF FAITH

It is often said that Judaism left belief free while it put conduct into fetters. Neither half of this assertion is strictly true. Belief was not free altogether; conduct was not altogether controlled. In the *Mishnah* (Sanhedrin, x. 1) certain classes of unbelievers are pronounced portionless in the world to come. Among those excluded from Paradise are men who deny the resurrection of the dead, and men who refuse assent to the doctrine of the Divine origin of the Torah, or Scripture. Thus it cannot be said that belief was, in the Rabbinic system, perfectly free. Equally inaccurate is the assertion that conduct was entirely a matter of prescription. Not only were men praised for works of supererogation, performance of more than the Law required; not only were there important divergences in the practical rules of conduct formulated by the various Rabbis; but there was a whole class of actions described as 'matters given over to the heart,' delicate refinements of conduct which the law left untouched and were a concern exclusively of the feeling, the private judgment of the individual. The right of private judgment was passionately insisted on in matters of conduct, as when Rabbi Joshua refused to be guided as to his practical decisions by the Daughter of the Voice, the supernatural utterance from on high. The Law, he contended, is on earth, not in heaven; and man must be his own judge in applying the Law to his own life and time. And, the Talmud adds, God Himself announced that Rabbi Joshua was right.

Thus there was neither complete fluidity of doctrine nor complete rigidity of conduct. There was freedom of conduct within the law, and there was law within freedom of doctrine.

But Dr. Emil Hirsch puts the case fairly when he says: 'In the same sense as Christianity or Islam, Judaism cannot be credited with Articles of Faith. Many attempts have indeed been made at systematising and reducing to a fixed phraseology and sequence the contents of the Jewish religion. But these have always lacked the one essential element: authoritative sanction on the part of a supreme ecclesiastical body' (*Jewish Encyclopedia*, ii. 148).

Since the epoch of the Great Sanhedrin, there has been no central authority recognised throughout Jewry. The Jewish organisation has long been congregational. Since the fourth century there has been no body with any jurisdiction over the mass of Jews. At that date the Calendar was fixed by astronomical calculations. The Patriarch, in Babylon, thereby voluntarily abandoned the hold he had previously had over the scattered Jews, for it was no longer the fiat of the Patriarch that settled the dates of the Festivals. While there was something like a central authority, the Canon of Scripture had been fixed by Synods, but there is no record of any attempt to promulgate articles of faith. During the revolt against Hadrian an Assembly of Rabbis was held at Lydda. It was then decided that a Jew must yield his life rather than accept safety from the Roman power, if such conformity involved one of the three offences: idolatry, murder, and unchastity (including, incest and adultery). But while this decision throws a favourable light on the Rabbinic theory of life, it can in no sense be called a fixation of a creed. There were numerous synods in the Middle Ages, but they invariably dealt with practical morals or with the problems which arose from time to time in regard to the relations between Jews and their Christian neighbours. It is true that we occasionally read of excommunications for heresy. But in the case, for instance, of Spinoza, the Amsterdam Synagogue was much more anxious to dissociate itself from the heresies of Spinoza than to compel Spinoza to conform to the beliefs of the Synagogue. And though this power of excommunication might have been employed by the mediaeval Rabbis to enforce the acceptance of a creed, in point of fact no such step was ever taken.

Since the time of Moses Mendelssohn (1728-1786), the chief Jewish dogma has been that Judaism has no dogmas. In the sense assigned above this is clearly true. Dogmas imposed by an authority able and willing to enforce conformity and punish dissent are non-existent in Judaism. In olden times membership of the religion of Judaism was almost entirely a question of birth and race, not of confession. Proselytes were admitted by circumcision and baptism, and nothing beyond an acceptance of the Unity of God and the abjuration of idolatry is even now required by way of profession from a proselyte. At the same time the earliest passage put into the public liturgy was the Shema' (Deuteronomy vi. 4-9), in which the unity of God and the duty to love God are expressed. The Ten Commandments were also recited daily in the Temple. It is instructive to note the reason given for the subsequent removal of the Decalogue from the daily liturgy. It was feared that some might assume that the Decalogue comprised the whole of the binding law. Hence the prominent position given to them in the Temple service was no longer assigned to the Ten Commandments in the ritual of the Synagogue. In modern times, however, there is a growing practice of reading the Decalogue every Sabbath day.

What we do find in Pharisaic Judaism, and this is the real answer to Harnack (*supra*, p. 15), is an attempt to reduce the whole Law to certain fundamental principles. When a would-be proselyte accosted Hillel, in the reign of Herod, with the demand that the Rabbi should communicate the whole of Judaism while the questioner stood on one foot, Hillel made the famous reply: 'What thou hatest do unto no man; that is the whole Law, the rest is commentary.' This recalls another famous summarisation, that given by Jesus later on in the Gospel. A little more than a century later, Akiba said that the command to love one's neighbour is the fundamental principle of the Law. Ben Azzai chose for this distinction another sentence: 'This is the book of the generations of man,' implying the equality of all men in regard to the love borne by God for His creatures. Another Rabbi, Simlai (third century), has this remarkable saying: 'Six hundred and thirteen precepts were imparted unto Moses, three hundred and sixty-five negative (in correspondence with the days of the solar year), and two hundred and forty-eight positive (in correspondence with the number of a man's limbs). David came and established them as eleven, as it is written: A psalm of David —Lord who shall sojourn in Thy tent, who shall dwell in Thy holy mountain? (i) He that walketh uprightly and (ii) worketh righteousness and (iii) speaketh the truth in his heart. (iv) He that backbiteth not with his tongue, (v) nor doeth evil to his neighbour, (vi) nor taketh up a reproach against another; (vii) in whose eyes a reprobate is despised, (viii) but who honoureth them that fear the Lord. (ix) He that sweareth to his own hurt, and changeth not; (x) He that putteth not out his money to usury, (xi) nor taketh a bribe against the innocent. He that doeth these things shall never be moved. Thus David reduced the Law to eleven principles. Then came Micah and reduced them to three, as it is written: 'What doth the Lord require of thee but (i) to do justice, (ii) to love mercy, and (iii) to walk humbly with thy God? Then came Habbakuk and made the whole Law stand on one fundamental idea, 'The righteous man liveth by his faith' (Makkoth, 23 b).

This desire to find one or a few general fundamental passages on which the whole Scripture might be seen to base itself is, however, far removed from anything of the nature of the Christian Creeds or of the Mohammedan Kalimah. And when we remember that the Pharisees and Sadducees differed on questions of doctrine (such as the belief in immortality held by the former and rejected by the latter), it becomes clear that the absence of a formal declaration of faith must have been deliberate. The most that was done was to introduce into the Liturgy a paragraph in which the assembled worshippers declared their assent to the truth and permanent validity of the Word of God. After the Shema' (whose contents are summarised above), the assembled worshippers daily recited a passage in which they said (and still say): 'True and firm is this Thy word unto us for ever.... True is it that Thou art indeed our God ... and there is none beside Thee.'

After all, the difference between Pharisee and Sadducee was political rather than theological. It was not till Judaism came into contact, contact alike of attraction and repulsion, with other systems that a desire or a need for formulating Articles of Faith was felt. Philo, coming under the Hellenic spirit, was thus the first to make the attempt. In the last chapter of the tract on the Creation (*De Opifico*, lxi.), Philo enumerates what he terms the five most beautiful lessons, superior to all others. These are—(i) God is; (ii) God is One; (iii) the World was created (and is not eternal); (iv) the World is one, like unto God in singleness; and (v) God exercises a continual providence for the benefit of the world, caring for His creatures like a parent for his children.

Philo's lead found no imitators. It was not for many centuries that two causes led the Synagogue to formulate a creed. And even then it was not the Synagogue as a body that acted, nor was it a creed that resulted. The first cause was the rise of sects within the Synagogue. Of these sects the most important was that of the Karaites or Scripturalists. Rejecting tradition, the Karaites expounded their beliefs both as a justification of themselves against the Traditionalists and possibly as a remedy against their own tendency to divide within their own order into smaller sects. In the middle of the twelfth century the Karaite Judah Hadassi of Constantinople arranged the whole Pentateuch under the headings of the Decalogue, much as Philo had done long before. And so he formulates ten dogmas of Judaism. These are—(i) Creation (as opposed to the Aristotelian doctrine of the eternity of the world); (ii) the existence of God; (iii) God is one and incorporeal; (iv) Moses and the other canonical prophets were called by God; (v) the Law is the Word of God, it is complete, and the Oral Tradition was unnecessary; (vi) the Law must be read by the Jew in the original Hebrew; (vii) the Temple of Jerusalem was the place chosen by God for His manifestation; (viii) the Resurrection of the dead; (ix) the Coming of Messiah, son of David; (x) Final Judgment and Retribution.

Within the main body of the Synagogue we have to wait for the same moment for a formulation of Articles of Faith. Maimonides (1135-1204) was a younger contemporary of Hadassi; he it was that drew up the one and only set of principles which have ever enjoyed wide authority in Judaism. Before Maimonides there had been some inclination towards a creed, but he is the first to put one into set terms. Maimonides was much influenced by Aristotelianism, and this gave him an impulse towards a logical statement of the tenets of Judaism. On the other side, he was deeply concerned by the criticism of Judaism from the side of Mohammedan theologians. The latter contended, in particular, that the biblical anthropomorphisms were destructive of a belief in the pure spirituality of God. Hence Maimonides devoted much of his great treatise, *Guide for the Perplexed*, to a philosophical allegorisation of the human terms applied to God in the Hebrew Bible. In his Commentary on the *Mishnah* (Sanhedrin, Introduction to Chelek), Maimonides declares 'The roots of our law and its fundamental principles are thirteen.' These are—(i) Belief in the existence of God, the Creator; (ii) belief in the unity of God; (iii) belief in the incorporeality of God; (iv) belief in the priority and eternity of God; (v) belief that to God and to God alone worship must be offered; (vi) belief in prophecy; (vii) belief that Moses was the greatest of all prophets; (viii) belief that the Law was revealed from heaven; (ix) belief that the Law will never be abrogated, and that no other Law will ever come from God; (x) belief that God knows the works of men; (xi) belief in reward and punishment; (xii) belief in the coming of the Messiah; (xiii) belief in the resurrection of the dead.'

Now here we have for the first time a set of beliefs which were a test of Judaism. Maimonides leaves no doubt as to his meaning. For he concluded by saying: 'When all these principles of faith are in the safe keeping of a man, and his conviction of them is well established, he then enters into the general body of Israel'; and, on the other hand: 'When, however, a man breaks away from any one of these fundamental principles of belief, then of him it is said that he has gone out of the general body of Israel and he denies the root-truths of Judaism.' This formulation of a dogmatic test was never confirmed by any body of Rabbis. No Jew was ever excommunicated for declaring his dissent from these articles. No Jew was ever called upon formally to express his assent to them. But, as Professor Schechter justly writes: 'Among the Maimonists we may probably include the great majority of Jews, who accepted the Thirteen Articles without further question. Maimonides must have filled up a great gap in Jewish theology, a gap, moreover, the existence of which was very generally perceived. A century had hardly lapsed before the Thirteen Articles had become a theme for the poets of the Synagogue. And almost every country can show a poem or a prayer founded on these Articles' (*Studies in Judaism*, p. 301).

Yet the opposition to the Articles was both impressive and persistent. Some denied altogether the admissibility of Articles, claiming that the whole Law and nothing but the Law was the Charter of Judaism. Others criticised the Maimonist Articles in detail. Certainly they are far from logically drawn up, some paragraphs being dictated by opposition to Islam rather than by positive needs of the Jewish position. A favourite condensation was a smaller list of three Articles: (i) Existence of God; (ii) Revelation; and (iii) Retribution. These three Articles are usually associated with the name of Joseph Albo (1380-1444), though they are somewhat older. There is no doubt but that these Articles found, in recent centuries, more acceptance than the Maimonist Thirteen, though the latter still hold their place in the orthodox Jewish Prayer Books. They may be found in the *Authorised Daily Prayer Book*, ed. Singer, p. 89.

Moses Mendelssohn (1728-1786), who strongly maintained that Judaism is a life, not a creed, made the practice of formulating Articles of Judaism unfashionable. But not for long. More and more, Judaic ritual has fallen into disregard since the French Revolution. Judaism has therefore tended to express itself as a system of doctrines rather than as a body of practices. And there was a special reason why the Maimonist Articles could not remain. Reference is not meant to the fact that many Jews came to doubt the Mosaic origin of the Pentateuch. But there were lacking in the Maimonist Creed all emotional elements. On the one hand, Maimonides, rationalist and anti-Mystic as he was, makes no allowance for the doctrine of the Immanence of God. Then, owing to his unemotional nature, he laid no stress on all the affecting and moving associations of the belief in the Mission of Israel as the Chosen People. Before Maimonides, if there had been one dogma of Judaism at all, it was the Election of Israel. Jehuda Halevi, the greatest of the Hebrew poets of the Middle Ages, had at the beginning of the twelfth century, some half century before Maimonides, given expression to this in the famous epigram: 'Israel is to the nations like the heart to the limbs.'

Though, however, the Creed of Maimonides has no position of authority in the Synagogue, modern times have witnessed no successful intrusion of a rival. Most writers of treatises on Judaism prefer to describe rather than to define the religious tenets of the faith. In America there have been several suggestions of a Creed. Articles of faith have been there chiefly formulated for the reception of proselytes. This purpose is a natural cause of precision in belief; for while one who already stands within by birth or race is rarely called upon to justify his faith, the newcomer is under the necessity to do so. In the pre-Christian Judaism it is probable that there was a Catechism or short manual of instruction called in Greek the *Didache*, in which the Golden Rule in Hillel's negative form and the Decalogue occupied a front place. Thus we find, too, modern American Jews formulating Articles of Faith as a Proselyte Confession. In 1896 the Central Conference of American Rabbis adopted the following five principles for such a Confession: (i) God the Only One; (ii) Man His Image; (iii) Immortality of the Soul; (iv) Retribution; (v) Israel's Mission. During the past few months a tract, entitled 'Essentials of Judaism,' has been issued in London by the Jewish Religious Union. The author, N. S. Joseph, is careful to explain that he is not putting forth these principles as 'dogmatic Articles of Faith,' and that they are solely 'suggestive outlines of belief which may be gradually imparted to children, the outlines being afterwards filled up by the teacher. But the eight paragraphs of these Essentials are at once so ably compiled and so informing as to the modern trend of Jewish belief that they will be here cited without comment.

According then to this presentation, the Essentials of Judaism are: '(i) There is One Eternal God, who is the sole Origin of all things and forces, and the Source of all living souls. He rules the universe with justice, righteousness, mercy, and love. (ii) Our souls, emanating from God, are immortal, and will return to Him when our life on earth ceases. While we are here, our souls can hold direct communion with God in prayer and praise, and in silent contemplation and admiration of His works. (iii) Our souls are directly responsible to God for the work of our life on earth. God, being All-merciful, will judge us with loving-kindness, and being All-just, will allow for our imperfections; and we, therefore, need no mediator and no vicarious atonement to ensure the future welfare of our souls. (iv) God is the One and only God. He is Eternal and Omnipresent. He not only pervades the entire world, but is also within us; and His Spirit helps and leads us towards goodness and truth. (v) Duty should be the moving force of our life; and the thought that God is always in us and about us should incite us to lead good and beneficent lives, showing our love of God by loving our fellow-creatures, and working for their happiness and betterment with all our might. (vi) In various bygone times God has revealed, and even in our own days continues to reveal to us, something of His nature and will, by inspiring the best and wisest minds with noble thoughts and new ideas, to be conveyed to us in words, so that this world may constantly improve and grow happier and better. (vii) Long ago some of our forefathers were thus inspired, and they handed down to us—and through us to the world at large—some of God's choicest gifts, the principles of Religion and Morality, now recorded in our Bible; and these spiritual gifts of God have gradually spread among our fellow-men, so that much of our religion and of its morality has been adopted by them. (viii) Till the main religious and moral principles of Judaism have been accepted by the world at large, the maintenance by the Jews of a separate corporate existence is a religious duty incumbent upon them. They are the "witnesses" of God, and they must adhere to their religion, showing forth its truth and excellence to all mankind. This has been and is and will continue to be their mission. Their public worship and private virtues must be the outward manifestation of the fulfilment of that mission.'

SOME CONCEPTS OF JUDAISM

Though there are no accepted Articles of Faith in Judaism, there is a complete consensus of opinion that Monotheism is the basis of the religion. The Unity of God was more than a doctrine. It was associated with the noblest hope of Israel, with Israel's Mission to the world.

The Unity of God was even more than a hope. It was an inspiration, a passion. For it the Jews 'passed through fire and water,' enduring tribulation and death for the sake of the Unity. All the Jewish martyrologies are written round this text.

In one passage the Talmud actually defines the Jew as the Monotheist. 'Whoever repudiates the service of other gods is called a Jew' (Megillah, 13 a).

But this all-pervading doctrine of the Unity did not reach Judaism as an abstract philosophical truth. Hence, though the belief in the Unity of God, associated as it was with the belief in the Spirituality of God, might have been expected to lead to the conception of an Absolute, Transcendent Being such as we meet in Islam, it did not so lead in Judaism. Judaism never attempted to define God at all. Maimonides put the seal on the reluctance of Jewish theology to go beyond, or to fall short of, what historic Judaism delivered. Judaism wavers between the two opposite conceptions: absolute transcendentalism and absolute pantheism. Sometimes Judaism speaks with the voice of Isaiah; sometimes with the voice of Spinoza. It found the bridge in the Psalter. 'The Lord is nigh unto all that call upon Him.' The Law brought heaven to earth; Prayer raised earth to heaven.

As was remarked above, Jewish theology never shrank from inconsistency. It accepted at once God's foreknowledge and man's free-will. So it described the knowledge of God as far above man's reach; yet it felt God near, sympathetic, a Father and Friend. The liturgy of the Synagogue has been well termed a 'precipitate' of all the Jewish teaching as to God. He is the Great, the Mighty, the Awful, the Most High, the King. But He is also the Father, Helper, Deliverer, the Peace-Maker, Supporter of the weak, Healer of the sick. All human knowledge is a direct manifestation of His grace. Man's body, with all its animal functions, is His handiwork. He created joy, and made the Bridegroom and the Bride. He formed the fruit of the Vine, and is the Source of all the lawful pleasures of men. He is the Righteous Judge; but He remembers that man is dust, He pardons sins, and His loving-kindness is over all. He is unchangeable, yet repentance can avert the evil decree. He is in heaven, yet he puts the love and fear of Him into man's very heart. He breathed the Soul into man, and is faithful to those that sleep in the grave. He is the Reviver of the dead. He is Holy, and He sanctified Israel with His commandments. And the whole is pervaded with the thought of God's Unity and the consequent unity of mankind. Here again we meet the curious syncretism which we have so often observed. God is in a special sense the God of Israel; but He is unequivocally, too, the God of all flesh.

Moses Mendelssohn said that, when in the company of a Christian friend, he never felt the remotest desire to convert him to Judaism. This is the explanation of the effect on the Jews of the combined belief in God as the God of Israel, and also as the God of all men. At one time Judaism was certainly a missionary religion. But after the loss of nationality this quality was practically dormant. Belief was not necessary to salvation. 'The pious of all nations have a part in the world to come' may have been but a casual utterance of an ancient Rabbi, but it rose into a settled conviction of later Judaism. Moreover, it was dangerous for Jews to attempt any religious propaganda in the Middle Ages, and thus the pressure of fact came to the support of theory.

Mendelssohn even held that the same religion was not necessarily good for all, just as the same form of government may not fit equally all the various national idiosyncrasies. Judaism for the Jew may almost be claimed as a principle of orthodox Judaism. It says to the outsider: You may come in if you will, but we warn you what it means. At all events it does not seek to attract. It is not strange that this attitude has led to unpopularity. The reason of this resentment is not that men wish to be invited to join Judaism; it lies rather in the sense that the absence of invitation implies an arrogant reserve. To some extent this is the case. The old-fashioned Jew is inclined to think himself superior to other men. Such a thought has its pathos.

On the other hand, the national as contrasted with the universal aspect of Judaism is on the wane. Many Jewish liturgies have, for instance, eliminated the prayers for the restoration of sacrifices; and several have removed or spiritualised the petitions for the recovery of the Jewish nationality. Modern reformed Judaism is a universalistic Judaism. It lays stress on the function of Israel, the Servant, as a 'Light to the Nations.' It tends to eliminate those ceremonies and beliefs which are less compatible with a universal than with, a racial religion. Modern Zionism is not a real reaction against this tendency. For Zionism is either non-religious or, if religious, brings to the front what has always been a corrective to the nationalism of orthodox Judaism. For the separation of Israel has ever been a means to an end; never an end in itself. Often the end has been forgotten in the means, but never for long. The end of Israel's separateness is the good of the world. And the religious as distinct from the merely political Zionist who thinks that Judaism would gain by a return to Palestine is just the one who also thinks that return is a necessary preliminary to the Messianic Age, when all men shall flow unto Zion and seek God there. Reformed Jews would have to be Zionists also in this sense, were it not that many of them no longer share the belief in the national aspects of the prophecies as to Israel's future. These may believe that the world may become full of the knowledge of God without any antecedent withdrawal of Israel from the world.

If Judaism as a system of doctrine is necessarily syncretistic in its conception of God, then we may expect the same syncretism in its theory of God's relation to man. It must be said at once that the term 'theory' is ill-chosen. It is laid to the charge of Judaism that it has no 'theory' of Sin. This is true. If virtue and righteousness are obedience, then disobedience is both vice and sin. No further theory was required or possible. Atonement is reversion to obedience. Now it was said above that the doctrine of the Unity did not reach Judaism as a philosophical truth exactly defined and apprehended. It came as the result of a long historic groping for the truth, and when it came it brought with it olden anthropomorphic wrappings and tribal adornments which were not easily to be discarded, if they ever were entirely discarded. So with the relation of God to man in general and Israel in particular. The unchangeable God is not susceptible to the change implied in Atonement. But history presented to the Jew examples of what he could not otherwise interpret than as reconciliation between God the Father and Israel the wayward but always at heart loyal Son. And this interpretation was true to the inward experience. Man's repentance was correlated with the sorrow of God. God as well as man repented, the former of punishment, the latter of sin. The process of atonement included contrition, confession, and change of life. Undoubtedly Jewish theology lays the greatest stress on the active stage of the process. Jewish moralists use the word Teshubah (literally 'turning' or 'return,' *i.e.* a turning from evil or a return to God) chiefly to mean a change of life. Sin is evil life, atonement is the better life. The better life was attained by fasting, prayer, and charity, by a purification of the heart and a cleansing of the hands. The ritual side of atonement was seriously weakened by the loss of the Temple. The sacrificial atonement was gone. Nothing replaced it ritually. Hence the Jewish tendency towards a practical religion was strengthened by its almost enforced stress in atonement on moral betterment. But this moral betterment depended on a renewed communion with God. Sin estranged, atonement brought near. Jewish theology regarded sin as a triumph of the *Yetser Ha-ra* (the 'evil inclination') over the *Yetser Ha-tob* (the 'good inclination'). Man was always liable to fall a prey to his lower self. But such a fall, though usual and universal, was not inevitable. Man reasserted his higher self when he curbed his passions, undid the wrong he had wrought to others, and turned again to God with a contrite heart. As a taint of the soul, sin was washed away by the suppliant's tears and confession, by his sense of loss, his bitter consciousness of humiliation, but withal man was helpless without God. God was needed for the atonement. Israel never dreamed of putting forward his righteousness as a claim to pardon. 'We are empty of good works' is the constant refrain of the Jewish penitential appeals. The final reliance is on God and on God alone. Yet Judaism took over from its past the anthropomorphic belief that God could be moved by man's prayers, contrition, amendment—especially by man's amendment. Atonement was only real when the amendment began; it only lasted while the amendment endured. Man must not think to throw his own burden entirely on God. God will help him to bear it, and will lighten the weight from willing shoulders. But bear it man can and must. The shoulders must be at all events willing.

Judaism as a theology stood or fell by its belief that man can affect God. If, for instance, prayer had no validity, then Judaism had no basis. Judaism did not distinguish between the objective and subjective efficacy of prayer. The two went together. The acceptance of the will of God and the inclining of God's purpose to the desire of man were two sides of one fact. The Rabbinic Judaism did not mechanically posit, however, the objective validity of prayer. On the contrary, the man who prayed expecting an answer was regarded as arrogant and sinful. A famous Talmudic prayer sums up the submissive aspect of the Jew in this brief petition (Berachoth, 29 a): 'Do Thy will in heaven above, and grant contentment of spirit to those that fear Thee below; and that which is good in Thine eyes do. Blessed art Thou, O Lord, who hearest prayer.' This, be it remembered, was the prayer of a Pharisee. So, too, a very large portion of all Jewish prayer is not petition but praise. Still, Judaism believed, not that prayer would be answered, but that it could be answered. In modern times the chief cause of the weakening of religion all round, in and out of the Jewish communion, is the growing disbelief in the objective validity of prayer. And a similar remark applies to the belief in miracles. But to a much less extent. All ancient religions were based on miracle, and even to the later religious consciousness a denial of miracle seems to deny the divine Omnipotence. Jewish theology from the Rabbinic age sought to evade the difficulty by the mystic notion that all miracles were latent in ordered nature at the creation. And so the miraculous becomes interconnected with Providence as revealed in history. But the belief in special miracles recurs again and again in Judaism, and though discarded by most reformed theologies, must be admitted as a prevailing concept of the older religion.

But the belief was rather in general than in special Providence. There was a communal solidarity which made most of the Jewish prayers communal more than personal. It is held by many that in the Psalter 'I' in the majority of cases means the whole people. The sense of brotherhood, in other relations besides public worship, is a perennial characteristic of Judaism.

Even more marked is this in the conception of the family. The hallowing of home-life was one of the best features of Judaism. Chastity was the mark of men and women alike. The position of the Jewish woman was in many ways high. At law she enjoyed certain privileges and suffered certain disabilities. But in the house she was queen. Monogamy had been the rule of Jewish life from the period of the return from the Babylonian Exile. In the Middle Ages the custom of monogamy was legalised in Western Jewish communities. Connected with the fraternity of the Jewish communal organisation and the incomparable affection and mutual devotion of the home-life was the habit of charity. Charity, in the sense both of almsgiving and of loving-kindness, was the virtue of virtues. The very word which in the Hebrew Bible means righteousness means in Rabbinic Hebrew charity. 'On three things the world stands,' says a Rabbi, 'on law, on public worship, and on the bestowal of loving-kindness.'

Some other concepts of Judaism and their influence on character will be treated in a later chapter. Here a final word must be said on the Hallowing of Knowledge.

In one of the oldest prayers of the Synagogue, repeated thrice daily, occurs this paragraph: 'Thou dost graciously bestow on man knowledge, and teachest mortals understanding; O let us be graciously endowed by Thee with knowledge, understanding, and discernment. Blessed art Thou, O Lord, gracious Giver of Knowledge.' The intellect was to be turned to the service of the God from whom intelligence emanated. The Jewish estimate of intellect and learning led to some unamiable contempt of the fool and the ignoramus. But the evil tendency of identifying learning with religion was more than mitigated by the encouragement which this concept gave to education. The ideal was that every Jew must be a scholar, or at all events a student. Obscurantism could not for any lengthy period lodge itself in the Jewish camp. There was no learned caste. The fact that the Bible and much of the most admired literature was in Hebrew made most Jews bilingual at least. But it was not merely that knowledge was useful, that it added dignity to man, and realised part of his possibilities. The service of the Lord called for the dedication of the reason as well as for the purification of the heart. The Jew had to think as well as feel He had to serve with the mind as well as with the body. Therefore it was that he was always anxious to justify his religion to his reason. Maimonides devoted a large section of his *Guide* to the explanation of the motives of the commandments. And his example was imitated. The Law was the expression of the Will of God, and obeyed and loved as such. But the Law was also the expression of the Divine Reason. Hence man had the right and the duty to examine and realise how his own human reason was satisfied by the Law. In a sense the Jew was a quite simple believer. But never a simpleton. '*Know* the Lord thy God' was the key-note of this aspect of Jewish theology.

SOME OBSERVANCES OF JUDAISM

The historical consciousness of Israel was vitalised by a unique adaptability to present conditions. This is shown in the fidelity with which a number of ancient festivals have been maintained through the ages. Some of these were taken over from pre-Israelite cults. They were nature feasts, and these are among the oldest rites of men. But, as Maimonides wisely said eight centuries ago, religious rites depend not so much on their origins as on the use men make of them. People who wish to return to the primitive usages of this or that church have no grasp of the value and significance of ceremonial. Here, at all events, we are not concerned with origins. The really interesting thing is that feasts, which originated in the fields and under the free heaven, were observed and enjoyed in the confined streets of the Ghetto. The influence of ceremonial is undying when it is bound up with a community's life. 'It is impossible to create festivals to order. One must use those which exist, and where necessary charge them with new meanings.' So writes Mr. Montefiore in his *Liberal Judaism* (p. 155).

This is precisely what has happened with the Passover, Pentecost, and the Feast of Tabernacles. These three festivals were originally, as has been said, nature feasts. But they became also pilgrim feasts. After the fall of the Temple the pilgrimages to Jerusalem, of course, ceased, and there was an end to the sacrificial rites connected with them all. The only sense in which they can still be called pilgrim feasts is that, despite the general laxity of Sabbath observance and Synagogue attendance, these three celebrations are nowadays occasions on which, in spring, summer, and autumn, a large section of the Jewish community contrives to wend its way to places of public worship.

In the Jewish Liturgy the three feasts have special designations. They are called respectively 'The Season of our Freedom,' 'the Season of the Giving of our Law,' and 'the Season of our Joy.' These descriptions are not biblical, nor are they found in this precise form until the fixation of the Synagogue liturgy in the early part of the Middle Ages. But they have had a powerful influence in perpetuating the hold that the three pilgrim feasts have on the heart and consciousness of Israel. Liberty, Revelation, Joy—these are a sequence of wondrous appeal. Now it is easily seen that these ideas have no indissoluble connection with specific historical traditions. True, 'Freedom' implies the Exodus; 'Revelation,' the Sinaitic theophany; 'Joy,' the harvest merry-makings, and perhaps some connection with the biblical narrative of Israel's wanderings in the wilderness. But the connection, though essential for the construction of the association, is not essential for its retention. 'The Passover,' says Mr. Montefiore (*Liberal Judaism*, p. 155), 'practically celebrates the formation of the Jewish people. It is also the festival of liberty. In view of these two central features, it does not matter that we no longer believe in the miraculous incidents of the Exodus story. They are mere trappings which can easily be dispensed with. A festival of liberty, the formation of a people for a religious task, a people destined to become a purely religious community whose continued existence has no meaning or value except on the ground of religion,—here we have ideas, which can fitly form the subject of a yearly celebration.' Again, as to Pentecost and the Ten Commandments, Mr. Montefiore writes: 'We do not believe that any divine or miraculous voice, still less that God Himself, audibly pronounced the Ten Words. But their importance lies in themselves, not in their surroundings and origin. Liberals as well as orthodox may therefore join in the festival of the Ten Commandments. Pentecost celebrates the definite union of religion with morality, the inseparable conjunction of the "service" of God with the "service" of man. Can any religious festival have a nobler subject?' Finally, as to tabernacles, Mr. Montefiore thus expresses himself: 'For us, to-day, the connection with the wanderings from Egypt, which the latest [biblical] legislators attempted, has again disappeared. Tabernacles is a harvest festival; it is a nature festival. Should not a religion have a festival or holy day of this kind? Is not the conception of God as the ruler and sustainer of nature, the immanent and all-pervading spirit, one aspect of the Divine, which can fitly be thought of and celebrated year by year? Thus each of the three great Pentateuchal festivals may reasonably and joyfully be observed by liberals and orthodox alike. We have no need or wish to make a change.' And of the actual ceremonial rites connected with the Passover, Pentecost, and Tabernacles, it is apparently only the avoidance of leaven on the first of the three that is regarded as unimportant. But even there Mr. Montefiore's own feeling is in favour of the rite. 'It is,' he says, 'a matter of comparative unimportance whether the practice of eating unleavened bread in the house for the seven days of the Passover be maintained or not. Those who appreciate the value of a pretty and ancient symbol, both for children and adults, will not easily abandon the custom.'

This is surely a remarkable development. In the Christian Church it seems that certain festivals are retaining their general hold because they are becoming public, national holidays. But in Judaism the hold is to be maintained precisely on the ground that there is to be nothing national about them, they are to be reinterpreted ideally and symbolically. It remains to be seen whether this is possible, and it is too early to predict the verdict of experience. The process is in active incubation in America as well as in Europe, but it cannot be claimed that the eggs are hatched yet. On the other hand, Zionism has so far had no effect in the opposite direction. There has been no nationalisation of Judaism as a result of the new striving after political nationality. Many who had previously been detached from the Jewish community have been brought back by Zionism, but they have not been re-attached to the religion. There has been no perceptible increase, for instance, in the number of those who fast on the Ninth of Ab, the anniversary of the destruction of the Temple. Hence, from these and other considerations, of which limited space prevents the specification, it seems on the whole likely that, as in the past so in the future, the Festivals of the

Synagogue will survive by changes in religious significance rather than by any deepening of national association.

Except that the Synagogues are decked with flowers, while the Decalogue is solemnly intoned from the Scroll of the Pentateuch, the Feast of Pentecost has no ceremonial trappings even with the orthodox. Passover and Tabernacles stand on a different footing. The abstention from leavened bread on the former feast has led to a closely organised system of cleansing the houses, an interminable array of rules as to food; while the prescriptions of the Law as to the bearing of palm-branches and other emblems, and the ordinance as to dwelling in booths, have surrounded the Feast of Tabernacles with a considerable, if less extensive, ceremonial. But there is this difference. The Passover is primarily a festival of the Home, Tabernacles of the Synagogue. In Europe the habit of actually dwelling in booths has been long unusual, owing to climatic considerations. But of late years it has become customary for every Synagogue to raise its communal booth, to which many Jews pay visits of ceremony. On the other hand, the Passover is *par excellence* a home rite. On the first two evenings (or at all events on the first evening) there takes place the *Seder*, (literally 'service'), a service of prayer, which is at the same time a family meal. Gathered round the table, on which are spread unleavened cakes, bitter herbs, and other emblems of joy and sorrow, the family recounts in prose and song the narrative of the Exodus. The service is in two parts, between which comes the evening meal. The hallowing of the home here attains its highest point.

Unless, indeed, this distinction be allotted to the Sabbath. The rigidity of the laws regarding Sabbath observance is undeniable. Movement was restricted, many acts were forbidden which were not in themselves laborious. The Sabbath was hedged in by a formidable array of enactments. To an outside critic it is not wonderful that the Jewish Sabbath has a repellent look. But to the insider things wear another aspect. The Sabbath was and is a day of delight. On it the Jew had a foretaste of the happiness of the world to come. The reader who wishes to have a spirited, and absolutely true, picture of the Jewish Sabbath cannot do better than turn to Dr. Schechter's excellent *Studies in Judaism* (pp. 296 *seq.*). As Dr. Schechter pithily puts it: 'Somebody, either the learned professors, or the millions of the Jewish people, must be under a delusion.' Right through the Middle Ages the Sabbath grew deeper into the affections of the Jews. It was not till after the French Revolution and the era of emancipation, that a change occurred. Mixing with the world, and sharing the world's pursuits, the Jews began to find it hard to observe the Saturday Sabbath as of old. In still more recent times the difficulty has increased. Added to this, the growing laxity in observances has affected the Sabbath. This is one of the most pressing problems that face the Jewish community to-day. Here and there an attempt has been made by small sections of Jews to substitute a Sunday Sabbath for the Saturday Sabbath. But the plan has not prospered.

One of the most notable rites of the Service of the Passover eve is the sanctification with wine, a ceremony common to the ordinary Sabbath eve. This rite has perhaps had much to do with the characteristic sobriety of Israel. Wine forms part of almost every Jewish rite, including the marriage ceremony. Wine thus becomes associated with religion, and undue indulgence is a sin as well as a vice. 'No joy without wine,' runs an old Rabbinic prescription. Joy is the hallmark of Judaism; 'Joyous Service' its summary of man's relation to the Law. So far is Judaism from being a gloomy religion, that it is almost too light-hearted, just as was the religion of ancient Greece. But the Talmud tells us of a class who in the early part of the first century were known as 'lovers of sorrow.' These men were in love with misfortune; for to every trial of Israel corresponded an intervention of the divine salvation. This is the secret of the Jewish gaiety. The resilience under tribulation was the result of a firm confidence in the saving fidelity of God. And the gaiety was tempered by solemnity, as the observances, to which we now turn, will amply show.

Far more remarkable than anything yet discussed is the change effected in two other holy days since Bible times. The genius of Judaism is nowhere more conspicuous than in the fuller meanings which have been infused into the New Year's Day and the Day of Atonement. The New Year is the first day of the seventh month (Tishri), when the ecclesiastical year began. In the Bible the festival is only known as a 'day of blowing the shofar' (ram's horn). In the Synagogue this rite was retained after the destruction of the Temple, and it still is universally observed. But the day was transformed into a Day of

Judgment, the opening of a ten days' period of Penitence which closed with the Day of Atonement.

Here, too, the change effected in a biblical rite transformed its character. 'It needed a long upward development before a day, originally instituted on priestly ideas of national sin and collective atonement, could be transformed into the purely spiritual festival which we celebrate to-day' (Montefiore, *op. cit.*, p. 160). But the day is none the less associated with a strict rite, the fast. It is one of the few ascetic ceremonies in the Jewish Calendar as known to most Jews. There is a strain of asceticism in some forms of Judaism, and on this a few words will be said later. But, on the whole, there is in modern Judaism a tendency to underrate somewhat the value of asceticism in religion. Hence the fast has a distinct importance in and for itself, and it is regrettable that the laudable desire to spiritualise the day is leading to a depreciation of the fast as such. But the real change is due to the cessation of sacrifices. In the Levitical Code, sacrifice had a primary importance in the scheme of atonement. But with the loss of the Temple, the idea of sacrifice entirely vanished, and atonement became a matter for the personal conscience. It was henceforth an inward sense of sin translating itself into the better life. 'To purify desire, to ennoble the will—this is the essential condition of atonement. Nay, it is atonement' (Joseph, *Judaism as Creed and Life*, p. 267; cf. *supra*, p. 45). This, in the opinion of Christian theologians, is a shallow view of atonement. But it is at all events an attempt to apply theology to life. And its justification lies in its success.

Of the other festivals a word is due concerning two of them, which differ much in significance and in development. Purim and Chanuka are their names. Purim was probably the ancient Babylonian Saturnalia, and it is still observed as a kind of Carnival by many Jews, though their number is decreasing. For Purim is emphatically a Ghetto feast. And this description applies in more ways than one. In the first place, the Book of Esther, with which the Jewish Purim is associated, is not a book that commends itself to the modern Jewish consciousness. The historicity of the story is doubted, and its narrow outlook is not that of prophetic Judaism. Observed as mediaeval Jews observed it, Purim was a thoroughly innocent festivity. The unpleasant taste left by the closing scenes of the book was washed off by the geniality of temper which saw the humours of Haman's fall and never for a moment rested in a feeling of vindictiveness. But the whole book breathes so nationalistic a spirit, so uncompromising a belief that the enemy of Israel must be the enemy of God, that it has become difficult for modern Judaism to retain any affection for it. It makes its appeal to the persecuted, no doubt: it conveys a stirring lesson in the providential care with which God watches over His people: it bids the sufferer hope. Esther's splendid surrender of self, her immortal declaration, 'If I perish, I perish,' still may legitimately thrill all hearts. But the Carnival has no place in the life of a Western city, still less the sectional Carnival. The hobby-horse had its opportunity and the maskers their rights in the Ghetto, but only there. Purim thus is now chiefly retained as a children's feast, and still better as a feast of charity, of the interchange of gifts between friends, and the bestowal of alms on the needy. This is a worthy survival.

Chanuka, on the other hand, grows every year into greater popularity. This festival of light, when lamps are kindled in honour of the Maccabean heroes, has of late been rediscovered by the liberals. For the first four centuries of the Christian Era, the festival of Chanuka ('Dedication') was observed by the Church as well as by the Synagogue. But for some centuries afterwards the significance of the anniversary was obscured. It is now realised as a momentous event in the world's history. It was not merely a local triumph of Hebraism over Hellenism, but it represents the re-entry of the East into the civilisation of the West. Alexander the Great had occidentalised the Orient. But with the success of the Judaeans against the Seleucids and of the Parthians against the Romans, the East reasserted itself. And the newly recovered influence has never again been surrendered. Hence this feast is a feast of ideals. Year by year this is becoming more clearly seen. And the symbol of the feast, light, is itself an inspiration.

The Jew is really a very sentimental being. He loves symbols. A good deal of his fondness for ritual is due to this fact. The outward marks of an inner state have always appealed to him. Ancient taboos became not only consecrated but symbolical. Whether it be the rite of circumcision, or the use of phylacteries and fringed praying garments, or the adfixture of little scrolls in metal cases on the door-posts, or the glad submission to the dietary laws, in all these matters sentiment played a considerable part. And the word sentiment is used in its best sense. Abstract morality is well enough for the philosopher, but men of flesh and blood want their morality expressed in terms of feeling. Love of God is a fine thing, but the Jew wished to do loving acts of service. Obedience to the Will of God, the suppression of the human desires before that Will, is a great ideal. But the Jew wished to realise that he was obeying, that he was making the self-suppression. He was not satisfied with a general law of holiness: he felt impelled to holiness in detail, to a life in which the laws of bodily hygiene were obeyed as part of the same law of holiness that imposed ritual and moral purity. Much of the intricate system, of observance briefly summarised in this paragraph, a system which filled the Jew's life, is passing away. This is largely because Jews are surrendering their own original theory of life and religion. Modern Judaism seems to have no use for the ritual system. The older Judaism might retort that, if that be so, it has no use for the modern Judaism. It is, however, clear that modern Judaism now realises the mistake made by the Reformers of the mid-nineteenth century. Hence we are hearing, and shall no doubt hear more and more, of the modification of observances in Judaism rather than of their abolition.

JEWISH MYSTICISM

Judaism is often called the religion of reason. It is this, but it is also the religion of the soul. It recognises the value of that mystic insight, those indefinable intuitions which, taking up the task at the point where the mind impotently abandons it, carries us straight into the presence of the King. Thus it has found room both for the keen speculator on theological problems and for the mystic who, because he feels God, declines to reason about Him—for a Maimonides and a Mendelssohn, but also for a Nachmanides, a Vital, and a Luria' (M. Joseph, *op. cit.*, p. 47). Used in a vague way, mysticism stands for spiritual inwardness. Religion without mysticism, said Amiel, is a rose without perfume. This saying is no more precise and no more informing than Matthew Arnold's definition of religion as morality touched with emotion. Neither mysticism nor an emotional touch makes religion. They are as often as not concomitants of a pathological state which is the denial of religion. But if mysticism means a personal attitude towards God in which the heart is active as well as the mind, then religion cannot exist without mysticism.

When, however, we regard mysticism as what it very often is, as an antithesis to institutional religion and a revolt against authority and forms, then it may seem at first sight paradoxical to recognise the mystic's claim to the hospitality of Judaism. That a religion which produced the Psalter, and not only produced it, but used it with never a break, should be a religion, with intensely spiritual possibilities, and its adherents capable of a vivid sense of the nearness of God, with an ever-felt and never-satisfied longing for communion with Him, is what we should fully expect. But this expectation would rather make us look for an expression on the lines of the 119th Psalm, in which the Law is so markedly associated with freedom and spirituality. Judaism, after all, allowed to authority and Law a supreme place. But the mystic relies on his own intuitions, depends on his personal experiences. Judaism, on the other hand, is a scheme in which personal experiences only count in so far as they are brought into the general fund of the communal experience.

But in discussing Judaism it is always imperative to discard all *a priori* probabilities. Judaism is the great upsetter of the probable. Analyse a tendency of Judaism and predict its logical consequences, and then look in Judaism for consequences quite other than these. Over and over again things are not what they ought to be. The sacrificial system should have destroyed spirituality; in fact, it produced the Psalter, 'the hymnbook of the second Temple.' Pharisaism ought to have led to externalism; in fact, it did not, for somehow excessive scrupulosity in rite and pietistic exercises went hand in hand with simple faith and religious inwardness. So, too, the expression of ethics and religion as Law ought to have suppressed individuality; in fact, it sometimes gave an impulse to each individual to try to impose his own concepts, norms, and acts as a Law upon the rest. Each thought very much for himself, and desired that others should think likewise. We have already seen that in matters of dogma there never was any corporate action at all; in ancient times, as now, it is not possible to pronounce definitely on the dogmatic teachings of Judaism. Though there has been and is a certain consensus of opinion on many matters, yet neither in practice nor in beliefs have the local, the temporal, the personal elements ever been negligible. In order to expound or define a tenet or rite of Judaism it is mostly necessary to go into questions of time and place and person.

Perhaps, then, we ought to be prepared to find, as in point of fact we do find, within the main body of Judaism, and not merely as a freak of occasional eccentrics, distinct mystical tendencies. These tendencies have often been active well inside the sphere of the Law. Mysticism was, as we shall see, sometimes a revolt against Law; but it was often, in Judaism as in the Roman Catholic Church, the outcome of a sincere and even passionate devotion to authority. Jewish mysticism, in particular, starts as an interpretation of the Scriptures. Certain truths were arrived at by man either intuitively or rationally, and these were harmonised with the Bible by a process of lifting the veil from the text, and thus penetrating to the true meaning hidden beneath the letter. Allegorical and esoteric exegesis always had this aim: to find written what had been otherwise found. Honour was thus done to the Scriptures, though the latter were somewhat cavalierly treated in the process; Philo's doctrine (at the beginning of the Christian era) and the great canonical book of the mediaeval Cabbala, the Zohar (beginning of the fourteenth century), were alike in this, they were largely commentaries on the Pentateuch. Maimonides in the twelfth century followed the same method, and only differed from these in the nature of his deductions from Scripture. This prince of rationalists agreed with the mystics in adopting an esoteric exegesis. But he read Aristotle into the text, while the mystics read Plato into it. They were alike faithful to the Law, or rather to their own interpretations of its terms.

But further than this,—a large portion of Jewish mysticism was the work of lawyers. Some of the foremost mystics were famous Talmudists, men who were appealed to for decisions on ritual and conduct. It is a phenomenon that constantly meets us in Jewish theology. There were antinomian mystics and legalistic opponents of mysticism, but many, like Nachmanides (1195-1270) and Joseph Caro (1488-1575), doubled the parts of Cabbalist and Talmudist. That Jewish mysticism comes to look like a revolt against the Talmud is due to the course of mediaeval scholasticism. While Aristotle was supreme, it was impossible for man to conceive as knowable anything unattainable by reason. But reason must always leave God as unknowable. Mysticism did not assert that God was knowable, but it substituted something else for this spiritual scepticism. Mysticism started with the conviction that God was unknowable by reason, but it held that God was nevertheless realisable in the human experience. Accepting and adopting various Neo-Platonic theories of emanation, elaborating thence an intricate angelology, the mystics threw a bridge over the gulf between

God and man. Philo's Logos, the Personified Wisdom of the Palestinian Midrash, the demiurge of Gnosticism, the incarnate Christ, were all but various phases of this same attempt to cross an otherwise impassable chasm. Throughout its whole history, Jewish mysticism substituted mediate creation for immediate creation out of nothing, and the mediate beings were not created but were emanations. This view was much influenced by Solomon ibn Gabirol (1021-1070). God is to Gabirol an absolute Unity, in which form and substance are identical. Hence He cannot be attributively defined, and man can know Him only by means of beings which emanate from Him. Nor was this idea confined to Jewish philosophy of the Greece-Arabic school. The German Cabbala, too, which owed nothing directly to that school, held that God was not rationally knowable. The result must be, not merely to exalt visionary meditation over calm ratiocination, but to place reliance on inward experience instead of on external authority, which makes its appeal necessarily to the reason. Here we see elements of revolt. For, as Dr. L. Ginzberg well says, 'while study of the Law was to Talmudists the very acme of piety, the mystics accorded the first place to prayer, which was considered as a mystical progress towards God, demanding a state of ecstasy.' The Jewish mystic must invent means for inducing such a state, for Judaism cannot endure a passive waiting for the moving spirit. The mystic soul must learn how to mount the chariot (Merkaba) and ride into the inmost halls of Heaven. Mostly the ecstatic state was induced by fasting and other ascetic exercises, a necessary preliminary being moral purity; then there were solitary meditations and long night vigils; lastly, prescribed ritual of proved efficacy during the very act of prayer. Thus mysticism had a farther attraction for a certain class of Jews, in that it supplied the missing element of asceticism which is indispensable to men more austerely disposed than the average Jew.

In the sixteenth century a very strong impetus was given to Jewish mysticism by Isaac Luria (1534-1572). His chief contributions to the movement were practical, though he doubtless taught a theoretical Cabbala also. But Judaism, even in its mystical phases, remains a religion of conduct. Luria was convinced that man can conquer matter; this practical conviction was the moving force of his whole life. His own manner of living was saintly; and he taught his disciples that they too could, by penitence, confession, prayer, and charity, evade bodily trammels and send their souls straight to God even during their terrestrial pilgrimage. Luria taught all this not only while submitting to Law, but under the stress of a passionate submission to it. He added in particular a new beauty to the Sabbath. Many of the most fascinatingly religious rites connected now with the Sabbath are of his devising. The white Sabbath garb, the joyous mystical hymns full of the Bride and of Love, the special Sabbath foods, the notion of the 'over-Soul'—these and many other of the Lurian rites and fancies still hold wide sway in the Orient. The 'over-Soul' was a very inspiring conception, which certainly did not originate with Luria. According to a Talmudic Rabbi (Resh Lakish, third century), on Adam was bestowed a higher soul on the Sabbath, which he lost at the close of the day. Luria seized upon this mystical idea, and used it at once to spiritualise the Sabbath and attach to it an ecstatic joyousness. The ritual of the 'over-Soul' was an elaborate means by which a relation was established between heaven and earth. But all this symbolism had but the slightest connection with dogma. It was practical through and through. It emerged in a number of new rites, it based itself on and became the cause of a deepening devotion to morality. Luria would have looked with dismay on the moral laxity which did later on intrude, in consequence of unbridled emotionalism and mystic hysteria. There comes the point when he that interprets Law emotionally is no longer Law-abiding. The antinomian crisis thus produced meets us in the careers of many who, like Sabbatai Zebi, assumed the Messianic role.

Jewish mysticism, starting as an ascetic corrective to the conventional hedonism, lost its ascetic character and degenerated into licentiousness. This was the case with the eighteenth-century mysticism known as Chassidism, though, as its name ('Saintliness') implies, it was innocent enough at its initiation. Violent dances, and other emotional and sensual stimulations, led to a state of exaltation during which the line of morality was overstepped. But there was nevertheless, as Dr. Schechter has shown, considerable spiritual worth and beauty in Chassidism. It transferred the centre of gravity from thinking to feeling; it led away from the worship of Scripture to the love of God. The fresh air of religion was breathed once more, the stars and the open sky replaced the midnight lamp and the college. But it was destined to raise a fog more murky than the confined atmosphere of the study. The man with the book was often nearer God than was the man of the earth.

The opposition of Talmudism against the neo-mysticism was thus on the whole just and salutary. This opposition, no doubt, was bitter chiefly when mysticism became revolutionary in practice, when it invaded the established customs of legalistic orthodoxy. But it was also felt that mysticism went dangerously near to a denial of the absolute Unity of God. It was more difficult to attack it on its theoretical than on its practical side, however. The Jewish mystic did sometimes adopt a most irritating policy of deliberately altering customs as though for the very pleasure of change. Now in most religious controversies discipline counts for more than belief. As Salimbene asserts of his own day: 'It was far less dangerous to debate in the schools whether God really existed, than to wear publicly and pertinaciously a frock and cowl of any but the orthodox cut.' But the Talmudists' antagonism to mysticism was not exclusively of this kind in the eighteenth century. Mysticism is often mere delusion. In the last resort man has no other guide than his reason. It is his own reason that convinces him of the limitations of his reason. But those limitations are not to be overpassed by a visionary self-introspection, unless this, too, is subjected to rational criticism. Mysticism does its true part when it applies this criticism also to the current forms, conventions, and institutions. Conventions, forms, and institutions, after all, represent the corporate wisdom, the accumulated experiences of men throughout the ages. Mysticism is the experience of one. Each does right to test the corporate experience by his own experience. But he must not elevate himself into a law even for himself. That, in a sentence, would summarise the attitude of Judaism towards mysticism. It is medicine, not a food.

ESCHATOLOGY

That the soul has a life of its own after death was a firmly fixed idea in Judaism, though, except in the works of philosophers and in the liberal theology of modern Judaism, the grosser conception of a bodily Resurrection was predominant over the purely spiritual idea of Immortality. Curiously enough, Maimonides, who formulated the belief in Resurrection as a dogma of the Synagogue, himself held that the world to come is altogether free from material factors. At a much earlier period (in the third century) Rab had said (Ber. 17 a): 'Not as this world is the world to come. In the world to come there is no eating or drinking, no sexual intercourse, no barter, no envy, hatred, or contention. But the righteous sit with their crowns on their heads, enjoying the splendour of the Shechinah (the Divine Presence).' Commenting on this in various places, Maimonides emphatically asserts the spirituality of the future life. In his *Siraj* he says, with reference to the utterance of Rab just quoted: 'By the remark of the Sages "with their crowns on their heads" is meant the preservation of the soul in the intellectual sphere, and the merging of the two into one.... By their remark "enjoying the splendour of the Shechinah" is meant that those souls will reap bliss in what they comprehend of the Creator, just as the Angels enjoy felicity in what they understand of His existence. And so the felicity and the final goal consists in reaching to this exalted company and attaining this high pitch.' Again, in his philosophical *Guide* (I. xli.), Maimonides distinguishes three kinds of 'soul': (1) The principle of animality, (2) the principle of humanity, and (3) the principle of intellectuality, that part of man's individuality which can exist independently of the body, and therefore alone survives death. Even more remarkable is the fact that Maimonides enunciates the same opinion in his Code (Laws of Repentance, viii. 2). For the Code differs from the other two of the three main works of Maimonides in that it is less personal, and expresses what the author conceives to be the general opinion of Judaism as interpreted by its most authoritative teachers.

There can be no question but that this repeated insistence of Maimonides has strongly affected all subsequent Jewish thought. To him, eternal bliss consists in perfect spiritual communion with God. 'He who desires to serve God from Love must not serve to win the future world. But he does right and eschews wrong because he is man, and owes it to his manhood to perfect himself. This effort brings him to the type of perfect man, whose soul shall live in the state that befits it, viz. in the world to come.' Thus the world to come is a state rather than a place.

But Maimonides' view was not accepted without dispute. It was indeed quite easy to cite Rabbinic passages in which the world to come is identified with the bodily Resurrection. Against Maimonides were produced such Talmudic utterances as the following: 'Said Rabbi Chiya b. Joseph, the Righteous shall arise clad in their garments, for if a grain of wheat which is buried naked comes forth with many garments, how much more shall the righteous arise full garbed, seeing that they were interred with shrouds' (Kethub. 111 b). Again, 'Rabbi Jannai said to his children, Bury me not in white garments or in black: not in white, lest I be not held worthy (of heaven) and thus may be like a bridegroom among mourners (in Gehenna); nor in black, lest if I am held worthy, I be like a mourner among bridegrooms (in heaven). But bury me in coloured garments (so that my appearance will be partly in keeping with either fate),' (Sabbath, 114 a). Or finally: 'They arise with their blemishes, and then are healed' (Sanh. 91 b).

The popular fancy, in its natural longing for a personal existence after the bodily death, certainly seized upon the belief in Resurrection with avidity. It had its roots partly in the individual consciousness, partly in the communal. For the Resurrection was closely connected with such hopes as those expressed in Ezekiel's vision of the re-animation of Israel's dry bones (Ezek. xxxvii.). Thus popular theology adopted many ideas based on the Resurrection. The myth of the Leviathan hardly belongs here, for, widespread as it was, it was certainly not regarded in a material light. The Leviathan was created on the fifth day, and its flesh will be served as a banquet for the righteous at the advent of Messiah. The mediaeval poets found much attraction in this idea, and allowed their imagination full play concerning the details of the divine repast. Maimonides entirely spiritualised the idea, and his example was here decisive. The conception of the Resurrection had other consequences. As the scene of the Resurrection is to be Jerusalem, there grew up a strong desire to be buried on the western slope of Mount Olivet. In fact, many burial and mourning customs of the Synagogue originated from a belief in the bodily Resurrection. But even in the orthodox liturgy the direct references to it are vague and idealised. Two passages of great beauty may be cited. The first is taken from the *Authorised Daily Prayer Book* (ed. Singer, p. 5):

'O my God, the soul which Thou gavest me is pure; Thou didst create it, Thou didst form it, Thou didst breathe it into me; Thou preservest it within me; and Thou wilt take it from me, but wilt restore it unto me hereafter. So long as the soul is within me, I will give thanks unto Thee, O Lord my God and God of my fathers, Sovereign of all works, Lord of all souls! Blessed art Thou, O Lord, who restorest souls unto dead bodies.' The last phrase is also extant in another reading in the Talmud and in some liturgies: 'Blessed art Thou, who revivest the dead,' but the meaning of the two forms is identical. This passage, be it noted, is ancient, and is recited every morning at prayer. The second passage is recited even more frequently, for it is said thrice daily, and also forms part of the funeral service. It may be found in the Prayer Book just quoted on p. 44: 'Thou, O Lord, art mighty for ever, Thou quickenest the dead, Thou art mighty to save. Thou sustainest the living with loving-kindness, quickenest the dead with great mercy, supportest the falling, healest the sick, loosest the bound, and keepest Thy faith to them that sleep in the dust. Who is like unto Thee, Lord of mighty acts, and who resembleth Thee, O King, who killest and quickenest, and causest salvation to spring forth? Yea faithful art Thou to quicken the dead.'

The later history of the doctrine in the Synagogue may be best summarised in the words of Dr. Kohler, whose theological articles in the *Jewish Encyclopedia* deserve grateful recognition. What follows may be read at full length in that work, vol. vi. p. 567: 'While mediaeval philosophy dwelt on the intellectual, moral, or spiritual nature of the soul to prove its immortality, the Cabbalists endeavoured to explain the soul as a light from heaven, after Proverbs xx. 27, and immortality as a return to the celestial world of pure light. But the belief in the pre-existence of the soul led the mystics to the adoption, with all its weird notions and superstitions, of the Pythagorean system of the transmigration of the soul.' Moses Mendelssohn revived the Platonic form of the doctrine of immortality. Thenceforth the dogma of the Resurrection was gradually discarded until it was eliminated from the Prayer Book of the Reform congregations. Man's future was thought of as the realisation of those 'higher expectations which are sown, as part of its very nature, in every human soul.' The statement of Genesis that 'God made man in His own image,' and the idea conveyed in the text (1 Samuel xxv. 29), 'May the soul ... be bound up in the bundle of life with the Lord thy God,' which as a divine promise and a human supplication 'filled the generations with comfort and hope, received a new meaning from this view of man's future; and the Rabbinical saying (Ber. 64 a): "The Righteous rest not, either in this or in the future world, but go from strength to strength until they see God in Zion," appeared to offer an endless vista to the hope of immortality.'

But quite apart from this indefiniteness of attitude as to the meaning of immortality, it is scarcely possible to speak of a Jewish Eschatology at all. The development of an Eschatology occurred in that section of Jewish opinion which remained on the fringe. It must be sought in the apocalyptic literature, which has been preserved in Greek. The whole subject had but a small attraction for Judaism proper. Naturally there was some curiosity and some speculation. The Day of the Lord, with its combination of Retribution and Salvation, was pictured in various ways and with some elaboration of detail. Paradise and Hell were mapped out, and the comfortable compartments to be occupied by the saints and the miserable quarters of sinners were specified with the precision of an Ordnance Survey. Purgatory was an institution not limited to the Roman Catholic Church; it had a strong hold on the mediaeval Jewish mind. The intermediate state was a favourite escape from the theological necessity of condemning sinners to eternal punishment. The Jewish heart could not suffer the pain of conceiving Gehenna inevitable. So, one by one, those who might logically be committed there were rescued on various pretexts. In the end the number of the individual sinners who were to suffer eternal torture could be named on the fingers of one hand.

By the preceding paragraph it is not implied that Jewish literature in Hebrew has not its full complement of fancies, horrible and beautiful, regarding heaven and hell. But such fancies were neither dogmatic nor popular. They never found their way into the tenets of Judaism as formulated by any authority; they never became a moving power in the life of the Jewish masses. It was the poets who nourished these lurid ideas, and poetry which has done so much for the good of religion has also done it many a disservice. Judaism, in its prosaic form, accepted the ideas of Immortality, Retribution, and so forth, but the real interest was in life here, not in life hereafter.

We can see how the two were bridged over by the Jewish conviction of human solidarity. For twelve months after the death of a father the son recited daily the Kaddish prayer (*Authorised Daily Prayer Book*, p. 77). This was a mere Doxology, opening: 'Magnified and sanctified be His great name in the world which He hath created according to His will. May He establish His kingdom during your life and during your days, and during the life of all the house of Israel, even speedily and at a near time, and say ye Amen.' As to the Messianic idea of the Kingdom of God, something will be said in the next chapter. But this Doxology was believed efficacious to save the departed soul when uttered by the living son. The generations were thus bound together, and just as the merits of the fathers could exert benign influence over the erring child on earth, so could the praises of the child move the mercy of God in favour of the erring father in Purgatory. It was a beautiful expression of the unbreakable chain of tradition, a tradition whose links were human hearts. In such conceptions, rather than in descriptive pictures of Paradise and Gehenna, is the true mind of Judaism to be discerned.

That the first formal sign of grief at the death of a parent should be a Doxology will not have escaped notice. God is the Righteous Judge. Thus, in the Eschatology of Judaism, this idea of Judgment predominates. A favourite passage was the Mishnic utterance (second century): 'Rabbi Eleazar said: They that are born are destined to die, and they that die to be brought to life again, and they that live to be judged.' (Aboth, iv. 29). But in another sense, too, there was judgment at death. The sorrow of the survivors, like the decease of the departed, was to be considered as God's doing, and therefore right. Hence in the very moment of the death of a loved one, when grief was most poignant, the survivor stood forth before the congregation and praised God. And so the Burial Service is named in Hebrew 'Zidduk Ha-din,' *i.e.* 'The Justification of the Judgment.' A few sentences in it ran thus (*Prayer Book*, p. 318): 'The Rock, His work is perfect.... He ruleth below and above, He bringeth down to the grave and bringeth up again.... Blessed be the true Judge.' And perhaps more than all attempts to analyse beliefs and dogmas, the following prayer, recited during the week of mourning for the dead, will convey to the reader the real attitude of Judaism (at least in its central variety) to some of the questions which have occupied us in this chapter. The quotation is made from p. 323 of the same Prayer Book that has been already cited several times above:

'O Lord and King, who art full of compassion, in whose hand is the soul of every living thing and the breath of all flesh, who killest and makest alive, who bringest down to the grave and bringest up again, receive, we beseech Thee, in Thy great loving-kindness, the soul of our brother who hath been gathered unto his people. Have mercy upon him, pardon all his transgressions, for there is not a righteous man upon earth, who doeth good and sinneth not. Remember unto him the righteousness which he wrought, and let his reward be with him and his recompense before him. O shelter his soul in the shadow of Thy wings. Make known to Him the path of life: in Thy presence is fulness of joy; at Thy right hand are pleasures for evermore. Vouchsafe unto him of the abounding happiness that is treasured up for the righteous, as it is written, Oh how great is Thy goodness, which Thou hast laid up for them that fear Thee, which Thou hast wrought for them that trust in Thee before the children of men!

'O Lord, who healest the broken-hearted and bindest up their wounds, grant Thy consolation unto the mourners: put into their hearts the fear and love of Thee, that they may serve Thee with a perfect heart, and let their latter end be peace.

'Like one whom his mother comforteth, so will I comfort you, and in Jerusalem shall ye be comforted. Thy sun shall no more go down, neither shall thy moon withdraw itself; for the Lord shall be thine everlasting light, and the days of thy mourning shall be ended.

'He will destroy death for ever; and the Lord will wipe away tears from off all faces; and the rebuke of his people shall he take away from off all the earth: for the Lord hath spoken it.'

THE SURVIVAL OF JUDAISM

The Messianic Hope has an intimate connection with Eschatology. Whereas, however, the latter in so far as it affirmed a Resurrection conceived of the immortality of Israelites, the former conceived the Immortality of Israel. It is not necessary here to trace the origin and history of the Messianic idea in Judaism. That this idea had a strong nationalistic tinge is obvious. The Messiah was to be a person of Davidic descent, who would be the restorer of Israel's greatness. Throughout Jewish history, despite the constant injunction to refrain 'from calculating the date of the end,' men have arisen who have claimed to be Messiahs, and these have mostly asserted their claim on nationalistic pleas. They were to be kings of Israel as well as inaugurators of a new regime of moral and spiritual life. But though this is true without qualification, it is equally true that the philosophers of the Middle Ages tried to remove all materialistic notions from the Messianic idea. It is very difficult to assert nowadays whether Judaism does or does not expect a personal Messiah. A very marked change has undoubtedly come over the spirit of the dream.

On the one hand the neo-Nationalists deny any Messianic hopes. When that great leader, Theodor Herzl, started a Zionistic movement without claiming to be the Jewish Messiah, he was putting the seal on a far-reaching change in Jewish sentiment. Dr. J. H. Greenstone, who has just published an interesting volume on the *Messianic Idea in Jewish History*, writes (p. 276): 'After the first Basle Congress (1897), when Zionism assumed its present political aspect, Dr. Max Nordau, the vice-president of the Congress, found it necessary to address an article to the Hebrew-reading public, in which he disclaimed all pretensions of Messiahship for himself or for his colleague Dr. Theodor Herzl.' We have thus this extraordinary situation. Many orthodox Jews stood aloof from the Zionistic movement because it was not Messianic, while many unorthodox Jews joined it just because of the movement's detachment from Messianic ideas.

It may be well to cite Dr. Greenstone's verdict on the whole question, as the reader may care to have the opinion of so competent an authority whose view differs from that of the present writer. 'Sacred as Zionism is to many of its adherents, it cannot and will not take the place of the Messianic hope. Zionism aims at the establishment of a Jewish State in Palestine under the protection of the powers of Europe. The Messianic hope promises the establishment, by the Jews, of a world-power in Palestine to which all the nations of the earth will pay homage. Zionism, even in its political aspect, will fulfil only one phase of the Jewish Messianic hope. As such, if successful, it may contribute toward the full realisation of the hope. If not successful, it will not deprive the Jews of the hope. The Messianic hope is wider than the emancipation of the Jews, it is more comprehensive than the establishment of a Jewish, politically independent State. It participates in the larger ideals of humanity, the ideals of perfection for the human race, but it remains on Jewish soil, and retains its peculiarly Jewish significance. It promises universal peace, an age of justice and of righteousness, an age in which all men will recognise that God is One and His name One. But this glorious age will come about through the regeneration of the Jewish people, which in turn be effected by a man, a scion of the house of David, sent by God to guide them on the road to righteousness. The people chosen by God to be His messengers to the world will then be able to accomplish their mission of regenerating the world. This was the Messianic hope proclaimed by the prophets and sages, and this is the Messianic hope of most Jews to-day, the difference between the various sections being only a difference in the details of the hope' (*op. cit.*, p. 278).

Dr. Greenstone surely cannot mean that the question of a 'personal Messiah' is a mere detail of the belief. Yet it is on that point that opinion is most divided among Jews. The older belief undeniably was what Dr. Greenstone enunciates. But for this belief, none of what Mr. Zangwill aptly terms the 'Dreamers of the Ghetto' would have found the ready acceptance that several of them did when they presented themselves as Messiah or his forerunners. And no doubt there are many Jews who still cling to this form of the belief.

On the other hand, there has been a slow but widespread tendency to reinterpret the whole intention of the Messianic hope of Judaism. In 1869, and again in 1885, American Conferences of liberal Rabbis adopted resolutions to the following effect: 'The Messianic aim of Israel is not the restoration of the old Jewish State under a descendant of David, involving a second separation from the nations of the earth, but the union of all children of God in the confession of the unity of God, so as to realise the unity of all rational creatures and their call to moral sanctification.' This view sees in the destruction of the Temple and the dispersal of Israel not a punishment but a stage in the fulfilment of Israel's destiny as revealed to Abraham. Israel is High-Priest, and can only fulfil his mission in the close neighbourhood of those to whom he is elected to minister.

This, no less than the non-Messianic Zionism, is a considerable change from older beliefs. As a Messianic hope it transcends the visions of Isaiah. The prophet looks forward to an ideal future, a reign of peace and felicity, but the nations are to flow to Zion. The significance of the change lies in this. The Messianic idea now means to many Jews a belief in human development and progress, with the Jews filling the role of the Messianic people, but only as *primus inter pares*. It is the expression of a genuine optimism. 'Character, no less than Career,' said George Eliot, 'is a process and an unfolding.' So with the Character of mankind as a whole. But this idea of development, unfolding, is quite modern in the real sense of the terms; it is something outside the range even of the second Isaiah. Judaism was never quite sure whether to join the ranks of the '*laudatores temporis acti,*' or to believe that man never is but always to be blest. On the one hand, the person of Adam was endowed with perfections such as none of his successors matched. On the other hand, the Golden Age of Judaism, as Kenan said, was thrown forward into the future. That on the whole Judaism has taken the prospective rather than the retrospective view, is the sole justification for the modern conception of the Messianic Age which is fast becoming predominant in the Synagogue. The Synagogue does not share the Roman poet's sentiment:

> '*A race of men baser than their sires*
> *Gave birth to us, a progeny more vile,*
> *Who dower the world with offspring viler still*';

but the English poet's trust:

> '*Yet I doubt not through the ages one increasing purpose runs,*
> *And the thoughts of men are widened with the process of the suns.*'

Denouncing the 'Calculators of the End,' a Rabbi said (Sanh. 97 b): 'All the computed terms have passed, and the matter dependeth now on repentance and good deeds' (cf. S. Singer, The Messianic Idea in Judaism, pp. 1 and 18)

If, however, Israel is not destined to a Restoration, if the Jewish Mission is the propagation of an idea, on what ground is the continued existence of Israel as a separate organisation defensible or justified? Israel is indestructible, said Jehuda Halevi in the twelfth century; certainly Israel is undestroyed. When Frederick the Great asked what should make him believe in God, he received in answer, 'the survival of the Jews.' Dr. Guttmann of Breslau not long since put forward a similar plea in vindication of the continued significance of Judaism. In nature all forms die when their utility is over; in history, peoples succumb when their work in and for the world is complete. Shall, he asks, we recognise Judaism as the solitary exception, as the unique instance of the survival of the unfit and the unnecessary?

The modern apologists for all religions rarely belong to the rank and file. Whether it be Harnack for Christianity or Mr. Montefiore for Judaism, the vindicators stand far above the average of the believers whose faith they are vindicating. The average man needs no defence for a religion which enables him to live and thrive, materially and spiritually. The importance of this consideration is very great. Restricting our attention to Judaism, it is clear that it still offers ideals to many, prescribes and enforces a moral law, teaches a satisfying doctrine of God. If so, then it is futile to discuss whether Judaism is still necessary. Can the world afford to surrender a single one of its forces for good? If there are ten millions of men, women, and children who live, and live not ignobly, by Judaism, can it be contended that Judaism is obsolete? The first, the main justification of Judaism is its continued efficiency, its proved power still to control and inspire many millions of human lives. There are more people living as Jews to-day, than there were at any previous moment in the world's history.

But, like many answers to questions, this reply does not satisfy those who raise the question. I refer exclusively to the doubters among the Jews themselves, for if Jews were themselves convinced of the justification of the Jewish separateness, the rest of the world would be convinced. Now, the Jews who ask this question are those who are not so completely given over to Judaism, that they are blind to the claims of other religions. To them the question is one not of absolute, but of comparative truth. Judaism may still be a power, but it may not be a desirable power. The further question therefore arises as to the mission of Israel in history to come as well as in history past. History seems contradicted by the claim made by Judaism. Jews are quick enough to see the weakness of the pretension made by certain sects of dogmatic Christianity that it is the last word of religion, that all saving truth was once for all revealed some nineteen centuries ago. History, says the Jewish controversialist, teaches no such lessons of finality. Forces appear, work their destined course, and then make way for other forces. The world does not stand still; it moves on. Then how can Judaism claim for itself a permanence, a finality, which it must deny to every other system, to every other influence which has in its turn moulded human destiny?

A favourite answer is: Judaism is the exception that proves the rule. It *has* been a permanent force in the world's history. It is argued that Jewish ideals have exercised recurrent influence at all important crises. Dr. Guttmann somewhat rhetorically makes this identical claim. He points to the birth of Christianity, the rise of Islam, the mediaeval Scholasticism, the Italian Renaissance, the German Reformation, the English and American Puritanism, the modern humanitarian movement, as exemplifications of the continued power of Judaism to mould the minds and souls of men. There is a sense in which this claim is just. It is a valuable support to the Jew's allegiance to Judaism. But even if Dr. Guttmann's claim were granted, and it is considerably exaggerated, how does it help? We are all agreed as to the debt which the world owes to Greece. That debt is a great one. Is it obsolete? Surely not. Greece has again and again revived its ancient power to inspire men. The world would be a poor one to-day without all that Greek culture stands for. Greece did not give men enough to live by; Hebraism did that. But Greece made life more worth living. Hellenism is an ever-recurrent force in human civilisation. Yet no one argues that because Hellenism is still necessary, Hellenes are also necessary. Who contends that for carrying on Greek culture you need Greeks? On the contrary, it was the case of Greece that gave rise to the profound observation that just as a man must die to live, so peoples must die that men may live through them. Renan, who, among the moderns, gave fullest value to this truth, included Judaea with Greece in the generalisation. Certainly as a nation, whether temporarily or irrevocably, Judaea perished no less than Athens, that a new world might be born. And a new Jewish nation would no more be the old Judaea of Isaiah than the Athens of to-day is the Athens of Pericles, or the Rome of to-day the Rome of Augustus. History does not retrace its steps.

Athens fell, and with it the Athenians. Why then, when Judaea fell, did the Jews remain? Greek culture does not need Greeks to carry it on; why does Jewish culture need Jews? The first suggestion to be offered is this:—Israel is the protestant people. Every religious or moral innovator has also been a protestant. Socrates, Jesus, Luther; Isaiah, Maimonides, Spinoza; all of them, besides their contributions—very unequal contributions—to the positive store of truth, assumed also the negative attitude of protesters. They refused to go with the multitude, to acquiesce in current conventions. They were all unpopular and even anti-popular. The Jews as a community have fulfilled, and are fulfilling, this protestant function. They have been and are unpopular just because of their protestant function. They refuse to go with the multitude; they refuse to acquiesce. Geiger used this argument very forcibly, from the spiritual point of view, in the early part of the nineteenth century, and Anatole Leroy-Beaulieu (in his book *Israel among the Nations*) even more forcibly used it at the end of the same century, from the historical point of view. This ingenious French observer cites a suspicion that 'the sons of Jacob, as compared with the rest of the human race, represent a higher state of evolution' (p. 232). No modern Jew would make so preposterous a claim. But when the same writer sees in the Jew a *different* stage of evolution, then he is on the right tack. Here is a passage which deserves to be quoted again and again: 'I have little taste, I confess, for uniformity; I leave that to the Jacobins. My ideal of a nation is not a monolith, nor a bronze formed at a single casting. It is better that a people should be composed of diverse elements and of many races. If the Jew differs from us, so much the better; he is the more likely to bring a little variety into the flat monotony of our modern civilisation' (p. 261). And the same argument applies to religions. There is a permanent value to the world in Israel's determined, protestant attitude. The handful of protestants who, in Elijah's day, refused to bow to Baal and to kiss him, were the real saviours of their generation. And though the world to-day is in no need of such salvation, still the Jew remains the finest exemplification of the truth that God fulfils Himself in many ways, lest one good custom should corrupt the world.

Then again, Judaism seems destined to survive because it represents at once the God-idea and the ethical idea. The liberal Jew, as well as the orthodox, believes that no other religion does this in the same way as does Judaism. Putting it crudely, the Jew would perhaps admit that Christianity has absorbed, developed, enlarged and purified the Hebrew ethics, but he would, rightly or wrongly, think that it has obscured by dogmatic accretions the Jewish Monotheism. On the other hand, the Jew would admit that Islam has absorbed and purified the Jewish Monotheism, but has done less of the flattery of imitation to the Hebrew ethics. Islam has certainly a pure creed; it freed itself from the entanglements of anthropomorphic metaphors and conceptions of God, which are apparent in the early strata of the Hebrew Bible, and from which Judaism, because of its reverence for the Bible, has not emancipated itself yet. But that it can emancipate itself is becoming progressively more clear. And even if we drop comparisons, Judaism stands for a life in which goodness and God are the paramount interests.

But, beyond all, the Jew believes himself to be a Witness to God. He thinks that on him, in some real sense, depends the fulfilment of the purposes of God. It may be an arrogant thought, but unlike most boasts it at once humiliates and ennobles, humiliates by the consciousness of what is, ennobles by the vision of what might be. After enumerating certain ethical and religious ideas which, he holds, Judaism still has to teach the world, the Rev. M. Joseph adds: 'But to the Jew himself, first of all, these truths are uttered. He is to help to win the world for the highest ideals. But if he is to succeed, he must himself be conspicuously faithful to them. He is the chosen, but his very election binds him to vigorous service of truth and righteousness. "Be ye clean, ye that bear the vessels of the Lord." Only when Israel proves by the nobility of his life that he deserves his holy vocation will the accomplishment of his mission be at hand. When all the peoples of the earth shall see that he is worthily called by the name of the Lord, the Divine name and law will be near to the attainment of their destined empire over the hearts of men' (*Judaism as Creed and Life*, p. 513).

A community that believes itself to fill this place in the Divine purpose deserves to live. Its separate existence is a means, not an end; for when all has been said, the one God carries with it the idea of one humanity. The Fatherhood of God implies the brotherhood of man. And so, amid all its trust that the long travail of centuries cannot fulfil itself in Israel's annihilation, amid all its particularism, there soars aloft the belief in the day when there will be no religions, but only Religion, when Israel will come together with other communions, or they with Israel. And so, thrice daily, in most Synagogues of Israel, this prayer is uttered: 'We therefore hope in Thee, O Lord our God, that we may speedily behold the glory of Thy might, when Thou wilt remove the abominations from the earth, and the idols will be utterly cut off; when the world will be perfected under the kingdom of the Almighty, and all the children of flesh will call upon Thy name, when Thou wilt turn unto Thee all the wicked of the earth. Let all the inhabitants of the world perceive and know that unto Thee every knee must bow, every tongue must swear. Before Thee, O Lord our God, let them bow and fall; and unto Thy glorious name let them give honour. Let them all accept the yoke of Thy kingdom, and do Thou reign over them speedily, and for ever and ever. For the Kingdom is Thine, and to all eternity Thou wilt reign in glory; as it is written in Thy Law, The Lord shall reign for ever and ever. And it is said, And the Lord shall be King over all the earth; in that day shall the Lord be One, and His name One.'

Modern Judaism, in short, claims no finality but what is expressed in that hope. It holds itself ready to develop, to modify, to absorb, to assimilate, except in so far as such processes seem inconsistent with this hope. Modern Jews think that in some respects the Rabbinic Judaism was an advance on the Biblical; they think further that their own modern Judaism is an advance on the Rabbinic. Judaism, as they conceive it, is the one religion, with a great history behind it, that does not claim the religious doctrines of some particular moment in its history to be the last word on Religion. It thinks that the last word is yet to be spoken, and is inspired with the confidence that its own continuance will make that last word fuller and truer when it comes, if it ever does come.

THE TALMUD

By Arsène Darmesteter

Arsène Darmesteter (1846-1888) was a distinguished French philologist and man of letters. Teacher at the *Ecole Rabbinique*, he co-founded the *Société des Etudes Juives*, and the *Revue des Etudes Juives*, to which he contributed several articles.

PREFATORY NOTE

THE following passage from the biography of Arsène Darmesteter, prefixed to Volume I of his *Reliques Scientifiques*, deserves quotation, both on account of its criticism of Emanuel Deutsch's brilliant article on the Talmud, which originally appeared in the *Quarterly Review* for October, 1867 (reprinted as No. 3 of this *Special Series*), and as an illustration of the phenomenon, often noted in the scientific world, that investigators, wholly independent and perhaps in ignorance of each other, publish work of similar import simultaneously, though the phase of the subject presented may have been completely neglected up to that time.

The biographer, Arsène's equally distinguished brother, James Darmesteter, says (page xv): "In that period falls his first essay, an essay on the Talmud, in which he undertook to give an idea of the contents of that vast compilation, of its formation and its history, and which, even leaving out of consideration the age of the author,"—he was then about nineteen years old—"is a marvel by reason of its precision, clearness, and grasp of the subject. That essay might have sufficed to establish the reputation of an Orientalist and an historian. Unfortunately, Arsène did not find the means to publish it. As he was about to finish it, there appeared in an English review an article on the Talmud, treating in reality of scarcely anything but the Mishna, and written with perfect appreciation of the public to which the journal appealed. It is the model of a superficial, popular, enjoyable exposition. Deutsch's article created a sensation in England, and was translated in France. Coming after it, Arsène's, superior though it was, would have appeared to be inspired by it. It therefore remained unpublished despite the efforts later, on made by M. Gaston Paris to effect its appearance in the French reviews. . . . Notwithstanding the great and happy changes brought about in France during the last fifteen years in studies of this kind, which have found a centre at the *École des Hautes-Études* and an organ in the *Revue des Études juives*, his article has preserved its originality unimpaired, and even now is unique in our language as a summing up of the vast Talmudic chaos."

In a foot-note, the biographer says: "My brother later retouched his article, and introduced the references to Deutsch contained therein." The essay, here translated from the *Reliques Scientifiques*, finally, in 1889, the year following the death of its author, found its way into the *Revue des Études juives*.

THE TRANSLATOR

THE TALMUD

THE Talmud, exclusive of the vast Rabbinic literature attached to it, represents the uninterrupted work of Judaism from Ezra to the sixth century of the common era, the resultant of all the living forces and of the whole religious activity of a nation. If we consider that it is the faithful mirror of the manners, the institutions, the knowledge of the Jews, in a word of the whole of their civilization in Judea and Babylonia during the prolific centuries preceding and following the advent of Christianity, we shall understand the importance of a work, unique of its kind, in which a whole people has deposited its feelings, its beliefs, its soul. Nothing, indeed, can equal the importance of the Talmud, unless it be the ignorance that prevails concerning it. For what is generally known of this book? At the utmost its name. People have a vague idea that it is a huge, strange, fantastic work, written in a still more fantastic style, in which bits of all sorts of more or less exact knowledge, together with dreams and fables, lie heaped up with the incoherency of complete disorder. But it has not yet been made plain, that it is the work of a nation, the expression of a social system, and that in virtue thereof it falls under the laws governing the progress of humanity. It is not understood that it is a human product, whose origin and development are human, capable of being resolved into laws, and therefore laying claim to scientific analysis. From a very different point of view it has heretofore been studied. Up to the present, this word Talmud has had the power of kindling passions and exciting acrimonious strife. The impartiality of which the author of the *Annals* boasts, *sine irâ et studio*, should not be expected of those who have written about this book. I have not in mind the last three centuries, during which its study was oftenest inspired by religious passion; Christian scholars for the most part looking upon it as a monstrosity, an infernal production, which damned the morality of the Jewish people, and the Jews hotly defending the sacredness of a work that was the bulwark of their faith and the embodiment of their religious life. Even in our days, when the demand for a more scientific treatment is justified, the Talmud has in general not been accorded impartial criticism, which, rising above polemics, should examine it dispassionately, and consider its nature and growth in the spirit that the physiologist carries into the study of an animal or the philologist into that of the characters of a language. The Jews of Germany alone in the European world of scholars have built up the science of the Talmud by the application of the critical method, which was unknown to the Jewish historians of the middle ages. About forty years ago, Jost, Zunz, and Rapoport by their learned researches inaugurated the great movement that continues with unabated vigor in our own time. Many names suggest themselves; among others those of Krochmal, Herzfeld, Graetz, Fränkel, and, above all, Geiger, who is remarkable for the assurance and the force of his bold criticism. Their influence is not confined to the Jewish world. Their work has succeeded in obtruding itself upon Protestant scholarship, both liberal and orthodox, forcing it to invite Talmudic research into the circle of the sciences. But outside of Germany their labors have met with only faint response. In France and England, they have been almost unknown up to the present time, and although special works are beginning to see the light of day, it is true that in the main nothing of these studies penetrates to the general public on this as on the other side of the Channel. For the benefit of this public, it is proposed in the following pages to give a cursory idea of the Talmud, by reviewing the principal results of German criticism. The first part shall be devoted to the analysis of the Talmud collection and to the examination of its two component elements, the *Halacha*[1] and the *Haggada*. The second part is reserved for the history of the development of the book and of the laws governing it. Finally, after a glance at its vicissitudes during the middle ages and in modern times, we shall indicate what remains for science to do with the Talmud, and what science may expect to find in it for the history of mankind at large.

---

1. *Ch* pronounced as in the German *Nacht*.

PART FIRST: ANALYTIC SKETCH OF THE TALMUD

GENERAL CHARACTERISTICS

IF one of the heavy folios that constitute the Talmud collection be opened at random, the eye will be met by a text in the square Hebrew characters, which is framed on the right and left by narrow columns, and above and below by wide bands, of a finer text, printed in the Rabbinic Characters. The frame is the work of French commentators of the middle ages; the portion framed is the TALMUD.

The Talmud, in turn, is composed of two distinct parts, the MISHNA and the GEMARA; the former the text, the latter the commentary upon that text. An analysis of the Talmud must therefore begin with that of the Mishna.

By the term Mishna we designate a collection of decisions and traditional laws, embracing all departments of legislation, civil and religious. This code, which was the work of several generations of Rabbis, received its final redaction towards the end of the second century at the hands of *Rabbi Jehuda the Holy*. It is divided into six sections, which in turn are subdivided into treatises, chapters, and paragraphs.[1]

Its language a Hebrew that has suffered a strong Chaldaic infusion, and has freely adopted Latin and especially Greek words, the Mishna is written in a simple style, so concise as sometimes to be obscure. Digressions are avoided, and the anecdotes met with here and there are introduced with the object of illuminating opinions with the light of facts.

It is useless to dwell on the legislation of the Mishna, which has so often been expounded and analyzed, recently again in an article in the *Quarterly Review*;[2] let us proceed at once to the Gemara. But a word must first be said concerning a collection called *Tosiftha*.

Rabbi Jehuda the Holy had not incorporated in the Mishna all the decisions of the Rabbis that had preceded him. A considerable number found no place in the code, either because in his eyes they were not vested with sufficient authority, or because they were useless repetitions of those published by him. Under the name *Boraïthoth (externæ)*, the greater part of the excluded decisions were collected a little later in the order of the Mishna, with the same divisions and subdivisions, and gave rise to a new book, the *Tosiftha*, or *addition*. The Tosiftha, the work of the Babylonian schools, was compiled by R. Hyya and R. Oshaya, and presents the same external characteristics as the Mishna—the same language and the same style—but anecdotes form a far more considerable element. The *Tosiftha* and the *Boraïthoth* incorporated neither in the Tosiftha nor in the Mishna are among the constituent elements of the Gemara.

This, then, brings us to the Gemara, the perpetual commentary following the Mishna in all its divisions and subdivisions.[3] It has come down to us in two different forms or redactions. The one is the work of the Palestinian schools, and was drawn up at Tiberias in about 380; the other emanates from the Babylonian academies at Sora, Nehardea, and Pumbeditha, and was reduced to writing by R. Ashi and his disciple Rabina, receiving its final shape from R. José in about 500. The Babylonian Gemara, improperly called the Babylonian Talmud, is clearer and more complete than the Palestinian Gemara, still more inaccurately called the Jerusalem Talmud. The former, therefore, was adopted by the synagogue, and the other, of higher importance to critical research by reason of its greater antiquity, was neglected by the Rabbis and the copyists of the middle ages, and has reached us in a much damaged condition and not without having lost many a page in its journey across the centuries. Unfortunately, too, there exists but one manuscript copy of the Jerusalem Talmud, that used for the *editio princeps*; no other manuscript by the aid of which its mutilated text might be corrected has been preserved. Its Babylonian rival has had a happier lot; manuscripts are not lacking, though for the most part fragmentary, and up to 1864 there had appeared forty-four editions of this Talmud, including the Mishna, the Gemara, and the commentaries, all paged alike, each edition numbering thousands of copies, each copy containing 2,947 leaves, divided up into twelve massive folios.

In the language of the Mishna the groundwork is Hebrew; of the Gemara the same cannot be said. Its language comes closer to the popular idiom, a sort of Aramean, more or less corrupt. However, specimens of the Hebrew of every age are met with, sometimes even of the classic Hebrew, according to the antiquity of the incorporated texts. After the return from the Captivity, Hebrew was an artificial language used by the Rabbis, degenerating little by little into low Hebrew, impregnating itself more and more with Aramaic elements, and finally merging into the dialect of the people. This explains how it happens that a single page of the Talmud contains three or four different languages, or rather specimens of one language at three or four different stages of degeneracy. It is not rare to find the redactor of the Talmud confirming the opinion of a Rabbi of the fourth century by quoting that of a teacher of the second, word for word the same as the former, except that it is written in Hebrew. The general principle may be enunciated, that purity of language is testimony to the antiquity of the texts reproduced in the Talmud.

Let us penetrate further into the Gemara, and consider its various features. The first striking characteristic is the extent of the commentary as compared with that of the text. Many a Mishna of five or six lines is accompanied by fifty or sixty pages of explanation. In so prolix an elaboration, of course, the lucid order of an adept's exposition must not be expected. The broad lines of a well-defined plan providing a proper place for each part of the Gemara would be sought in vain. The modern scholar with his habits of order and method would find himself singularly out of his element there. Usually the Gemara presents the appearance of a boundless sea of discussions, digressions, narratives, legends, wherein the Mishna awaiting explanation is completely submerged. The reader of its pages, in which the most widely separated objects are as a matter of course placed in close juxtaposition, in which all things mix and clash with each other in the magnificence of barbaric disorder, might readily imagine himself a spectator at the enactment of an endless dream, subject to no laws but those of the association of ideas. Not even the most circumscribed discussions fail to give room to this characteristic disorder. For instance, to elucidate a point under discussion a quotation is needed—a quotation of a line. Let it not be supposed that it is considered sufficient to indicate the new argument incidentally. It is developed quite at length with all its ramifications, so that, to grasp its whole extent, it becomes necessary to forget the first and chief object that suggested it. Nor is this all. This argument in turn calls up another, not in the least germane to the principal question, and after the mind has been straying among unrelated digressions for the space of five or six pages, it must, in order to reach the starting point, painfully retrace the successive series of arguments, extricating as it goes along details useful in the discussion, if any there be. Worse still when the commentary by the essential nature of its object lacks stability and precision. In the explanation of a Mishna the opinion of a Rabbi is quoted; the Mishna is put aside in order to reproduce all the opinions bearing this Rabbi's name. Among them are moral dicta or principles of hygiene. In consequence, a whole page of maxims or of medical formulas defile before the reader. Then follow incantations, tales of demons, popular legends. Often the connecting link is not visible. Chance has brought together two absolutely irrelevant fragments—sufficient reason for the redactor of the Gemara to join them to each other. In this flood of digressions, the Mishna seems forgotten; the reader at all events has lost it from sight, so completely have his thoughts been borne away on this meandering course, directed, it seems, by fancy alone. But suddenly it meets his eye as at a turn in the road. The thread is resumed, the explanation proceeds. But how many digressions are needed to make a Mishna exhaust its Gemara!

"It is only after a time," says the author of the *Quarterly Review* article on the Talmud, "that the student learns to distinguish between two mighty currents in the book—currents that at times flow parallel, at times seem to work upon each other, and to impede each other's action; the one emanating from the brain, the other from the heart—the one prose, the other poetry—the one carrying with it all those mental faculties that manifest themselves in arguing, investigating, comparing, developing, bringing a thousand points to bear upon one and one upon a thousand; the other springing from the realms of fancy, of imagination, feeling, humor, . . . The first named is called *Halachah (Rule, Norm)*, a term applied both to the process of evolving legal enactments and the enactments themselves. The other, *Haggadah (Legend, Saga)*, not so much in our modern sense of the word, though a great part of its contents comes under that head, but because it was only a 'saying,' a thing without authority . . ."

In fact, precise as are the boundaries of the domain of the Halacha, so vague and ill-defined are those of the Haggada. It is elusive, varying from the fantastic legend to the moral maxim, from the magic formula to historical narratives and chronological records. It is an accurate definition to say that it is what is not Halacha. The latter, on the other hand, is clearly defined; for everything called Halacha has a sacred character, compelling the respect of the believer. Halacha is LAW in all its authority; it constitutes dogma and cult; it is the fundamental element of the Talmud, and with it we ought to begin our investigation of the Gemara.

---

1. The section is called *Seder*; the treatise, *Massecheth*, literally *web*; the chapter, *Pérek*; the paragraph, the simplest element of the code, bears the name of the code itself, *Mishna*.

    The following summary of the contents of the six sections will enable the reader to appreciate the extended variety of the subjects embraced by the legislation of the Mishna.

    Section I: Seeds.—After a chapter devoted to the benedictions, it treats of tithes, first fruits, sacrifices, and gifts due from the produce of the land to the priests, the Levites, and the poor; of the cessation of agricultural labor during the Sabbatic year; and of the prohibited mixtures in seeds and in grafting.—In all eleven treatises.

    Section II: Feasts.—Of the Sabbath and Sabbath rest, of feasts and fasts: Passover, Tabernacles, New Year, the Day of Atonement, and the Fasts; of work forbidden, ceremonies to be observed, and sacrifices to be brought on those days.—Twelve treatises.

    Section III: Women.—The legislation concerning marriage, divorce, the levirate marriage, and adultery; vows and the regulations for the Nazirite.—Seven treatises.

    Section IV: Fines.—Civil legislation, besides a tractate on idolatry, and one called *A both*, consisting of a collection of the ethical sentences of the Rabbis. This section treats of commercial transactions, purchases, sales, mortgages, prescriptions, etc.; of legal procedure, of the organization of tribunals, of witnesses, oaths, etc.—Ten treatises.

    Section V: Sacred Things.—The legislation concerning sacrifices, the first-born, clean and unclean animals; the description of Herod's Temple.—Eleven treatises.

Section VI: Purifications.—Laws concerning Levitical cleanness and uncleanness; clean and unclean persons and things, objects capable of becoming unclean by contact. Purifications.—Twelve treatises.
2. Emanuel Deutsch, *The Talmud, Quarterly Review*. October, 1867.
3. Not in absolutely all. Certain parts of the Mishna lack their Gemara, either because the discussions relating to them were not committed to writing, or because, though edited, they have not reached us. Thus, in the first and in the last section, a single treatise has its commentary. In the fifth, that on sacred things, two treatises are bereft of their commentaries.

THE HALACHA

THE name Halacha applies, not only to the special laws established by the Rabbis, but also to the discussions that result in the establishment of such laws. The schools did not stop at the text fixed by Rabbi Jehuda; they used it as the point of departure, and with the aid of various *Boraïthoth* and the *Tosiftha*, they went on to explain and develop the Mishna and render new decisions. The Mishna, in fact, could not be considered a final text. When earlier decisions are adduced, it usually fails to indicate their source; sometimes the name of the author is added, but only in order to oppose another authority cited in the same way; and in the latter case, though sometimes a decision between the two antagonistic opinions is made, the question is most frequently left suspended. All this must be taken up again; the discussions begun must be finished, the points under debate determined with precision, order and light introduced everywhere: this is the work of the Gemara. It first devotes itself to the laws set down as established, inquires into their origin, and rejects the various explanations offered, until one is found holding its own against all objections. Often it shows that the decision reached by the Mishna is incomplete, obscure, contradictory, and that it cannot be made to apply to all the cases that ought apparently to come under it. In other places the Gemara quotes against the Mishna a Tosiftha or a

Boraïtha of equal or of greater antiquity, one, therefore, invested with as much or with more authority. Thence arises a great variety of hypotheses; the discussions grow in extent and depth until an exhaustive explanation of the text is reached. Naturally, free play is granted to infinite variations in form. To give an accurate idea of the discussions would be difficult. It is preferable for us to venture upon a quotation, which will convey more than could be said about it. Opening at random a volume of the Talmud, we make choice of one example among a thousand. Here is what we read on folio 37[b] of the treatise *Gittin*, or *Divorces:*

MISHNA: A slave taken captive and ransomed by a third party to be a slave, is a slave; ransomed to be set free, he cannot be made a slave. R. Simeon, son of Gamaliel, says that in any case he may be made a slave.[1]

GEMARA: Of what case does the Mishna speak? Has he been ransomed by the third party before the first owner has renounced his right of possession? Ransomed to become free, why should he not be made a slave? Is it after that renunciation? Ransomed to be a slave, why should he not be free?

Abaïa answers: The Mishna should be explained thus: We are dealing with the case in which the first owner has not renounced his right, and the slave ransomed to remain a slave returns to serve his first master; ransomed to be free, he serves neither the second, who ransomed him to set him at liberty, nor the first, who might have permitted him to remain in captivity. R. Simeon, son of Gamaliel, says: In any case he remains the slave of the first master, because it is everybody's duty to ransom slaves equally with free men (and consequently it cannot be supposed that the first master would have allowed his slave to remain in captivity).

Raba answers: This is the way to understand the Mishna: We are dealing with the case in which the first owner has renounced his right upon the slave. And the Mishna declares that, ransomed in order to remain a slave, the slave serves his second master; ransomed to be set free, he serves neither the first, who has renounced his right, nor the second, who ransoms him to set him at liberty. And R. Simeon, son of Gamaliel, says that in any case he remains a slave, because he admits Hiskia's principle, namely, that if liberty could be obtained thus, slaves would deliver themselves up to the enemy in the hope of being ransomed and becoming free.

But in a Boraïtha it is said: R. Simeon, son of Gamaliel, says to the Rabbis: "As it is a duty to ransom free men, so it is a duty to ransom slaves." The explanation of the Mishna given by Abaïa agrees with the Boraïtha, since Abaïa attributes to R. Simeon ben Gamaliel precisely this reason. But how can the Boraïtha be understood in the explanation by Raba, since Raba can justify R. Simeon ben Gamaliel's opinion only by Hiskia's principle?

Raba answers: This Boraïtha is incomplete, and itself needs the following interpretation: R. Simeon ben Gamaliel, not knowing the opinion of the Rabbis exactly, says to them: If you speak of the case in which the first master has not renounced his right, I admit the principle, "As it is a duty to ransom, etc." If of the opposite case, Hiskia's principle must be admitted.

But how can Raba, who admits that the slave ransomed to be a slave belongs to him that has ransomed him, not to his first owner, who has renounced his rights,—how can Raba justify the second owner's rights of possession? Through whom does he hold them?

Through the captors who took the slave prisoner.

But the captors themselves, whence do they derive their rights? etc.

And the discussion on this Mishna of three lines continues for seven whole pages.

It appears, from the above passage, that in its Halachic portions the Gemara uses the dialogue form. But it will not do to think of Plato's animated dialogues, in which the reader sees not only thoughts conflicting and clashing, but souls with their passions, their sentiments, with all that makes them human. Here we have dialectics in its driest and most laborious development. The disputants are not men, but names and arguments. And the style!—if the language in which the discussions are clothed can be dignified with the name style. At times the phraseology is diffuse, and, swathed in a score of words when six or eight would suffice, the idea drags painfully. Again, at other times, the language is exasperatingly concise, a letter standing for a word, a word for a clause. Questions whose complete statement would take lines are indicated by a single term, from which, as it were, they hang suspended. There are peculiar formulas in which whole ideas seem to have deposited themselves and become crystallized. The two words *Alama thenan* (*verum cur docent*) mean: "*But* if you maintain that only the thesis contrary to the one upheld by me is true, *why is it taught?*"—The word *Minalan* (*unde nobis?*), found at the beginning of a number of Gemaras, means: "What is the origin of the decision of the Mishna?" But as one Mishna ordinarily comprises several, only the answer and the objections made to the answer can clear up the thought. Suppress the commentary by Rashi, that masterpiece of precision and clearness, and the Talmud becomes almost enigmatic even to a proficient Talmudist. Put Buxtorf's Talmudic Dictionary (I do not mention a grammar; there exists none of the language of the Gemara) into the hands of a scholar that has a fair knowledge of Hebrew and Aramaic, but has never seen the Talmud; it will be impossible for him to decipher a page. We say *decipher*, and the figure of speech is not exaggerated; he truly has before him a text of hieroglyphs or inscriptions in unknown characters. So true is this that even the Jews, who find the study of the Talmud easier than others, speak only of deciphering it. Suppose the teaching of the Talmud suddenly interrupted during the life of a generation; the tradition once lost, it would be well nigh impossible to recover it. The difficulties are of diverse kinds, growing out of the language and the subjects. The linguistic perplexities are certainly not lessened by the methods of teaching employed up to the present time. The inadequacy of the books compels the student to have recourse to the peculiar method of traditional teaching, that painful method which effects mastery of the language only by means of long habit. But a good grammar, a complete lexicon, a table of Talmudic formulas—they are not excessively numerous—would greatly curtail the labor. Yet, the greatest difficulties would remain to be conquered, difficulties almost insuperable, because inherent in the very nature of Talmudic argumentation. The lucid French mind would be hard put to it to reconcile itself to these discussions, which wind in and out through endless labyrinths of subtlest reasoning. It were absolutely necessary to assume the Oriental habit of mind, that ease and force of imagination which bear thought beyond the limits of our systematic, straitlaced logic, and enable it to grasp the intangible relations between the most widely separated things. It is necessary to accustom oneself to that refinement of reasoning which penetrates to the innermost depths of an idea, and analyzes its most delicate, most evanescent shades, until the feeling of reality fades away. The influence such a book can wield upon the intelligence of a nation is patent. The daily study of the Talmud, which among Jews began with the age of ten to end with life itself, necessarily was a severe gymnastic exercise for the mind, thanks to which it acquired incomparable subtlety and acumen. Reasoning accustomed itself to accuracy, thinking to logic; in a word, intelligence grew in depth. In depth, mark you, not in extent. Discipline a well-endowed mind with Talmudic study, and you will produce a dialectician, forceful by reason of his logic and his penetration; you will have the unequalled scholars of the French, German, or Polish schools, who spend all their ability on casuistic commentaries; you will have a Spinoza, who carries Talmudic acuteness and profundity into philosophy. But do not expect to find largeness of view, breadth of outlook, expansiveness of ideas. The Halacha ignores all that. It is ratiocination, deductive reasoning raised to the highest power, and takes no account of inductive reasoning.

This characteristic of the Halacha naturally suggests another monument raised by learned men to the glory of religion, and one is tempted to pronounce the name of Scholasticism. In fact, the comparison is seductive. Scholasticism, like the Halacha, is the work of schools; like the Halacha, it rests upon deduction; and like it, employs the deductive method. But though Scholasticism with the Syllogism, and the Talmud with its hermeneutic laws, with the seven rules of Hillel, with R. Ishmael's thirteen principles, or Akiba's method, seek to do but one thing, namely, to demonstrate, they differ absolutely as to the aim of their demonstrations. The one wishes by reasoning to establish the reality of dogmatic principles; the other tries only to remember, to recall half forgotten or badly reported legal decisions, and, by an effort of reasoning memory, to rediscover them in their entirety. Scholasticism is a philosophic system, very limited, to be sure, very petty, an enslaved system, *ancilla theologiæ;* but as human reason is not called upon to do its full part, this philosophy will some day dominate and overthrow theology. Talmudic Halacha is anything but this. Philosophy it knows not even by name, and cannot know it; moreover, it ought not to know it, since it aspires to but one thing: to establish for Judaism a *Corpus Juris Ecclesiastici.*

If the nature of the Halacha has been made clear, and if besides it is remembered that it embraces all departments of religious and civil legislation, it will be seen how limited a construction must be put upon the word encyclopædia, which has been freely applied to the Talmud. The Talmud is indeed an encyclopaedia in the sense that it contains information on all subjects of knowledge cultivated in the epoch of its composition, all of which have left in it some trace or reminder of themselves. But one must not expect to see the Rabbis treat the sciences as such. Cast a glance at the summary of the contents of the Mishna given at the beginning of this article. The first section deals with the laws having reference to the products of the field. Some among them bear on the mixing of seeds. Thus the Rabbis are led to speak incidentally of botany and to adduce certain botanic facts previously acquired with the sole aim of making them subserve the establishment of the Halacha. The second section treats of the Sabbath and the feasts. With regard to the Sabbath, one of the great questions is that of Sabbath repose. It is prohibited to go beyond a radius of two thousand steps from one's house on that day. But in order to determine the limits in despite of the accidents of the ground, of valleys, hills, watercourses, certain geometric facts must be considered, and hence our Rabbis are obliged to talk geodesy. The fixing of the dates of the festivals presupposes that of a calendar, which again requires astronomical knowledge. Hence our doctors now turn to astronomy, and demand of her guidance in the establishment of the legislation for the feasts. Elsewhere, the discussion turns on prohibited animal food. Meat is forbidden when derived from animals presenting specific characteristics that render them unclean, or from clean animals tainted by certain diseases causing their prohibition. To determine these specific characteristics or these morbid conditions, some knowledge of anatomy and physiology is necessary. This part of Halachic legislation, then, displays the results of natural history studies without permitting the assertion that natural history is specifically treated. Finally, in another place, in the laws on the causes of uncleanness in persons (issues, menses, etc.), the lawmakers take up physiology and medicine, inasmuch as they apply to religious legislation the results of physiologic and medical observation. Thus the Rabbis are led to speak of all the departments of knowledge cultivated in their time, in order to abstract from them principles available for the establishment of the Halachoth. Moreover, this miscellaneous knowledge was acquired, not for its own sake, but to press it into the service of the Halacha. Science was not the end, merely the instrument permitting the attainment of the end.

Nevertheless it took protracted study to compass the Halacha in all its extent and diversified manifestations. The title of Rabbi was not to be gained in a few years, and at a period in which books were rare, in which, particularly, tradition might not be reduced to writing, a long pupilage was necessary to entitle one to participation in the discussions of the sages. One is almost tempted to take literally the Talmudic accounts that tell of twenty years passed by some of the eminent doctors of the Halacha in the apprenticeship to the Law.

To complete our examination of the various characteristics of the Halacha, the method of instruction remains to be considered. The Rabbis kept schools (*Beth ha-Midrash, house of study*) in the localities in which they lived, and numerous disciples gathered in them. Some doctrinal point was assigned to the students for elaboration, and on the day of the discussion they presented themselves with their arguments all prepared. The master catechised them, and by a series of questions skilfully put led them to find the answers themselves. The instruction, then, was not technically such; it was a protracted conversation into which the Rabbis decoyed their disciples, and from which they boasted that they derived as much profit as the latter. The disciples, in turn, spread the doctrine of their master abroad. Thence the expression met with at every step in the Talmud: "Such a one says in the name of so-and-so, who had it from such another." As for the discussions that were to result in the fixation of the Law, they took place in the following way. The Rabbis met in the tribunal or synhedrin, often accompanied by their pupils, who listened in silence behind a bar. After a public discussion, the point of doctrine was decided by a plurality of the votes of the Rabbis. The session was presided over by the *Nassi*, or *prince*, and by the president of the tribunal (*Ab Beth Din, the chief of the house of justice*), the two religious heads of the nation. The Talmud asserts that these two dignities date back to the institution of the Great Synagogue, and perpetuated themselves without interruption from Simeon the Just, contemporary of Alexander the Great and last member of that assembly. The Mishna cites a series of *couples* (*zugoth*) of Rabbis succeeding each other in the instruction of the oral Law from Simeon the Just to Hillel and Shammar, and seems to confer the title of *Nassi* on the first, and *Ab Beth Din* on the second, of each couple. Hillel and Shammaï were the last of the series of couples, and their successors explicitly bear the two titles. As instruction was obligatory and schools were numerous in Palestine, every man, no matter of what rank, could aspire to the highest dignities. Outside of the priesthood, knowledge alone constituted nobility. Witness Akiba, who from the estate of a simple shepherd rose to be the great doctor of the Mishna, "the second Moses." The *Talmid Chacham* (student), if he distinguished himself, received the title of doctor from his masters, and though gratitude and the admiration of the public reserved the title of *Nassi* for the illustrious family of Hillel, at least the Rabbis could choose the *Ab Beth Din* from among those most deserving of the office. When the student was judged worthy of the title of doctor, Rabbinical authority was conferred upon him by a peculiar ceremony called *Semicha* or *Imposition* (*of the hands*). This ordination was absolutely necessary to give him the right to decide and to forbid, to invest him actually with the power to which his knowledge entitled him morally. The ceremony was of the utmost importance for the Jews, since it was efficacious in insuring the perpetuity of tradition, as was well illustrated during the persecutions of Hadrian, at the time of Bar-Cochba's revolt. Wishing to destroy the Jewish nation, Hadrian condemned to death every Rabbi convicted of having given or received the *Semicha*. "One day," the Talmud tells, "a government decree condemned to the rack both him that gave and him that received the *Semicha*. The city in which the ceremony took place with its environs in a radius of two thousand steps, was to be destroyed. What did Judah ben Baba do? He placed himself in a valley between two large towns, Usha and Shepharam, and ordained five disciples, R. Meïr, R. Judah, R. Simeon, R. José, and R. Nehemiah. Scarcely was the ceremony completed when the enemy perceived them. R. Judah ben Baba had time only to say to the Rabbis: 'Flee, my sons!'—'And thou, O master?'—'I am like a stone that lies immovable.' And it is said that the Roman soldiers did not abandon his body until they had riddled it like a sieve with three hundred lance-thrusts." Later, when the right of Semicha was irrevocably taken from the Jews of Palestine, the work of the schools stopped, and the chain of tradition was broken. The constantly growing power of the Church thus led to the closing of the *Bathé-Midrashim,* and in about 370 the critical condition of the school of Tiberias forced the Rabbis to reduce to writing the Palestinian Gemara (*Talmud Jerushalmi*).

---

1. The above translation of the text being somewhat of a paraphrase, it seems to us of interest to give a Latin translation, whose absolute literalness is the excuse for its strange barbarity.

    Mishna: Servus, in captivitatem ductus, et redemptus, in servi nomine, serviet; in liben i nomine non serviet. R. Simeo ben Gamaliel dicit: seu hic, seu illic serviet.

    Gemara; De quo agimus? An ante repudiationem? In servi nomine, cur non serviet?—Verum post repndiationem? In servi nomine, cur serviet?

    Dicit Abaia: ante quidem repudiationem; in servi nomine, serviet priori hero; in liben i nomine, nec priori hero, nee pasteriori hero serviet. Posteriori hero non, quia in liberi nomine redemit; priori hero non, ne renuerit eum redimere. R. Simeo ben Gamaliel dicit: seu hic seu illic serviet. Censet, ut officium ingenuos liberare, sic servos officium esse liberare.

    Dicit Raba: post quidem; et, in servi nomine, posteriori hero serviet; in liberi nomine serviet nec priori hero nec posteriori hero; posteriori hero non, quia in liberi nomine redemit eum; priori hero non, quia post repudiationem est. R. Simeo ben Gamaliel dicit seu hic seu illic serviet, ut τὸ Hiskiae; quia dicit Hiskias: cur dixere seu hic seu illic serviet, ne singulus ultro hostibus se offerat et e manu heri vindicet.

    Quæstio: dicit eis R. Simeo ben Gamaliel ut officium ingenuos in libertatem vindicare, sic servos esse officium. Quoad Abaïam, qui dicit ante repudium, hoc est quod dicit τὸ ut. Sed quoad Rabam, quid τὸ ut? Ob τὸ Hiskiae est?

    Tibi dicit Raba: R. Simeo ben Gamaliel ignorabat quid dixissent Doctores et sic eis locutus est: si ante repudiationem dicitis, hoc est τὸ ut; si post repudiationem dicitis, ut τὸ Hiskiae.

    — Et Raba qui dicit post et posteriori hero, posterior herus a quo acquirit?

    — A captantibus?—

    — Captantes ipsi, quis eis acquirit? etc. . . .

    Now, in this peculiar Latin suppress the hyphens, commas, and periods. Beginning with the word *Gemara*, let all the sentences form only a long string of words placed one after the other, neither the beginning nor the end of a proposition being distinguishable, and you will have an almost exact facsimile of the text, which may be reckoned among the easiest to decipher.

THE HAGGADA

WE have now arrived at the second current whose existence in the "sea of the Talmud," to employ the expression of the Rabbis, was mentioned above. The question, What is the Haggada, we answered by saying that whatever in the Talmud does not appertain to the legal discussions, and does not bear upon the explanation of the Halacha, belongs to the realm of the Haggada. It embraces not only homilies, preaching, and edifying explanations of the Bible—all that addresses itself to the heart to touch it, to the mind to persuade it—but also history and legend, the most varied information of a scientific character in mathematics, astronomy, physics, medicine, and natural history. The Haggada is *talk* in all its wide play and vague generality, the daily *on dit*, simple conversation or moral instruction, interrupting or following the learned and painful discussions of the school and resting the weary spirit. It is evident, then, that the Haggada cannot have authority, and though it may elicit veneration from the crowd, because it issues from the mouth of official teachers whose words are respected, its characteristic is not legality; it does not legislate. "Objections are not raised to a Haggada," is one of the rules of the Talmud. Elsewhere it is said, "A decision is not rendered according to the Haggada." The Rabbis specially devoted to the study of the Halacha, maliciously applying to the Aggadist a verse from Ecclesiastes, called him, *A man to whom God hath given riches, yet giveth him not power to enjoy them,* because "he can make use of his Haggadistic knowledge neither to permit nor to forbid, neither to declare clean nor to declare unclean."

In the immense field of the Haggada the Oriental mind unfolds in all its wealth and fulness. Here especially we must seek the beliefs, ideas, sentiments that animated the Jewish, indeed the Asiatic, world, in the productive centuries that saw the enormous expansion of the superstitions of the Empire and the germination and growth of the religion of Jesus and the apostles; that saw the rich development of Oriental mysticism and the supreme effort of Greek philosophy shedding a last and brilliant gleam. This treasury, where the noblest beliefs the world has been able to conceive, as well as the most fantastic thoughts that have ever crossed human brain, lie promiscuously heaped up, is a sort of microcosm, in which that submerged civilization reappears in its most salient features. Add all that is characteristic of Judaism, and gives it its distinctive stamp—its religious and moral beliefs, its customs and usages springing from its religious doctrines, or, if borrowed from neighboring nations, so completely transformed and so well marked by the Jewish impress as to appear Jewish—and you will understand the profound charm exercised by the Haggada over the thinker and the scholar that investigate the manifestations of human thought under whatever form they appear. A great piece of work might be done—the sifting and co-ordinating of the Haggada's heterogeneous wealth. It would be necessary to go over the whole ground, and make a systematic classification, such as we of modern times demand; show what the Haggada knew of the exact and what of the natural sciences; present the allotment of truths which it has been able to discover and of errors which it harbors. It would be necessary to scrutinize its morality and its religious philosophy (the only philosophy it knows), and see to what level it was able to rise. And it were specially important to study the oddities, the fables, the superstitions of the Haggada, since in the history of the human mind nothing is more instructive than the study of the diseases of the intellect, which enable us the better to understand the mind in its healthy state, on the principle that sends physiology to the examination of morbid phenomena. The stranger the customs of other nations appear to us, the odder their manner of feeling and of regarding things, the more fruitful a source are observation and research for the philosopher. Nothing, therefore, may be neglected, and without fearing the outrage to our habits or the shock to our modern taste, we should accept the pebble as well as the precious stone, mud and slime as well as the pure and limpid waters; in a word, bring together all the productions of the popular imagination, whatever they may be, in which nature expresses herself in all her *naïveté*, and displays herself in her nakedness. This is the work, not without dignity and charm, that awaits performance, and that might tempt a mind at once patient and bold. But it is easy enough to trace out a plan or point out a *desideratum*. The important thing is to realize both.

We make no pretense of giving even a sketch of the work indicated. We content ourselves with putting together some few features that convey at least an idea of the Haggada.

In the exact sciences, the Haggada presents the singular characteristic of a mixture of truths and errors, thus seeming to prove the acceptance of certain scientific traditions from alien sources, rather than the existence of a method of investigation. Everywhere in the Talmud the ratio of the circumference to the diameter is as three to one, although four or five centuries earlier Archimedes had found it to be 22/7. The method indicated by the Mishna for measuring the width of a hill is most primitive. Two men measure it with a chain about four cubits in length, one of them holding one end against his stomach, the other holding the other end with his feet. The Talmud says: "The circumference of the world (that is, the length of the orbit described by the sun in his course from rising to setting) is about six thousand *Peras*, and the thickness of the firmament (that is, the distance from the sun to the earth) is about one thousand *Peras*." The first of these statements is an old tradition; the second is an inference from R. Jochanan's saying: A man walking at the ordinary pace can take thirty thousand steps a day, five thousand from the beginning of dawn to the first rays of the sun, and five thousand from sunset to the appearance of the stars. Thus the time taken by the sun to send us his light, namely, the period of the five thousand steps during dawn or twilight, is the sixth part of that devoted to the illumination of the world, the period of the thirty thousand steps. Then the thickness of the firmament is one-sixth of the length of the solar orbit. By the side of such puerilities, statements like the following are found: R. Gamaliel says: "There is a tradition in my grandfather's family that the new moon sometimes is ahead of her time, sometimes is delayed; in no case does she appear before the lapse of 29 1/2 days plus 2/3 and 73 parts of an hour." The hour in the Talmud is divided into 1080 parts—in passing, notice the happy choice of a number divisible by every digit except 7. All reductions being made, we have 29 days, 12 hours, 44 minutes, 3.3 + seconds. The mean length of a synodic revolution being 29 days, 12 hours, 44 minutes, 2.8 seconds, the approximation is seen to be very close. Here is a curious assertion: "The sages of Israel maintain that the sphere is motionless, and that it is the planets that move; the learned men of other nations maintain that the planets are fixed to the sphere, which turns." But what is one to say about the following? "The sages of Israel maintain that during the day the sun rolls under the firmament, and during the night above it (which renders him invisible); the sages of other nations maintain the contrary." It seems that R. Joshua (towards the end of the first century) knew how to calculate the period of the comet to which Halley's name is attached. The Talmud speaks of the profound astronomical learning of Samuel the Babylonian, who made a special study of the moon. He is the one who asserted that he was as well acquainted with the paths of the heavenly bodies as with the streets of Nehardea; but he was wholly unable to explain the nature of comets. "We know only by tradition," he added, "that the comets do not cross Orion, else they would shatter the world, and if they appear to cross it, it is the light they cast that traverses the constellation, not they themselves." These quotations, in which the word *tradition* occurs several times, seem to prove that, though some of the Rabbis devoted themselves specially to the exact sciences, the others were totally unacquainted with them. Had they a scientific method of research? We do not think so; we rather incline to the opinion that the greater part of these scientific facts were borrowed either from the inhabitants of Irak or from the Greeks.

In natural history and in anatomy the Haggada is clearer. Here the Rabbis made observations, doubtless because the Halacha is more particularly interested in these departments, having, for instance, to legislate on agricultural subjects, classify the mammals, the fish, and the birds as clean and unclean, and study the diverse diseases that can attack the clean animals. Therefore, facts were collected, animals dissected, their organs studied: the brain, whose superior and inferior membrane are known; the cerebellum, whose diseases may cause impotence; the spinal cord, which is the prolongation of the cerebellum, and whose lesions in certain cases are fatal, in others do not bring on death; the heart, with its two ventricles, its two auricles, and the pericardium. The lungs and the stomach are the objects of special study. By the side of ingenious observations, general principles are found: "Every horned animal is clovenfooted." "The presence of scales proves the existence of fins." The form of the egg indicates the class of the bird. The Rabbis observed that the milk of an unclean animal does not curdle; that animals cast their young by day or by night, according as they copulate by day or by night; that the union of animals with the same mode of copulation and the same period of pregnancy is fruitful. They know the amianthus that whitens in the fire. But they assert, agreeing in this respect with Lucretius, Pliny, and the whole ancient world, that the lion is afraid of the crowing of the cock; nor do they contradict another of Pliny's statements, that the salamander extinguishes fire. They look upon apes of the larger kinds as half men, and they know the *Shamir*, created, says the Mishna, during the twilight of the sixth day, a worm as large as a barley grain, whose look cleaves rocks; therefore, as the Temple was to be constructed with stones untouched by iron, the *Shamir* was used to cut them.

Natural history leads us to medicine, which was always cultivated among the Jews, and remained a scientific tradition with them up to modern times. It is, therefore, not surprising to find fairly extended information on the subject in the Haggada. Whole pages are taken up with the explanation of medical formulas and pharmaceutic prescriptions. There are hygienic lessons and series of injunctions as to the use of simples. Our ignorance of these matters forbids our making a selection and giving extracts. We believe, however, that it would be interesting to investigate whether the Haggada contains a collection of personal observations and true experiments, as they were considered to be by the Jewish scholars of the middle ages. The author of the *Cozari*, Jehuda Halevi, maintains that the Talmud boasts knowledge not to be found in either Aristotle or Galen. Perhaps, too, its notions are connected by general systematic views, in which case it would be necessary to investigate whether the medical theories were not borrowed from, or at least influenced by, the schools of Hippocrates, Galen, and Soranus. At all events, in our opinion, we have here an interesting problem in the history of medicine.

Did the Rabbis look with favor upon magical medicine, that mass of superstitious practices with which Chaldea flooded Asia and Europe? Knowing their disposition to be what it is, we can boldly answer, No. Somewhere in the Talmud it is told that King Hezekiah hid and destroyed a medical book, and the act is praised, because, says Maimonides, the book contained talismanic remedies. It is, nevertheless, not astonishing to find a large part of the Haggada given over to magic. Yet among the masters of the black art figures neither Samuel the Babylonian nor Theodosius the Palestinian, of whose medical science the Talmud makes boast. There are Rabbis that recall with more or less credulity the popular superstitions, the study of which, it must be conceded, is not without interest, for it is very curious to see how pseudo-medical practices, common to the whole of Asia, among the Jews take on forms in which their peculiar genius is revealed. According to Pliny, the quartan fever is cured by suspending from one's neck the longest tooth of a black dog, or some dust in which a sparrow has wallowed, tied up in a piece of linen attached by a red thread. R. Huna is more exacting: "One must take seven thorns from seven palm trees, seven splinters from seven beams, seven pegs from seven bridges, seven cinders from seven ovens, seven grains of dust from seven door pivots, seven kinds of pitch from seven ships, seven caraway seeds, and, finally, seven hairs from seven old dogs." You recognize, do you not, in the multiplication of ingredients, the riotous imagination of the Oriental, and in the use of *seven* the Jewish tendency to make this number sacred? Perhaps, however, it is proper to look upon this prescription by R. Huna as hidden irony against the popular prejudices, which he is secretly combating even while appearing to lower himself to them.. The following advice is characteristic, and leaves no room for uncertain interpretations: "Against a burning fever," says R. Jochanan, "take a knife made entirely of iron, go into the underbrush and tie a white hair to it; on the first day cut a notch into a thorn while saying the verse from Exodus: 'The angel of the Lord appeared unto Moses,' etc. (in the burning bush). The next day make another incision in the thorn, and say: 'The Lord saw that Moses turned aside to see.' The third day return, and say: 'God said to Moses, Draw not nigh hither.' That done, bend to the ground, and pronounce these words: 'Bush! Bush! it is not because thou art the greatest, but because thou art the humblest of the trees that the Holy One, blessed be He, has made His glory to descend upon thee, and as the fire was lighted before Hanania, Mishael, and Azaria, and fled before them, so may the fever which burns in me flee before me!'" If this practice was inspired by alien customs, Judaism has transformed it in a singular way, and given it its own impress. Means are found of turning popular superstitions to edifying uses and of reading an elevated lesson of morality into a good wife's prescription.—Elsewhere Abaïa reports numerous formulas in the name of his mother, a woman celebrated in Talmudic demonology: three madder-colored threads (the red thread of Pliny?) around one's neck arrest disease, five drive it away, seven are a safeguard against spells.—"Yes," says R. Aha bar Jacob, "if the wearer of the threads sees neither the sun, nor the moon, nor rain, and hears not the noise of iron, nor that of the forge, nor the crowing of a cock."—"Why, then, the virtues of thy madder-colored threads fall to the ground," answers R. Nachman, "for thou demandest the impossible."

Turn a page, and from magic receipts we pass to pure magic. The Haggada unveils strange mysteries. It tells at great length of demons, who like mortals eat and drink, live and die, and reproduce themselves, in these respects partaking of human weakness, but who are winged, transport themselves in an instant over the whole universe, know the future, and invisible can assume any form they please. You are informed that some are charged with the mission of rubbing up against you without your knowledge, and that is the reason your garments wear out; that others delight in destroying unoccupied dwellings, but leave them at the sight of a man. Therefore, the owner of a deserted house ought to be grateful to him who takes up his residence in it. Some perch on the roofs, and are on the lookout for passers-by to cast a spell on them; others sit down on the parings of nails incautiously thrown on the ground; then woe to the woman with child who walks over them; others on onions, or on garlic with the outside skin taken off: beware of swallowing them along with those vegetables! Others hide themselves in water during the night; therefore, precautions must be taken when one is thirsty at night! Thus:

"Do not drink at night. The demon *Shabriri*, who takes up his abode in water, is to be feared; he strikes blind those who drink. If, however, you are thirsty, awaken your companion, and say, Let us drink together. The demon will keep himself quiet. If you are alone, make a noise with your pillow, and say aloud, Thou so-and-so, son of so-and-so, *thy mother* has told thee: Beware of Shabriri, *briri, riri, iri, ri, i,* in white vases."

We might continue our quotations endlessly. The reader sees a phantasmagoria pass before his eyes, sometimes strange, odd, ridiculous, sometimes impish, bold, audacious, seeming to mock at the laws of nature and bid defiance to the rules of good sense or taste. Under the conjuring wand of the Haggada, new life animates the universe. The human soul seems to have transfused nature with her sentiments, her passions, her language. Trees, animals, stones are endowed with speech. The souls of the dead converse with one another in the graveyards. The infinitely great and the infinitely small are intermingled and confounded; by the side of the *Shamir*, the marvellous worm whose look cleaves rocks, are gigantic monsters: the *Behemoth*, which every day browses on the grass of a thousand mountains, but which God castrated that its progeny might not destroy the whole of terrestrial vegetation; and the *Leviathan*, whose female, killed from a similar precaution, girdles the earth with her carcass. It is the unrolling of a vast fairy world, in which reason must perforce yield to riotous imagination.

Who shall tell the history of these poetic or singular legends and their successive transformations in Mahometan and Christian mythology? Who shall tell the history of the tales of Asmodeus, Lilith, Sammael, originating doubtless in the depths of Chaldea and preserved by pious tradition throughout the centuries up to our day? Go to the remote parts of Alsace, or to Germany, or Poland; enter Jewish homes in which old customs have scarcely been encroached upon by modern civilization, and there, in the intimate intercourse of winter evenings, some good wife will tell you with pious terror the fantastic tales that mayhap her captive ancestors heard two thousand years ago on the banks of the Euphrates.

Between legend and history the boundary line is not well marked, especially not in the imagination of an Oriental. Let us cross it, and inquire into the value of the Haggada as an historic authority. This question admits of two contradictory answers, for, according to the point of view, it is equally just to concede and to refuse value to it. To hope to find in the Haggada precise and detailed chronicles, scrupulously exact and circumstantial narratives of events, is to run the risk of complete disappointment. The Haggada is totally ignorant of what is properly called history. Reality and dream mingle in nebulous vagueness. It does not seem to have an accurate idea of time. The Orient, in fact, immobile in its unchangeable existence, cannot have the precise notion of time so clearly conveyed to the Occidental mind by perpetual mutations. Thus the various epochs of the past seem to be put upon the same plane. Edom, Nebuchadnezzar, Vespasian, Titus, Hadrian, all the enemies of the Jewish race, merge into one type, and one is substituted for the other in the long martyrology of its history. If, for instance, there is any event that should have left deep traces in the memory of the nation, it assuredly is the destruction of Jerusalem and the "Holy House." Yet, concerning the various phases of the struggle, the men that took part in and directed it, and the final catastrophe, clear and accurate data are sought in vain. Aside from some vague details, in which the element of truth they may contain waits to be set free by criticism, absolutely nothing can be found. But what the Haggada does know, are the poetic legends that thrill the populace, and go straight to one's heart. It tells the story of Martha, the wife of the high priest Joshua ben Gamala, the elegant, fastidious lady to whom were applied the words of Deuteronomy: "The tender and delicate woman among you, which would not adventure to set the sole of her foot upon the ground for delicateness and tenderness," and who dies of hunger in the streets of Jerusalem, or, according to another version, is dragged across country bound by her hair to the tail of a wild horse. It tells the story of that Zadok who bewails the misery of his land, and in his grief condemns himself to a forty years' fast. "He ate only one fig a day, and he grew so thin that this fig could be seen to pass down his throat." It recounts with all possible precision the fortunes of the son and the daughter of the high priest Ishmael ben Elisha after the sack of the Holy City. They were sold as slaves to two neighboring masters.—Said the first, I have a slave of incomparable beauty.—And I, said the other, possess the most beautiful maiden imaginable. Let us join them in marriage, and share their children.—In the evening they locked them up together in a chamber. The youth remained in one corner, the maiden in another. The former said: I, a priest, the son of a high priest, should take to wife a slave! The latter said: I, the daughter of a high priest, should marry a slave! Thus they lamented all night. With the dawn came recognition, and each leaping towards the other, they stood clasped in close embrace until their souls took flight. And, stirred to his depths, the narrator, recalling the verse in Lamentations, exclaims, "For these things I weep: mine eye, mine eye runneth down with water."—Such are the recollections that remain of the catastrophe—legends and tales. This is no longer history, or, if you will, it is still history, but of the kind made by the people.

Assuredly, it will not do to require of the Haggada the exactitude of an historic chronicle. And if perchance we find here and there, buried under a thick layer, a few precise data, a few accurate notes, a few lines of history, the *Seder Olam* (*Chronicle of the World*), the *Megillath Taanith* (*Roll of Fasts*), it must nevertheless be conceded that the Haggada has nearly no value at all as a documentary source.

But precisely because the narrative of facts is merged into legend, the Haggada ought to yield all the interest of legendary chronicles. It will not do to turn up one's nose at legend; it is the absolutely necessary complement of history, which usually presents facts in all their nudity and dryness. But facts are far from being all that is essential. There is the idea hiding beneath the facts and dominating them, as vital force animates the skeleton of an animal. Now this idea, which only with great difficulty can be abstracted from a series of facts, appears in all its clearness in legend. By means of legends, a people expresses its desires, its aspirations, its ideal, later translated into facts, and expresses them with precision so much the greater as the form of the legend is vague and its web loose. In legend we have first a narrative, in itself without historic value, and then the idea, which is crystallized in the narrative form, and which answers to a real sentiment, reproduced with the greatest clearness, and therefore of considerable value to the historian. In this sense legend should be invested with authority of a certain kind, and this is the authority that the Haggada may lay claim to. In the Haggada, we find *local color;* it conveys Jewish manners, customs, and beliefs, the spirit of the institutions and the religion, in a word, the soul and the life of the nation.

To complete this all too superficial examination of the Haggada, there remains for us to speak of its moral and religious philosophy. The *Quarterly Review* writer, with the warmth characteristic of his fine plea for the Talmud, has given an eloquent exposition of the system, reproducing Abraham Nager's substantial contribution to the subject. We shall give a *resumé* of the same work, supplying certain features that were omitted and that to us appear important.

In the beginning there was nothing. God, by an act of His will, created matter or the first substance, according to some, water, according to others, water, air, and fire, and organizing these elements, He formed, "in His own good time," the world as it is. God, then, is at once "creator and architect."—What was the process of creation? That is a mystery. Certain it is that the angels had naught to do with it, for they were formed at the earliest on the second day of creation, "that it might not be said: Michael stretched out the firmament to the north, and Gabriel to the south." But the world once created, Providence brought nothing to pass "without consulting the celestial household." Besides, there is an angel, "the master of the world," who is the intermediary between heaven and earth, *Metatron*, that is, the one seated near the heavenly throne (*meta thronos*). Each nation, nevertheless, has its special tutelary angel, as well as its guardian constellations, with the exception of Israel, who has "neither angel nor constellation, so long as he observes the divine law." Israel stands under the eye of God Himself.

At the same time with the world, God *created* miracles, which thenceforth fall under the immutable laws of nature regulating the universe despite the evil that may result. Creation has for its end man, who in turn is to use the world to execute the will of God on earth, the aim of creation thus being the realization of the divine here below. "If Israel accepts the Law (all other nations having refused it), God will maintain the world; if not, He will cause it to drop back into nothingness." The aim of man on earth, then, is the knowledge and the practice of the Law, "without which there were neither heaven nor earth"— the Law "on which God had His eye fixed when He created the universe, as the mason that builds a house has in mind the plans and the external appearance." Man endowed with free will, "created last on the eve of the Sabbath, that he might at once take his place at the holy banquet," ought therefore to strive endlessly for perfection, which eventually renders him superior to the angels, for, in spite of their eternal and infinite perfection, they are without liberty, and neither earn commendation nor incur censure.

How is this perfection reached? By the practice of the Law and the doing of good deeds. Useless to give examples of the morality of the Pharisees. The subject is too familiar. It is well known that the Talmud may lay claim to the most exalted ideals of goodness that human mind can conceive of, and that all the moral ideas incorporated in the Gospels had long before passed from mouth to mouth in the streets of Jerusalem. Glance through the Mishnic treatise *A both*, and you will find all that the most delicate charity, the most refined and intelligent kindliness can inspire into souls naturally disposed to the good. Human dignity, the sacredness of manual labor, the superiority of good works over learning, the equality of men before the divine tribunal, no matter what religion they may profess,—these are the great principles asserted and preached by the Haggada on every page.

The Talmud, says Nager, has its peculiar psychology. In a number of passages the Platonic theory of the pre-existence of souls is stated, but nowhere does metempsychosis appear. Plato's doctrine appealed to the poetic imagination of the Rabbis more than the Aristotelian theory, which made of the soul the entelechy of the body. All the souls called to terrestrial life were created in the beginning, and kept in reserve. They have all-embracing knowledge of the Law up to the moment in, which they unite with a body. Then an angel closes the mouth of the child, and the soul forgets all it knew.—No original sin: "As God is pure, so the soul is pure."—Every child on leaving its mother's womb is made to swear by an angel that it will be just. "Be assured," he says to it, "that God is pure, that His servants are pure, and that the soul given to thee is also pure." In one passage, however, a teacher speaks of the crime of Adam, which recoils on the whole of mankind. "When the serpent tempted Eve, it corrupted her with its venom. Israel, by being witness of the Revelation at Sinai, was cured of the disease; "the idolaters could not be cured." But in general the story of the first sin has not found an echo in the teachings of the sages. Elsewhere it is expressly said: "No death without sin, no grief without fault." It is also said that children dying in infancy or at birth may enter into the future life.

Whence, then, comes sin? From man's free will. "Everything is foreseen," says Akiba, "but liberty is granted." And elsewhere: "Everything is in the power of God except the fear of God."

Human destiny is not fulfilled here below; the other world is the soul's true home, This earth is but "the caravansary by the wayside," in which a brief rest is taken. The dogmas of the immortality of the soul and a future life are energetically asserted by the Rabbis, who regard their negation as veritable heresy. But how is one to understand the entrance into the future life? Do you understand the entrance into this life? Death and birth resemble each other, say the Rabbis. Suppose a child in its mother's womb to know that after the lapse of a few months it will leave the place it occupies. That would seem to it the most grievous event that could happen. It is so comfortable in the element that surrounds it, and protects it against outside influences! However, the time of separation approaches; with terror it sees the protecting envelopes torn asunder, and it believes that the hour of death has arrived. But the moment of leaving its little world marks the beginning of a nobler, more beautiful, more perfect life, which lasts until a voice again sounds at its ear proclaiming: Thou must leave earth, as thou didst leave thy mother's womb, and, stripping off this earthly vesture, thou must once more die, once more begin life.

A new life opens for man, a life wholly spiritual, in which he receives the recompense or the chastisement for his conduct here below. "In the world to come, there is neither eating, nor drinking, nor any material pleasure; but the just sit there with crowns on their heads, and delight in the glory of the Divine Presence."—"The souls of the just, at the foot of the celestial throne, contemplate the splendor of God." Those of the impious are condemned to the torments of the nether world. Eternal punishment is reserved for well-defined classes of sinners, as, for example, those who knowing the Law have entirely abjured it, and those who not only sin themselves, but draw others into crime. The description of these tortures is vague and contradictory, as is that of the lower regions themselves. In fact, the Talmud gives us, not so much a system, as a series of individual opinions. The fire in the *Valley of Hinnôm* (*gé-Hinnôm, gehenne*) plays the principal rôle. As the Rabbis incline more or less to the popular beliefs, the descriptions are more or less material. The same holds good in the descriptions of future rewards. For instance, we have the peculiar belief that the flesh of the Leviathan, preserved in salt since the first days of creation, will be divided among the just, and that from its tanned hide tents will be made whose brilliancy will fill the universe. Such fantastic features, equally characteristic of the hell and the paradise of the middle ages, do not affect the elevated spirituality pervading these beliefs. Thus we have one Rabbi denying the very existence of hell. "There is no hell in the future world," says R. Simon ben Lakish. "But the Most Holy makes to shine His sun, whose splendor fills the righteous with happiness, and causes the wicked to suffer." Thus the soul finds reward or punishment within itself. The student recognizes, to use the expression of the schools, the subjective character of the sanction attached to the moral law.

Such are the teachings transmitted by the Haggada, and spread among the people by popular preaching. They were conveyed in a peculiar and rather original form well worthy of description. All of them were connected with the Bible, to which the Rabbis considered themselves obliged to trace the ideas they developed. It is the application to the Haggada of the method created by R. Akiba for the Halacha. The orator took a verse, which he commented on in a thousand ingenious ways, educing from it all sorts of moral lessons. It mattered little to him, if he did violence to the words, or abused a grammatical construction, or changed letters or words according to his caprice. Equally little it concerned his listeners, who, however, were not deceived, knowing as well as himself the fantastic character of his explanations. But nothing equals the ease with which they accepted them, for they craved only edification. Yet the preacher called to his aid allegory, parable, legend, which accompanied the commentary on the text, and sometimes even were confused with it. And as he had the powerful and facile imagination of the Oriental, he needed only the gift of fluent speech to charm an audience disposed to yield to his fascinations, convinced in advance, and happy to hear another give utterance to the feelings hidden in their hearts. The orator might be one of the doctors of the Halacha that addressed the congregations assembled in the synagogues on days of reunion, Sabbaths or holidays. In such cases true homilies were pronounced. But usually the speaker was any chance person that gathered a crowd about him on the street, and held it under the spell of his improvisations. Such were Judah, the son of Seripheus, and Matathias, the son of Margaloth, those victims of Herod of whom Josephus speaks, those beloved orators endowed with the gift of inspiring crowds and enkindling popular risings. "Who wishes to live, to live long?" cries an Aggadist in the open street. "Who wishes to buy happiness?" The original questions attract a crowd demanding to know the orator's secret. "Thou desirest to live many days," he answers, "thou wishest to enjoy peace and happiness? Keep thy tongue from evil, and thy lips from speaking guile. Seek peace, and pursue it. Depart from the evil, and do good." And paraphrasing these words of the Psalmist (Ps. xxxiv, 13–15), he develops his ideas in the midst of the attentive crowd.

What, in fact, was the importance of Aggadistic teaching? Assuredly it had considerable value. The study of the Halacha could have appealed only to a restricted part of the Jewish population. The schools and the academies doubtless were frequented by a large number of disciples, eager to listen to the instruction of the Rabbis. But they by no means constituted the kernel of the population, and what was there for the people outside of this popular preaching, these moral lessons given by men that spoke its simple language, and put themselves on a level with it? The Rabbis themselves, whose erudition raised the great monument of the Halacha, did not disdain to speak to the populace and, dropping all scientific apparel, array themselves in the simplicity of heart and the ingenuousness of the humble men they addressed. A number of names might be cited. One will suffice, that of Akiba, the first redactor of the Mishna, whom the admiration of his contemporaries placed by the side of Moses, and who, says the Talmud, was great in the Halacha and equally great in the Haggada. Nevertheless, it is easy to recognize two well-marked tendencies, two distinct movements, and at first sight it is evident that, though these two movements were sometimes parallel, they might sometimes contradict each other. Were all the Halachist doctors Aggadists? Obviously not. The Halacha and the Haggada demanded opposite gifts; they illustrate the natural opposition between science and poetry. Again, the Haggada was calculated to bring about by insensible degrees the predominance of inner religion over external forms and the depreciation of observances and ceremonies—an instinctive tendency bound to work its effect upon logical minds; a germ of dissidence apt to grow and lead to the separation of Halachists and Aggadists.

These inferences find full confirmation in the study of facts. We are fortunate to be able to shelter ourselves behind the authority of the learned author of the *Essay on the History of Palestine:* "The inhabitants of Galilee," says M. Derenbourg (p. 350), "in ill repute on account of their ignorance of legal affairs, seem to have replaced subtlety of mind by ardor of heart, and supplied lack of ability for brilliant tilts in scholastic discussions by excessive energy of feeling and tricks of expression, original rather than delicate. One always ends by attaching little value to what one is ignorant of, and has not been able to learn, especially if success comes in despite of ignorance, and seems to come precisely from a quarter despised by the informed and instructed. The merchant Hanania, who converted the young prince of Adiabene to Judaism, did not scruple to absolve him from the duty of circumcision, considering it binding only on the seed of Abraham. The Aggadists, indeed, learned from Isaiah and even Jeremiah a certain disdain for ceremonial observances, which naturally reacted on the Halachists occupied with hairsplitting casuistry on the subject of those very ceremonies. . . .

"Doubtless there were men who, though devoted to Rabbinic science, still occupied themselves with the instruction of the people at the synagogues in religious truths, which they sought to support with texts from the poetic portions of the Scriptures. But it is equally certain that others, by reason of temperament or inclination, gave themselves up to the one or the other development of Judaism exclusively. A glance at the Talmuds and the Midrashim suffices to reveal many names that figure in the *Halacha*, and are never met with in the *Agada*, as likewise Aggadists are found that are never mentioned in the Halachic discussions. To become an Aggadist only ardent conviction, lively imagination, and facility of invention were necessary—qualities not rare in times when oppression by aliens revives national zeal, and among a people that receives impressions rapidly, and promptly translates them into words. An Aggadist, then, could be produced without great difficulty, but long and serious study was necessary to penetrate to the depths of the Halacha. As the value of a thing is usually measured by the difficulties surmounted in its acquisition, the Halachists in their turn underrated the preachers or Aggadists, who, as said above, were not always charmed with the deductions of the Rabbis.

"The Talmuds have preserved numerous indications of the slight repute in which the Aggadists were held by the Rabbis. If, however, the passages relating to this subject contradict each other, and if a Rabbi who but now extolled preaching speaks of it scornfully, we must not be surprised; they are judgments rendered under the influence of an Agada recently heard, and are determined by the more or less respectful attitude assumed in it towards Rabbinic studies. Disdain for the Halacha has found a place particularly in Christian writings and in the school of St. Paul. We think that we do not err in maintaining that at its birth the Aggadists were the most powerful auxiliaries of Christianity."

The results of historic criticism, then, establish the justness of the deductions reached by psychologic observation. Human nature is too feeble to attain to a complete expansion of all its faculties; one of them at least is sacrificed to the cultivation of the others. Some pursue the ideal of the good, others that of the true, and only in rare instances is the perfection at once of knowledge and of goodness reached. Surely what is true of the individual is with greater force true of the crowd, in which tendencies realize and assert themselves more powerfully. Judaism is proof thereof, but not the only proof. Without going far afield, we find an illustration of a similar phenomenon in the Catholicism of the middle ages. It likewise offers the spectacle of these two opposite currents swaying the minds of men in the rivalry of its two monastic orders, the Benedictine and the Franciscan, the learned order and the mendicant order, which epitomize their duties, the one, in the pursuit of the true, the other, in the pursuit of the good, and which—to conclude with an expression of the Rabbis—might have said, the former, truth saves from death, the latter, charity saves from death.[1]

A number of Midrashim on the Prophets have been lost, or are still reposing on the shelves of various European libraries. In the twelfth century, a Rabbi, Simeon, conceived the idea of making a compilation of diverse Midrashim. This compilation, which bears the name *Yalkut Shimeoni*, or *Simeon's Collection*, has preserved a number of Midrashim that would otherwise not have reached us.

---

1. It may be useful to give here a list of the books composing the Haggada literature. This literature comprises only exegetic explanations or Scripture interpretations given in the synagogues or in popular homilies. The epithet *Midrash*, or *explanation*, was applied to them. The chief collections of Midrashim are the following:

    The great *Pesikta*, or *Pesikta Rabbathi*, of Palestinian origin, attributed to R. Cahana.

    The Midrash *Rabba*, Haggadistic commentary on the Pentateuch and the books of Esther, Ecclesiastes, Song of Songs, Ruth, and Lamentations.

    The Midrash *Yelamdenu* and the *Tanchuma* on the Pentateuch.

    The Midrash *Shokher Tob* on the Psalms and the Proverbs.

    The compilation of these Midrashim, most of them very ancient, cannot be traced back further than the sixth century.

PART SECOND: THE FORMATION OF THE TALMUD—THE SPIRIT OF ITS FORMATION

THE HALACHA ACCORDING TO THE SYNAGOGUE

I T is a cardinal principle of Judaism that, along with the code comprised in the Pentateuch, Moses received from God oh Mount Sinai an oral Law, which is the commentary developed from the written Law. Not a precept, not a decision, not a ceremonial injunction was left unaccompanied by oral explanations, which Moses was to transmit by word of mouth. These explanations, moreover, were of the same sacred character as the written Law. In its conciseness, the latter often is obscure; it is incomplete, for usually it proceeds by examples; sometimes even it consists of apparent contradictions, sometimes of seemingly useless repetitions. Examples abound: "At the mouth of two witnesses, or at the mouth of three witnesses shall the matter be established," it says in Deuteronomy XIX, 15. Is it two? Is it three? In Leviticus XXI, 12, the high priest is forbidden to go out of the sanctuary. Under what circumstances? Is he to be shut up in it all his life? Elsewhere it is said: "Thou shalt kill animals as I have commanded thee." Where is this command? A second passage relative to this ordinance would be sought in vain in the whole Pentateuch. The obligation to "lay Tephilin," one of the essential observances of Judaism, is barely indicated by a word. On the other hand, the following is found in three different places: "Thou shalt not seethe a kid in its mother's milk." Elsewhere historic facts in complete contradiction to the Law are told, although the men to whom they are attributed are charged with the duty of teaching the Law.

The pious king Hezekiah celebrates the Passover in the second month, although Moses fixes it on the fifteenth day of the first month. The prophet Elijah offers a sacrifice on Carmel, in spite of the law in Deuteronomy forbidding sacrifices outside of the Temple. Finally, in another sphere of ideas, a striking feature of the Books of Moses is their unbroken silence concerning primary dogmas of the Jewish religion, the dogmas of the immortality of the soul and the future life. These are not the only examples. A considerable number of similar facts, of obscure laws that cannot do without explanation, of important omissions, and of apparent contradictions, might be collated. It is evident, then, that the written Law stands in need of a perpetual commentary. This is the commentary received by Moses on Mount Sinai. Thence its name: *The Law of Moses from Sinai* (*Halacha le-Moshé mis-Sinaï* = *lex ad Mosem e Sinaï*). This Law descended orally from generation to generation. "Moses," says the Mishna, "received the (traditional) Law on Sinai, and transmitted it to Joshua; Joshua transmitted it to the Elders; the Elders transmitted it to the Prophets, and the Prophets to the Men of the Great Assembly." The Great Assembly, to which the last three prophets, Haggaï, Zechariah, and Malachi, belonged, finally transmit the oral Law to the teachers that succeed each other from the coming of the Seleucidæ into Syria to the second century of the Christian era.

The oral Law was never to be entrusted to writing, but was to remain in the memory of men and form a living tradition. But when the misfortunes that began to break in upon the people in the days of the last Maccabees imperilled the preservation of the sacred pledge; when Titus had destroyed the Temple, and Hadrian had scattered the Jewish people, and proscribed the study of the Law, it was feared that the chain of tradition might be ruptured, and the oral Law disappear in the cataclysm that swept away Jewish nationality. For the sake of the welfare of Judaism, R. Judah the Holy decided to violate the prohibition and reduce the oral Law to writing. This was the origin of the *Mishna*.

The synagogue declares that from the Sinaitic revelation until the rebuilding of the Temple, after the return from the Captivity, even until within a short time before the Christian era, the oral Law maintained itself intact, without uncertainty or obscurity. After the return, the novel conditions surrounding the nation brought up new problems for which tradition offered no solution. What were the Rabbis to do? Obviously classify them by means of certain ratiocinative processes under cases provided for by tradition. These exegetic processes themselves are taught by tradition. God had foreseen that a day would come when certain religious prescriptions would sink into oblivion, when new questions would obtrude themselves, and He gave unto Moses a hermeneutic system, by virtue of which the decisions of the oral Law might be rediscovered in the written Law, all the teachings of tradition might be brought into connection with the text, and general principles confidently applied to new details and unforeseen cases. The only thing to be done, therefore, was to make the points under discussion submit to these hermeneutic processes. But differences of opinion might thus arise. For, though the applicability of certain principles might be so obvious as to force immediate and unanimous assent, sometimes there might, on the other hand, be reason for hesitation and discussion. In these cases a vote was decisive, likewise in accordance with a principle established by the Scriptures, that, to employ the biblical expression, the multitude ought to be followed. A majority makes the law. The following account from the Mishna is a curious illustration. "Akabia ben Mahalalel maintained four propositions. The Rabbis said to him: Abandon them, and we shall give you the title of the chief of the Great Council. He replied: I prefer to be considered a fool all the days of my life to appearing infamous for a single instant before God by surrendering my convictions in exchange for honors . . . Nevertheless, at the point of death, he said to his son: Abandon the four propositions that I have taught thee.—And why didst thou pot yield?—*Because I had received them from teachers as numerous as those who had taught my adversaries the opposite opinions, and I supported what I had learnt as firmly as they maintained their traditions. But as for you, you have learned the four decisions only from me, and an individual's opinions ought to give way before those of a number.*—To this principle add the other that numbers being equal, the opinions of the older teachers prevail over those of the more recent ones. And that is just. For truth is subject to change as the distance from its origin across the ages lengthens; and though divergence of opinions began to manifest itself only very late, and Hillel and Shammaï, at the beginning of the Christian era, were at variance on only three points, yet in the space of three centuries differences multiplied so extensively as to produce the vast "sea of the Talmud." It is natural, then, that an opinion which has come down to us through few intermediaries should have more weight than one that has passed through many mouths. An *Amora*, or teacher of the Law posterior to the compilation of the Mishna, cannot prevail against a *Tana*, or teacher of the Mishna, no more than a *Tana* can enforce an opinion opposed by the *Dibré Sopherim*, the words of the Scribes.

With these principles regulating the discussion, the development was most simple; nothing was left to arbitrary chance. Discussion reduced itself to a deductive process. New laws were sacred by the same warrant as the revealed laws, since the latter enjoined the former by implication. The work of the Rabbis consisted simply in educing them, and we arrive at the explanation of the Talmudic sentence: "The Scriptures, Tradition, the decisions of the Rabbis, and all that a reverent disciple of the Law may teach, were given to Moses on Sinai."

Such is this theory of tradition, a theory remarkable for simplicity and consistency, and based upon a profoundly true view. Even if criticism cannot throw brilliant light upon the history of tradition in its primitive stages, it cannot fail to confirm the correctness of the view, that the development of the Halacha was logical and necessary, as we propose to demonstrate in the following pages.

HISTORY OF THE EORMATION OF THE HALACHA

ONE of the most curious problems in the history of religions assuredly is that presented by the state of the Jews on their return from the Captivity. Up to the last moments of the monarchy, the minds of the people are controlled by one of two religious currents. On the one side is popular superstition, the grossly sensual idolatry borrowed from Phenicia, against which the Jeremiahs and the Ezekiels thundered, often in vain. On the other side is the elevated, austere spirituality of the Prophets, who seek to lead back the multitude to the feet of Jehovah's altars, and energetically struggle against the depraving tendencies of paganism. On the return from the Exile, two changes have taken place. The whole people has rallied about the religious chiefs, and the latter are no longer Prophets, but Scribes. Thenceforth the streets of Jerusalem do not resound with the eloquent invectives of the *Nebiim*. Instead, the explanations and the commentaries of the *Sopherim* fill the schools and the synagogues. We no longer have dealings with an inconstant people hesitating between Baal and Jehovah, but with a nation that has made its choice, and enthusiastically accepts and develops a cult, that is, a well co-ordinated system of beliefs, laws, and practices. Its literature suits itself to this transformation. No longer the rich and vigorous efflorescence to which we owe such masterpieces as the Psalms, Isaiah, Job, it has become severe, dogmatic, scholastic instruction, which after eight laborious centuries will result in the Talmud. In a word, Hebraism is at an end, Judaism is born. What are the causes of the transformation? What series of circumstances could have effected it in so limited a period as the Captivity? Dark questions, the answers to which may be guessed at, but the elements of an unimpeachable solution are lacking. This is not the place to examine and discuss the problem; the statement of the change must suffice.

A new era begins for Israel. The whole nation crowds about the *Sopherim* to hear the explanation of the Law. It is learnt by heart, it is commented upon. Schools of Rabbis spring up, which charge themselves with the duty of teaching and explaining the sacred word. The Bible, the Book, especially the Pentateuch, *Mikra*, that is, *Reading*,—this is the only mental nourishment indulged in by the people. It is the aim of all science, and it is science itself. For all things flow from the Bible, as all converge towards it. The admonition addressed to Joshua, "Thou shalt meditate therein day and night," has become a reality. In a word, it is the axis on which turns the whole activity of the Jewish mind.

Thus originates and grows the study of the Law, which is called to play so considerable a rôle, and whence springs the body of traditional laws that will constitute the Talmud.

How do these traditional laws originate? Unless we accept the theory of their Sinaitic origin, affirmed, but not demonstrated, by the Synagogue, the historic documents fail to make direct answer to this question. The first traces of these traditions are met with late, in the Septuagint, in the Books of the Maccabees, in the Book of Daniel, contemporary with the Maccabees; but they suffice to put it beyond a doubt that as early as the time of Antiochus Epiphanes a number of decisions were definitely established; that even then the ceremonies connected with the cult and not indicated in the Pentateuch were regulated; in a word, that a rather extensive system of observances and laws existed. Doubtless it was during the long period of more than 250 years from Ezra to the Maccabean rebellion that this system grew up, and imposed itself upon the Jewish nation. Josephus passes over this religious development with profound silence; but it is well known that for this historian, more or less scrupulous concerning facts, the history of beliefs, ideas, and religious institutions was almost as though non-existent. However, it is beyond question that the Men of the Great Synagogue developed the Mosaic prescriptions, and especially by their personal authority raised "a hedge" about the Law. It is not possible to trace the traditional system further back with any degree of certainty. The critical study of several Mishnic traditions beginning with Hasmonean times enables us to follow the development of Jewish legislation, at once religious and civil. The searching investigation of juridic points led to its gradual extension. In the civil law the extension presents no peculiar features, its only object being the protection of the interests of the individual and the promotion of the intercourse and the transactions of the citizens with each other. But with the religious law the case was different. Eminently restrictive in character, it was developed to the point of burdening daily life with numerous observances. Its decisions multiplied indefinitely, and each became the fountainhead for others. Some, laid down as principles, were to bring forth, when fecundated by ratiocination, a close-linked chain of endless prescriptions embracing every moment of human life. To be clear, let us take examples.

A Pentateuch verse says: "Thou shalt not seethe a kid in its mother's milk." An old tradition, first expressed in the Septuagint, explains this verse by the prohibition to cook meat with milk food. This prohibition, universally recognized, the Rabbis take as their point of departure. They deduce therefrom a group of special laws, which, in-turn, will prove no less fruitful. For instance, it will give rise to the prohibition of eating meat with milk food, of eating milk food immediately after meat, of using the same vessel for meat and milk, and many others. And the logical deductions will go on to the bitter end, nor shrink from the consideration of the minutest details connected with the kitchen.—In the Pentateuch we read: "Thou shalt not eat flesh that is torn of beasts in the field." From this prohibition an entire code will be developed. In fact, what matters it whether it was torn in the city or in the field, so long as it is the carrion of an animal killed by a wild beast or dead of a disease? The purpose evidently is to forbid eating the flesh of a sick or unhealthy animal. But when is an animal *sick* or *unhealthy?* Thence so and so many new laws to determine all the cases falling under the interdiction. Again, the prohibition of working on the Sabbath. What is meant by the word *work?* Some more new laws to demonstrate what is forbidden and up to what limits.—Nor is this all. To these laws, logically and unavoidably deduced from more general, long recognized laws, must be added ordinances of recent institution. One Rabbi maintains somewhere in the Talmud that certain ones of these ordinances were later considered traditional, Sinaitic laws. Besides, there are measures and decrees (Tekanoth, Gezeroth) passed by the Synhedrin at the dictate and under the stress of circumstances, which, from the moment of their promulgation, had the authority of religious laws. Thus is woven an intricate web of prescriptions, ceaselessly reproducing others of their kind, which, enthusiastically accepted by a people enamored of its religious system, are at once consecrated by usage. Such is the work to which the schools devote themselves, especially in the century preceding and in that following the destruction of the second Temple. By that time the multiplicity of laws was so great that the links connecting a particular law with the primitive law, biblical or traditional, from which it was derived, could be grasped only with difficulty. Recourse was therefore had to artificial methods for the purpose of establishing a direct connection between the Pentateuch text on the one hand, and the early traditional laws, the deduced laws of whatsoever derivation, and the laws of recent institution, on the other. There were first Hillel's seven rules of interpretation, from which R. Ishmael evolved thirteen. Then came the curious, bold method that Akiba has the distinction of having applied and developed with undaunted consistency. It is based on the principle that in the Scriptures nothing is superfluous, neither phrase, nor word, nor particle, nor letter; that down to the most insignificant detail everything has peculiar value, and that besides the obvious meaning of the text the intelligent mind ought to discover a thousand hidden meanings, a thousand occult hints. Such and such a word, contrary to usage, is written with a *waw;* in another the *waw* is lacking apparently without reason; here the word *and* is redundant, there the conjunction is suppressed—all indications of half-revealed things, of laws, if the verse has a legal bearing, of facts, if the verse is of another character. The book of Genesis, for example, opens with the words: "In the beginning God created heaven and earth." The word "heaven" in Hebrew is preceded by the particle *eth*, usually the sign of the accusative, but sometimes also meaning *with*. That particle must have some meaning, says Akiba, and he explains the verse in the following manner: "God created *with* (the celestial hosts, that is, the stars) heaven and earth." This method, which in principle was recognized by the Fathers of the Church, St. Basil, St. Jerome, St. Chrysostom, was applied to all the religious prescriptions established by the Rabbis. Thenceforth the ordinances of the Rabbis and the practices sanctified by time, but lacking a sure foundation, were clothed with a sacred character, and animated with new life, by contact with the Holy Scriptures. The importance of the method is patent. In modern society the law preserves its character for majesty in the eyes of the people. Yet it is considered a human work, subject to error, capable of modification or amelioration according to changing needs. It is respected, because it has been freely assented to by all, and the people honor in it the wish and work of all. In a society pre-eminently religious, like that of the Jews, the same feeling cannot prevail. A number of Rabbinic prescriptions could doubtless have been shown to originate in ancient and venerable traditions, but many were of recent institution. How could they be urged upon the people and made to influence their manners, if they were not clothed with a sacred character, and in whatsoever way possible justified by the very letter of the Scriptures? This method, likewise, by providing the shelter of the Law, opened the way to the modifications and the useful reforms made necessary by circumstances. Thus Judaism accommodated itself to the constantly shifting needs of a society constantly in a state of upheaval, and, consecrating the aspirations of each new generation, it could develop and progress boldly on the path of reforms. This method secured the religion against the inert worship of the word and the letter, snatched it away from stagnation, and, by the flux and movement it produced, vivified and fortified faith. Thus it sanctioned at once tradition, which thenceforth was fixed, and future innovations that might crop up. Did the people understand immediately the immense import of the procedure? We do not know, but certainly they conceived profound admiration for the man able to educe "bushels of decisions from every stroke of a letter." Arbitrary as the method may seem to us, the favor it met with may be explained by the ardent desire of the people, pointed out above, to find everything in the Holy Scriptures. They are looked upon by the people as the source of all knowledge. The Rabbis invent nothing; they merely rediscover in the Sacred Writings the laws that they establish. Far from setting out on the search for the unknown, they repeat tradition. They are the *Tanaïm*, "the repeaters," and the work taught by them in the schools is the *Mishna*, that is, "the repetition." The aspirations of the crowd, then, are satisfied by this method, which, moreover, appeals to its admirers by its boldness and ingenuity; hence its triumph.

However, the work of the teachers was not approved by the entire nation. One class of society was outspoken in its opposition to the doctrines and the instruction of the Pharisees. The aristocracy, the rich priestly families, saw with displeasure the growth of an inconvenient legislative system, which compelled them to a life of austerities and sacrifices far from charming to their taste. The party of the *Sadducees* can be traced back to the establishment of the sacerdotal royalty of the Hasmoneans, to the day on which an aristocracy began to form about the reigning family. The Sadducees admitted all the religious traditions that time had consecrated up to their day. But they were opposed to the development of traditional legislation, and as Akiba's method was its most powerful instrument, they combated it with all their ability. Though living up to traditions that could not be explained by the Pentateuch, they insisted that they abided only by the pure and simple meaning of the text; they followed, or at least pretended to follow, scrupulously the letter of the Law, and observed its explicit injunctions, refusing to modify them by the ordinances of recent institution. They had no schools whose disciples might have been recruited from among the people. But the priests formed a college, and among themselves they propagated their traditions, which, however, were rejected by the people. During the great upheaval that terminated in the catastrophe of the year 70, the Sadducees, who were sincere Jews, and repudiated only the exaggerations of the Pharisaic system, fused with the people, and all dissension was forgotten in the face of the common danger. But after the destruction of the Temple, when the Rabbis established their schools at Jabne, in the north of Palestine, the priests, whose services had become superfluous, exiled themselves to the *Darôma*, or the South, and there established rival schools, in which they taught the sacerdotal tradition. While Akiba's numerous disciples developed the word of the master, R. Ishmael ben Elisha, high priest, taught in the Darôma. Rigorously confining to its narrowest limits the system of interpretation adopted by Akiba, he explained the Pentateuch according to its simplest sense. He thrust out of the Books of Moses the lessons that the school of the north made dominant, and preserved the variants that ancient priestly tradition had sanctified. We owe to him commentaries on all the Books of the Pentateuch except Genesis. They are the *Mechilta* (*measure*), commentary on Exodus; *Sifra* (*book*), commentary on Leviticus, also called *Torath Cohanim*, or *Law of the Priests*, on account of the numerous Levitical prescriptions which form the object of the third Book of Moses; finally, *Sifré* (*books*), the commentaries on Numbers and Deuteronomy. These are the only works bequeathed by the school of Darôma. The school, in fact, soon vanished into darkness, being each day more and more obscured by the brilliant light irradiating from its northern rival. The mentioned works, moreover, were preserved only because the Pharisaic schools adopted them after having modified them by touches changing their character. However, the alterations were not so radical but that under the Pharisaic layer traces remained of the Sadducean, or at least sacerdotal, method. Thanks to these vestiges, the historic science of our day has succeeded in rediscovering the spirit of the original work by a circumstantial study of the language, of the Halachoth, and the Pentateuch injunctions involved in them. By re-establishing the text three-fourths effaced, a species of palimpsest, it not only restored the work of Ishmael ben Elisha's school, but demonstrated the permanence of Sadducean instruction.

Akiba, however, had not yet finished his work. To have connected all the traditional and recently instituted laws with the Pentateuch was not sufficient. It was necessary to co-ordinate and unite them into a sort of code. In fact, in the schools the commentaries and the instruction of the Rabbis had at first followed the text of the Law, and the order of its chapters and verses determined the order of the Halachoth. But when the Halachoth, by the successive labors of the schools, had multiplied extensively, it became impossible to teach them in that order. Each verse was accompanied by a commentary of infinite length; the text disappeared, buried under the notes. A classification thus became necessary, and this again was Akiba's work. His master mind succeeded in putting order into the vast chaos of decisions. But he could do no more than trace the outlines. The Roman hangman prevented him from finishing the work, which his school continued, and a disciple of his followers, R. Judah the Holy, of the illustrious family of Hillel, had the glory of making the final compilation of the Mishna and attaching his name thereto.

It was an important achievement, this codification of the oral law, and one big with results. Once taught from the written word in the Mishna, Tradition received its final consecration. It ceased to be tradition to become a new Law—a Law completer, preciser, and clearer than the ancient Law, which found itself relegated to the background. "It is better to be occupied with the Mishna than with the Law," said the Rabbis; "the Law may be compared to water, but the Mishna is wine." Why, in fact, should one lose time in puzzling over the original text, when complete explanation is within reach of all, when the Mishna contains both text and commentary? So tradition, from being a commentary on the Law, itself becomes a second law, a Deuterosis, to use the expression of the Fathers of the Church, and takes the place of the first. Thereafter, the work of the schools, thought to be at an end, will be resumed. The long labor expended on the Pentateuch and terminating in the Mishna will be applied to the Mishna to produce finally the Gemara. The text of the Mishna will be taken up again and discussed. Every Rabbinic opinion, whether anonymous, that is, admitted by all, or cited with its author's name, that is, with every possible reservation, will be argued, debated, developed, explained. Obscure points will be illuminated, and so again new decisions will be arrived at. And after three centuries of discussion, the Gemara will be finished, and the Talmud closed. Thus a new era begins with the compilation of the Mishna. But a new era must have a new name. The doctors of the Mishna had been *Tanaïm, repeaters;* the teachers of the epoch upon which we are about to enter are called *Amoraïm, discoursers* —two well chosen names, in each case characterizing exactly the nature of the instruction. For if, on the one hand, the Tanaïm only taught tradition, only reproduced and repeated decisions received from ancient times to transmit them to disciples, then, on the other hand, this tradition once fixed, there remained nothing more than to discuss the Law and to discourse.

This work of the teachers of the Gemara does not withdraw itself wholly from foreign influences. While they are building up the code on the solid basis of the Mishna, a neighboring nation, whose formidable power they know only too well, is engaged about a similar task, and with incomparable force and marvellous genius raises the monumental *Corpus Juris civilis*, on which will be propped the legal systems of Europe. How was it possible for the Rabbis to escape the influence that Roman legislation, whose rigor and formalism they should have been the first to admire, could exercise upon them? In point of fact, the civil law of the Talmud is impregnated in almost all its parts with the spirit of the Roman system. Even formulas and expressions borrowed from Rome can be found in it. Certain departments of legislation, such as the laws on slavery and prescription, for which the Pentateuch furnishes not a hint, or sketches barely the shadow of a theory, are almost entirely inspired by Roman legislation. But all they borrow takes on modifications under the manipulation of the Rabbis. The Jewish mind transformed the alien elements by impressing upon them its peculiar character. And from this vast crucible, in which three centuries had melted down the materials of diverse origin gathered by the schools, was to emerge the essentially uniform and homogeneous work of Talmudic legislation.

INFLUENCE OF EVENTS ON THE DEVELOPMENT OF THE HALACHA

IN the preceding pages, we studied only the internal development of the Halacha. It is now time to consider whether external circumstances exercised influence upon this development; whether and up to what point they trammelled or favored it.

Although its first traces are found only in the Maccabean epoch, it is well known that the work of the Jewish schools resulting in the Talmud began on the return from the Captivity. From that period until the time of the final redaction of the Talmud, four great events mark the history of Judea: the persecutions of Antiochus Epiphanes, followed by the re-establishment of the kingdom by the Hasmoneans; the birth of Christianity; the destruction of the Temple, and the last revolt of the Jews under Hadrian. We shall examine the influence upon the formation of the Halacha attributable to each of these events.

In the long and tranquil years of the Persian domination, Judaism, under the direction of the Men of the Great Synagogue, could grow unshackled, and instruction, little by little penetrating the mass of the people, formed the national mind. The persecutions of Antiochus, therefore, were nothing more than a passing storm, which, we may well believe, effected a revival and strengthening of religious feeling. We say, we may well believe, for we possess no documents to acquaint us with the precise nature of their influence. The triumph of the

Maccabees again insured a certain tranquillity for the Jews, thanks to which the Rabbis, as under the Persian domination, could calmly prosecute their long continuing work. But Rome enters upon the scene. Pompey takes possession of Jerusalem, and desecrates the Sanctuary. Soon Judea falls under the iron yoke of the procurators, whose odious tyranny leads to the terrible insurrection of the year 65. The history of the heroic, superhuman struggle ending with the burning of the Temple and the annihilation of the Jewish state, is well known. It would seem that a revolution like this ought to react powerfully upon religious conditions. The results, however, do not correspond to the greatness of the catastrophe; for the influence was material rather than moral. With the destruction of the Temple disappeared a part of the cult and a whole set of ceremonies. All connected with the sacrifices was abrogated by the force of circumstances. But the rest of the cult remained intact, no cause, moreover, presenting itself to modify its spirit. The fact is that, though the Jewish nationality was crushed, the religion was not persecuted. The political mold shattered, the religious mold remained perfect, and preserved the hope of the re-establishment of national independence. This is what Vespasian did not understand, and in permitting R. Jochanan ben Zakkar to transport his school to Jabne, he did not realize that he was allowing a fire to be kindled on a new hearth of insurrection. Sixty years after the fall of Jerusalem, in fact, the grandsons of those who saw the ruin of the "Holy House," rise at the call of Akiba, rush to arms, chase the Romans out of Palestine, reconquer their land, summon all their brethren of the Empire, and for an instant re-erect the kingdom of their ancestors. It is a grave moment, for this struggle is to decide, not only upon Israel's fate, but also upon that of the new sect that Israel has permitted to go forth from his midst. The Christianity of about the year 70 had not acquired sufficient power to feel the consequences of the catastrophe. A little sect without influence, it found protection in its own feebleness. But from that time until Hadrian, it grew and extended itself, and the germs of dissidence present from its birth in the antagonism of Peter and Paul developed. The Church was divided into two chief sects: the Judeo-Christians, disciples of Peter, and the adepts of Paul. The Judeo-Christians still count themselves as Jews, and accept all the religious teachings of the Rabbis, adding only the article of faith that the

Messiah had come in the person of Jesus. Paul and his disciples reject all the ceremonies, all the traditional laws, more than that, even the Law of Moses, and profess a new doctrine, whence Catholicism was later to issue. This is the situation when Bar Coziba, the Son of the Star, the new Messiah whom Akiba salutes, stirs up the Jews in revolt against Tinnius Rufus. The Judeo-Christians, mindful of the Master's word, "My kingdom is not of this world," refuse to fight at the side of the Jews. Coziba, by threats of punishment, forces them to take up arms. But when Severus triumphs, and Bethar falls into the power of the Romans, the most terrible vengeance strikes all who bear the name Jew. Hadrian does not fall into Vespasian's error: he perceives that the Jews are to be feared so long as anything recalls the memory of their nationality, and religious ceremonials are proscribed on pain of death. "Why art thou condemned to death?" says a Talmudic text. "Because I observed the law of circumcision.—Why art thou led away to punishment?—Because I was faithful to the Sabbath.—Why art thou scourged?—Because I obeyed the injunction of the *Lulab*." In the face of these consequences, the Judeo-Christians break the last bond uniting them with the Jews, and throw themselves into the arms of the Paulinians. The Church, which preaches the abolition of ceremonies, sees her triumph assured.

But if the result of this war is to precipitate the Church along the road upon which she has just entered so resolutely, it ought to have the opposite influence on Judaism, plunging it deeper into Pharisaism. And that for two reasons. The first, producing an effect only during a limited period, is the religious persecution which Hadrian himself enforces against the Jews. For, the more the ceremonies are persecuted, and the more the people feels its lot bound up with them, the greater grows their importance in the eyes of the believer, the more do they tend to become absolute. Then, when the persecutions abated, and the people began to breathe more freely, it was necessary to institute a separation from the Church, which gained territory day after day. The differences dividing the two religions had to be marked more clearly. And the more unreservedly growing Christianity opened its ample bosom to the pagan nations, the more Judaism inclined to retreat, jealously withdrawing into itself and multiplying its practices and observances from day to day, from hour to hour. The abyss parting it from the Christians and the pagans deepened. It remained isolated in the midst of hostile nations, and this isolation constituted its strength. Thus became possible the strange phenomenon, unique in history, I believe, of a people dispersed to the four corners of the earth, yet one, of a nation without a land, yet living. The miracle was accomplished by a book, the Talmud. The Talmud was the ensign which served as a rallying point for the dispersed of Israel. The thousand austere and minute practices that it enjoins were so many strong bonds attaching one to the other. Thus, by a curious series of actions and reactions, the religious movement that gave birth to the Mishna brought about the national uprising under Hadrian. Through its influence on Christianity, this rebellion reacted indirectly on the religious movement that produced the Talmud. And the Talmud, in turn, maintained the unity of the people, conquered and crushed, yet none the less living and resisting.

SPIRIT OF THE HALACHIC DEVELOPMENT

LET us now cast a glance backwards, and take a bird's-eye view of this effective development of Pharisaic formalism. We are at once struck by its system of observances having relation to every moment of life. The believer finds himself enmeshed in a net-work of prescriptions, which close in upon him on all sides, and reduce him to never-ending slavery—slavery accepted freely and with joy, for this sacred, a thousand times blessed yoke is the condition of happiness. Chained down by the many links that his religion has forged into a system around him, he has only to follow without fatigue or effort the divine commandments. He has no need for long reflection upon his duties and for much reasoning on the rules of conduct, absolved as he is by religion, which has done all this work for him. Each day, each hour, is unalterably arranged by regulations from on high. In the morning, prayers and thanksgivings; at noon, prayers and thanksgivings; in the evening, prayers and thanksgivings; benedictions before the meal; after the meal, benedictions. At sight of the imposing phenomena of nature, of a storm, the sea, the first spring blossoms, thanksgivings. Thanksgivings for a new enjoyment, for unexpected good fortune, on eating new fruits, at the announcement of a happy event. Prayers of resignation at the news of a misfortune. At the tomb of a beloved being, set prayers; words all prepared to console the sorrowstricken, who have just been overtaken by affliction. Every emotion and every feeling, the most fugitive as well as the most profound, are foreseen, noted, and embodied in a formula of prayer or of benediction. In the most solemn moments of life as in the most vulgar, when the soul forgets itself and allows itself to drop into the prose of daily routine, or when, crushed under the load of lively emotions, it gives way, yielding to its powerlessness, the believer finds himself in the presence of a commandment, of a *Mitzwa* to be accomplished, recalling him to heavenly things, sanctifying the present hour, and keeping him in perpetual communication with the divine. If he wishes to breathe forth his feelings and give them definite shape, he finds ready-made formulas at hand, which he has but to repeat with fervor in order to pour out his soul before God. The Israelite, then, has no need of painful efforts in seeking the road to salvation. It is wide open to him, thanks to his religion, that tender, provident mother who convoys him to happiness, provided he obeys the divine prescriptions, and with docility goes whither God leads him. Such is the system the rearing of which the Talmud has pursued with the force of bold logic. Curiously enough, nowhere can the precisely formulated expression of this system be found. Moreover, it is well known that the Synagogue has never summoned a Council to decree a dogma and impose it upon the faith of the nation. But whether a precise formula embodying their system was present in the minds of the Rabbis, or whether they unconsciously followed it out, it may none the less be abstracted in all its clearness from the very spirit of Halachic development: namely, impotence of human reason to direct itself in the search for truth, and the duty imposed upon religion to teach it truth.

In fact, is not this the system of all religions? Do they not one and all recognize the powerlessness of human reason to arrive at truth without assistance from above? Are they not all sent down from heaven to lead man to salvation? Judaism, then, has followed out a natural evolution, and perhaps this is the point of view to be assumed in explaining its derivation from Hebraism. Every religion is at first based upon ideal principles, principles of justice and charity, which for some time, in a vague and indeterminate form, satisfy certain ardent, religious spirits. But it cannot long persist in this indeterminate form; it clothes itself with a body, becomes a dogma, and is transformed from moral instruction, which it first was, into a positive religion. Then, if it is logical, it condemns itself to pursue the course boldly taken by Pharisaism. That is what we are taught by the theoretic conception of the religious idea, and that is what is proved by history. History tells us that every religion rests upon formalism. It tells us that Mahometanism, like Judaism, has arrived at a cult burdened with ceremonies. It shows us in Italic polytheism an infinite multiplicity of divinities directing the conduct of men. It shows us the Roman peasant trembling before the *four thousand* gods that presided over every act and moment of life and Lucretius delivering men from the *chains* of religion. It tells us that the Brahmins arrive at scholasticism comparable with the Talmud; that the doctrine of St. Paul itself, the doctrine founded on the rejection of every external observance, later gives birth to the *Summa Theologiæ* of St. Thomas Aquinas and to the system of ceremonies from which Protestantism was a reaction. It tells us, finally, that, if Protestantism alone has hitherto escaped this law, it is because it is a compromise between religion and philosophy, and that logic condemns it to end up either in formalism or in deism. Judaism, then, could not but pursue this course, and urged by the logic of things, which was favored by an array of circumstances destructive of the political existence of the nation, beneficent for its religious work, it pursued it to the end. Accordingly, the Talmud is the completest expression of a religious movement, and this code of endless prescriptions and minute ceremonials represents in its perfection the total work of the religious idea. In our eyes, this is its greatest title to the respect and the consideration of thinkers; this is its greatest merit. Certainly, Judaism may be regarded as austere and arid. It has not the splendor and brilliant exuberance of Greek or Hindoo polytheism. We are far removed from the superabundant, vigorous poetry pervading the dazzling efflorescence of Aryan mythologies. Herein lies the great advantage of polytheism and pantheism over monotheism. But we are now not considering religions from the point of view of art; we are investigating only their dogmatic development, in so far as it can be abstracted and extricated from the rest of human faculties. Taken in this way, that of Judaism has been most logical, since without hesitation it has proceeded to extreme consequences. If these consequences incur condemnation, then the system as a whole must be condemned, for the starting point is wrong. If the starting point is accepted, it is necessary to go to the bitter end, and endorse all the consequences. At all events, the Talmud has done so, and thanks to it we have in Judaism the completest, and consequently the most perfect, expression of the religous idea.

THE TALMUD IN THE MIDDLE AGES AND MODERN TIMES

CONCLUSION

WE have arrived at the end of our task. Endeavoring to apply the critical method to the investigation of the Talmud, we have demanded from an analytic study information on the elements composing it, and from an historic study the supreme law or idea governing its formation. Before we close this article, it may be proper to cast a glance at the fortunes of the book in the middle ages and in modern times and to indicate cursorily what science may still demand of it for the general history of humanity.

When, a century after the compilation of the Palestinian Gemara, the Babylonian Talmud, in its turn, received its final shape, it was universally adopted in the Jewish schools, and the chiefs of the Academies, the *Saboraim* (*opinion givers*, from the sixth to the eighth century), declaring the text fixed, decided that no more modifications could be introduced into it. Despite the persecutions of Jezdegerd II, Firuz, and Kobad, who closed the schools in Persia for a period of sixty-three years, and interrupted the teaching of the tradition, the Talmud became a classic to be studied and commented. The Saborarm occupied themselves more especially with grammar, fixing the system of vowel points for the Bible, while the *Geonim* (*excellencies*, from the eighth to the ninth century), along with lexicographic work, devoted themselves especially to the study of the Talmud. Under their influence, this book formed the basis of instruction, and became for the schools what the Mishna had been for the Amorarm. To that epoch belongs the redaction of the *Great Decisions* (*Halachoth Gedoloth*), a work in which the principal decisions of the Talmud are classified in the order of the 613 commandments of the Pentateuch to which they had been attached. With the conquests of the Arabs, Jewish studies spread over Africa and Spain. A little later the movement takes possession of the Provence and of Italy, then of the regions to the north of the Loire as far as the German provinces on the Rhine. On all sides schools are opened, and remarkable works of various kinds published. R. Hananel undertakes an abridgment of the Halachic parts of the Talmud, which inspires, and in turn is displaced by, the similar work of R. Isaac of Fez (1013–1103). At the same time appears the complete Commentary by R. Solomon Isaaci, called Rashi, of Troyes in the Champagne, a masterpiece of brevity, precision, and clearness. In the following century, Maimonides, "the eagle of the Synagogue," publishes his Arabic commentary on the Mishna and the masterly work called *Mishne Torah*, "the second law," in which, embracing the whole domain of the Halacha, he seeks to systematize the vast mass of decisions. In France, Rashi created a school. With him directly is connected the galaxy of French Rabbis in the twelfth and thirteenth centuries, to whom the world owes the Talmudic glosses called *Tosaphoth*, or *Additions*. It is this work of the Tosaphists together with Rashi's commentary, become a classic, that frames the text of the Mishna and the Gemara in all the editions. From France the movement spreads to north-western Germany, which in the thirteenth and the fourteenth century furnishes its contingent of commentaries and supercommentaries. These diverse works bear the same character. In all, the various decisions reached by the Gemara in the different cases discussed are compared; one is sought to be explained by the other, the import and extent of each are determined, and in all, the order or rather the disorder of the Gemara, somewhat palliated, is followed. With the exception of Maimonides, no one thought of introducing the light of method into this vast chaos and of classifying all the Halachoth logically. The German, Jacob ben Asher, in the fourteenth century, taking the *Mishne Torah* as his model, undertakes a methodic piece of work. For a century the attempt remains without imitation; the fifteenth century produces nothing for the Halacha. But in the sixteenth century appears the Polish school, whose works, though not characterized by the breadth of conception that distinguishes Maimonides' *Mishne Torah*, are remarkable for penetration and depth, perhaps lacking in that book. This school has for its aim the completion of R. Jacob ben Asher's work, and in 1567 Joseph Karo publishes his *Shulhan Arukh* (*the prepared table*), in which all the religious and civil laws of the Jews, article by article, are classified according to subjects. The codification of the Halacha is thereby completed, but not the work of the commentators, which continues upon the text of the Code during the eighteenth century, and in our day is not at an end in Bohemia, in Hungary, and in all the sections of the world where the Jews have most faithfully preserved the customs and usages of past times.

While Judaism in the whole of Europe is employing all its intelligence and all its activity in the completion of its great Talmud work, what is the fortune of the book among Christians? The Jews were persecuted; the work that was the soul of the unfortunate nation was not to be spared. "It has been proscribed, and imprisoned, and burnt, a hundred times over," says the author of the *Quarterly Review* article. "From Justinian, who, as early as 553 A.D., honored it by a special interdictory Novella (Novella 146), down to Clement VIII and later—a space of over a thousand years—both the secular and the spiritual powers, kings and emperors, popes and anti-popes, vied with each other in hurling anathemas and bulls and edicts of wholesale confiscation and conflagration against this luckless book." In 1239, Gregory IX has it burnt in France and in Italy; in 1264, Clement IV renews the prohibition, and condemns to the stake those who harbor manuscripts of it. Two centuries later the interdict is not yet removed, and it took from 1484 to 1519, that is, thirty-six years, to print twenty-three treatises—the publication was secret. In 1520, Leo X abrogates the decree. But in 1553, at the instigation of the apostate Jew, Solomon Romano, Julius III again imposes the interdict, and has the Talmud burnt at Rome and at Venice. Paul IV, incited by Vittorio Eliano, the worthy brother of Romano, imitates Julius III in 1559. Four years later, the Council of Trent permits the publication of the Talmud, but under so close a surveillance by the censor that at first the Jews refuse to profit by the authorization. Not until 1578 does the Basle edition appear, "so expurgated that it might be read with profit even by Christians." But, though Pius VI in 1566 and Clement VIII in 1592 and 1599 renew the decrees of prohibition in spite of the Council, the editions of the Talmud multiply rapidly, and the sixteenth century, under the influence of the Reformation, sees Jewish studies in honor with Christian scholars, who seek the instruction of Rabbis. The most celebrated scholar of the sixteenth century is Reuchlin, the impartial *savant*, the intrepid champion of the Talmud. Among others, there is Maximilian I's physician, Paul Riccio, the first, I believe, to attempt a Latin compilation of the Talmud. In the following century works abound. Above all should be cited those of the two Buxtorfs, who for more than seventy years occupy in succession the chair of Hebrew at Basle, and publish Hebrew grammars and lexicons, translate Jewish authors of the middle ages, and instruct their contemporaries in Rabbinic studies. Next, Latin translations of diverse Talmudic texts are attempted. Constant l'Empereur translates and annotates the treatises *Baba Kamma* and *Middoth;* Cocceius, the treatises *Makkoth* and *Synhedrin;* Surenhusius, the Mishna, which had been translated before into Spanish and Latin by the Jew Jacob and his brother Isaac Abendana. Selden publishes his learned studies on *The Jewish Woman, the Civil Year, Natural Law according to the Hebrews, the Tribunals;* Lightfoot issues his *Hebraic and Talmudic Hours;* Shickard his *Royal Law among the Hebrews,* "snatched from Rabbinic Darkness;" Bartolocci, finally, his "great Rabbinic library." In the eighteenth century, we have among others the works of Wagenseil, Danz, Schœtggen, Rheinfeld, Egger. But though these authors in various respects deserve commendation, the greater part of them write under the influence of religious prejudice or the narrowest fanaticism, and wittingly or unwittingly sacrifice truth to party spirit. Often religious passion is openly displayed, and has the frankness to announce itself in the very titles. Wagenseil, the learned translator of *Sota*, gives us his *Fiery Datts of Satan, or, the Secret and Horrible Books of the Jews against Jesus Christ and the Christian Religion,* and later, his *Christian Denunciation of the Blasphemies of the Jews against Jesus Christ*. Danz, the author of *Rabbinism Explained,* publishes, *The Jews slain with their own Sword;* Eisenmenger, *Judaism Unmasked, or the*

Complete Account of the Calumnies, Blasphemies, Errors, and Fables of the Jews. Have such studies, inspired solely by ardent and malignant fanaticism, the rights of citizenship in the Republic of Letters?

The science of our day owes to itself the duty of studying the Talmud impartially. It will judge worthy of its attention this monument of a religion and a civilization whose influence has not been void in the world, and, whatever its absolute value may be adjudged to be, science will understand it, and study its formation and development. It will demand of the Talmud instruction, or at least information, almost as varied as the subjects coming within the compass of science. The historian will address himself to it for light upon the history of the early centuries of the Christian era and of the centuries immediately preceding it, and though not seeking in it precise data, which it cannot furnish, he will be sure to find a faithful picture of the beliefs and ideas of the Jewish nation, of its moral and spiritual life. The naturalist will ask of it numerous questions concerning the sciences, physical, natural, or medical. Has it ever occurred to any one to compile, if not the fauna, at least the flora of the Talmud, that is, of the Palestine and Babylonia contemporary with the Empire? It were easy with it as a basis to furnish a second edition of Pliny's *Natural History*, certainly as valuable as the first. The lawyer will question it on the history of its jurisprudence, will investigate whether, how, and by what intermediaries Roman law and Persian customs influenced it, and it will be a curious study to compare the results that two different civilizations, directed by opposite principles, have reached in the *Jus civile* and the *Jus Talmudicum*. The mythologist will dive into its legends, and, by a wise application of the comparative method, determine the history of Midrashic mythology. The philologist will devote himself to the language—that abrupt, rough language, by means of which the Talmud seems to please itself in heaping up obscurities of form over those of the thought, and he will be sure to make more than one happy find. For, says the author of the *History of the Semitic Languages*, "the lexical spoliation and grammatic analysis of the Talmudic language, according to the methods of modern philology, remain to be made. . . . That language fills a hiatus in the history of Semitic idioms." Finally, the philosopher will demand of the Talmud the explanation of Judaism and the history of Jewish institutions, and as the Talmudic books offer the completest expression thereof, and as he has at hand all the component elements, a scrupulous analysis will give him the law of the development of the Jewish religion.

JEWISH MYSTICISM

By Joshua Abelson

Joshua Abelson (1873–1940), ordained at Jews' College in London, was principal of the Jewish theological preparatory school Aria College in Portsmouth and became minister to the United Hebrew Congregation of Leeds.

PREFACE

THE following pages are designed to give the reader a bird's-eye view of the salient features in Jewish mysticism rather than a solid presentation of the subject as a whole. The reason for this will be apparent when one thinks of the many centuries of variegated thought that have had to be packed within the small number of pages allotted to the book. It is this very fact, too, that will possibly give the present treatment of the subject a fragmentary and tentative appearance. Thus Chapter V. follows immediately upon the contents of Chapter IV., without the least attempt to show any of the numerous intervening stages of development. Similarly, Chapter VI., dealing with the *Zohar*, should have been preceded by an exposition of the evolution of Jewish theological thought in the many centuries which divide that chapter from the matter contained in the previous chapter. But lack of space made these omissions inevitable. Should the reader be stimulated to a deeper study of the subject, he will be easily led to the missing parts by the aid of the bibliography at the end of the book.

I should add that the translated extracts from the *Zohar* are only in some cases made by me from the original Hebrew-Aramaic. I owe many of them to the French and German translations to be found in the works of the scholars from whom I have drawn much of my material.

J. ABELSON.
ARIA COLLEGE, PORTSMOUTH.

INTRODUCTION

IT might strike the average reader as exceedingly odd that any attempt should be made at writing a book on Jewish mysticism. The prevailing opinion--among theologians as well as in the mind of the ordinary man--seems to be that Judaism and mysticism stand at the opposite poles of thought, and that, therefore, such a phrase as Jewish mysticism is a glaring and indefensible contradiction in terms. It is to be hoped that the contents of this little book will show the utter falsity of this view.

What is this view, in the main, based upon? It is based upon the gratuitous assumption that the Old Testament, and all the theological and religious literature produced by Jews in subsequent ages, as well as the general synagogue ritual, the public and private religious worship of the Jew--that all these are grounded on the unquestioning assumption of an *exclusively transcendent God*. The Jews, it is said, never got any higher than the notion of the old Jehovah whose abode was in the highest of the seven heavens and whose existence, although very very real to the Jew, was yet of a kind so immeasurably far away from the scenes of earth that it could not possibly have that significance for the Jew which the God of Christianity has for the Christian. The Jew, it is said, could not possibly have that inward experience of

God which was made possible to the Christian by the life of Jesus and the teaching of Paul.

This is one erroneous assumption. A second is the following: The Pauline anti-thesis of law and faith has falsely stamped Judaism as a religion of unrelieved legalism; and mysticism is the irreconcileable enemy of legalism. The God of the Jew, it is said, is a lawgiver pure and simple. The loyal and conscientious Jew is he who lives in the throes of an uninterrupted obedience to a string of laws which hedge him round on all sides. Religion is thus a mere outward mechanical and burdensome routine. It is one long bondage to a Master whom no one has at any time seen or experienced. All spirituality is wanting. God is, as it were, a fixture, static. He never goes out of His impenetrable isolation. Hence He can have no bond of union with any one here below. Hence, further, He must be a stranger to the idea of Love. There can be no such thing as a self-manifestation of a loving God, no movement of the Divine Spirit towards the human spirit and no return movement of the human spirit to the Divine Spirit. There can be no fellowship with God, no opportunity for any immediate experiences by which the human soul comes to partake of God, no incoming of God into human life. And where there is none of these, there can be no mystical element.

A third false factor in the judgment of Christian theologians upon Judaism is their insistence upon the fact that the intense and uncompromising national character of Judaism must of necessity be fatal to the mystical temperament. Mystical religion does, of course, transcend all the barriers which separate race from race and religion from religion. The mystic is a cosmopolitan, and, to him, the differences between the demands and beliefs and observances of one creed and those of another are entirely obliterated in his one all-absorbing and all-overshadowing passion for union with Reality. It is therefore quite true that if Judaism demands of its devotees that they should shut up their God in one sequestered, watertight compartment, it cannot at the same time be favourable to the quest pursued by the mystic.

But as against this, it must be urged that Judaism in its evolution through the centuries has not been so hopelessly particularist as is customarily imagined. The message of the Old Testament on this head must be judged by the condition of things prevailing in the long epoch of its composition. The message of the Rabbinical literature and of much of the Jewish mediæval literature must similarly be judged. The Jew was the butt of the world's scorn. He was outcast, degraded, incapacitated, denied ever so many of the innocent joys and advantages which are the rightful heritage of all the children of men, no matter what their distinctive race or creed might be. He retaliated by declaring (as a result of conviction), in his literature and in his liturgy, that his God could not, by any chance, be the God of the authors of all these acts of wickedness and treachery. Idolatry, immorality, impurity, murder, persecution, hatred--the workers of all these must perforce be shut out from the Divine presence. Hence seeing that, in the sight of the Jew, the nations were the personification of these detestable vices, and seeing that the Jew, in all the pride of a long tradition, looked upon himself as invested with a spirit of especial sanctity, as entrusted with the mission of a holy and pure priesthood, one can quite easily understand how he came to regard the God of Truth and Mercy as first and foremost his God and no one else's.

But with all this, there are, in all branches of Jewish literature, gleams of a far wider, more tolerant, and universalist outlook. Instances will be quoted later. The fact that they existed shows that the germs of the universalism implied in mysticism were there, only they were crushed by the dead-weight of a perverse worldly fate. The Jew certainly did, and could, find God in his neighbour (a non-Jew) as well as in himself. And this ability is, and always was, a strong point of the mystics. Further, even if it be granted that there are in Judaism elements of a nationalism which can hardly be made to square with a high spirituality, this is no necessary bar to its possession of abiding and deeply-ingrained mystical elements. Nationalism is an integral and vital part of the Judaism of the Old Testament and the Rabbinical literature. It is bone of its bone, spirit of its spirit. It is so interfused with religion that it is itself religion. You cannot take up the old Judaism and break it up into pieces, saying: Here are its religious elements; there are its national elements. The two are inextricably combined, warp and woof of one texture. And thus it came about that--strange as it may appear to the modern mind--a halo of religious worth and of strong spirituality was thrown over beliefs and practices which, considered in and for themselves, are nothing more than national sentiments, national memories, and national aspirations. Such, then, being the case, the relation of Judaism to Jewish nationalism is the relation of a large circle to the smaller circle inscribed within it. The larger embraces the smaller.

To come now to mysticism; the mystic differs from the ordinary religionist in that whereas the latter knows God through an objective revelation whether in nature or as embodied in the Bible (which is really only second-hand knowledge, mediate, external, the record of other people's visions and experiences), the mystic knows God by contact of spirit with spirit; *cor ad cor loquitur*. He has the immediate vision; he hears the still small voice speaking clearly to him in the silence of his soul. In this sense the mystic stands quite outside the field of all the great religions of the world. Religion for him is merely his own individual religion, his own lonely, isolated quest for truth. He is solitary--a soul alone with God.

But when we examine the lives and works of mystics, what do we usually find? We usually find that in spite of the intensely individualistic type of their religion, they are allied with some one particular religion of the world's religions. Their mystical experiences are coloured and moulded by *some one* dominant faith. The specific forms of their conceptions of God do not come from their own inner light only, but from the teachings which they imbibe from the external and traditional religion of their race or country. Thus, Christian mysticism has characteristics which are *sui generis*; so has Mohammedan mysticism; so has Hindu mysticism; and likewise Jewish mysticism. The method, the temperament, the spirit are very much the same in all of them. But the influence wielded over them by the nature and trend of each of the great dominant religions is a decisive one, and stamps its features on them in a degree which makes them most easily distinguishable from one another. Thus Judaism, whatever be its composition or spiritual outlook, can certainly be a religion of mysticism. Its mysticism may be of a different order from that which we commonly expect. But this we shall see into later.

I have thus far dealt with the misconstructions put upon Judaism and its mysticism by theologians outside the Jewish fold. I must now say something about the erroneous judgments passed upon the subject by some Jewish theologians. Jewish mysticism is as old as the Old

Testament--nay, as old as some of the oldest parts of the Old Testament. It prevailed in varying degrees of intensity throughout the centuries comprised in the Old Testament history. The current flowed on, uninterrupted, into the era covered by the Rabbinic period. The religious and philosophical literature, ritual, worship, of Jewish mediævalism became heirs to it, developing and ramifying its teachings and implications in ways which it is the purport of this book partially to tell.

Now, more than one Jewish writer has categorically asserted that the origins of Jewish mysticism date back not, as is the fact, to the mists of antiquity, but to the period of European-Jewish history beginning with the 12th century. The German-Jewish historian, H. Graetz (1817-1891), one of the best-known upholders of this view, ascribes the origin of Jewish mysticism to a French Rabbi of the 12th and 13th centuries, by name Isaac ben Abraham of Posquières, more generally known as Isaac the Blind. He regards him as the father 'of the Kabbalah'--the latter term being the general name in Jewish literature for every kind or school of mystical interpretation. Isaac is the reputed author of the Hebrew mystical treatise written in dialogue form and called *Bahir* ('Brightness')--the book which, more than all its predecessors in this domain, anticipates the style and contents of the *Zohar* ('Shining'), which is *par excellence* the mediæval textbook of Jewish mysticism, and belongs to the 14th century. Graetz regards the appearance of this mysticism as some sudden, unexplained importation from without, a plant of exotic origin, "a false doctrine which, although new, styled itself a primitive inspiration; although un-Jewish, called itself a genuine teaching of Israel" (*History of the Jews*, English Trans., vol. iii. p. 565).

But a perusal of the Old Testament, the New Testament (much of which is Hebraic in thought and the work of Jews), and the Rabbinic records will not, for one moment, lend countenance to such a theory. It is in these early monuments of Judaism that the origins will be found. Of course, in saying that the Old Testament holds elements of mysticism--and in saying the same thing of the New Testament--it must be understood that the mysticism is of an implicit and unconscious kind and not the type of religion historically known as 'mysticism.' It is ever so far removed from the mysticism of a Plotinus or an Eckhart or an

Isaac Luria (Jewish mystic, 1533-1572). But taking mysticism in its broader connotation as meaning religion in its most acute, intense, and living stage (Rufus Jones, *Studies in Mystical Religion*, p. xv.), an immediate and first-hand experience of God, then the ascription of mysticism to the Old and New Testaments is perfectly correct. And, as will be obvious from our coming pages, the most highly-elaborated mystical doctrines of Jews in all ages subsequent to the Old Testament are, after allowing for certain extraneous additions, an offshoot of the latter's teachings.

Another type of ill-considered and unjust judgment often passed on Jewish mysticism by Jewish authorities, is to be found in the sneering and condemnatory attitude they adopt towards it in their writings. This, of course, is a phenomenon by no means confined to Jews. One need only think of the hostility of men like Ritschl, Nordau, and Harnack towards all mysticism, in-discriminately. The antagonism springs, in all cases, from an inability to appreciate the subjectivity and individualism of the mystical temperament. While rationalism attempts to solve the ultimate problems of existence by the application of the intellect and the imagination, mysticism takes account of the cravings of the heart and of the great fact of the soul. Pure philosophy will never avail to give the final answer to the questions, "what is above, what is below, what is in front, what is behind" (Mishna, Ḥaggigah, ii. 1). The world, to man's pure intellect, consists only of that which is seen and which is temporal. But there is an-other world transcending it, a world invisible, incomprehensible, but yet both visible and comprehensible to the soul's craving for communion with the Divine. No ratiocination, no syllogism of logic, can strip off the veil from this elusive world. The pathway to it lies through something quite other than intellectuality or sense-experience. It can be grasped only by those inward indefinable movements of feeling or emotion which, in their totality, constitute the soul.

From all this it follows that scholars who, whether congenitally or by mental training, have no sympathy with the subjectivity of the emotions, should be incapable of appreciating the paraphernalia of mysticism.

But in the case of Jewish theologians there is something more to be said. As will be seen in the course of our coming pages, mystical speculation among the Jews clustered largely round the cosmological sections of the Bible. This is true of the earlier as well as of the later mysticism. It is to be found in the Enoch literature, a product of the first pre-Christian century (see Charles, *The Book of the Secrets of Enoch*, 1896, p. xxv.), as well as in the Kabbalistic works produced in France, Spain, Germany, and Poland from the 12th to the 18th century. Combined with this cosmological speculation--or rather as an outcome of it--there went an anthropomorphism which cannot be described otherwise than as being gross. And, in addition to this, a mysterious power was ascribed to the permutations and combinations of the letters of the Hebrew alphabet. By some of the most extraordinary feats of verbal jugglery these letters are made to prove all sorts of things in heaven and earth. They are purely fantastic, and no one can possibly take them seriously. The treatment of the question of the soul, too, gave rise to many curious beliefs about the transmigration of the soul and the appearance of the soul of the Messiah.

All these aspects of Jewish mysticism, tainted as they undoubtedly are by many unlovely characteristics, have been eagerly seized upon by the critics in order to show the unedifying nature of the whole teaching. But it is really an unfair criticism, seeing that it leaves totally out of account the preponderating mass of true poetry and spirituality which inhere in all parts of Jewish mystical speculation. We shall have occasion to give many illustrations of this statement in pages to follow. Nowhere in Jewish literature is the idea of prayer raised to such a pitch of sublimity as it is in the lives and writings of the Jewish mystics. If it is true to say that Judaism here and there suffers from too large an element of formalism and legalism and externalism, it is equally true to say that many of these drawbacks are corrected, toned down, by the contributions of mysticism. And although its treatment of the soul is in many ways overwrought and far-fetched, it is good to know that there is a side of Judaism which laid stress not only on the importance of our securing happiness or reward in this earthly life but also in the life beyond. Jewish mysticism can congratulate itself in having, at one momentous epoch of Jewish history, achieved for Judaism a boon, which Christian mysticism in quite another way, but in an equally important degree, achieved for Christianity. Systematic Christian mysticism began in the late 14th and early 15th centuries. Its foremost exponent was Meister Eckhart, the Dominican monk. What Eckhart and his followers achieved may be summarised by saying that they relieved Christendom of the heavy load of arid scholasticism under which it had for long been oppressed, and, by introducing ideas of religion at once more simple, more practical, more social, and more spiritual, paved the way for the New Learning--for the new discoveries in science and philosophy which were to revolutionise the world. In other words, this Christian mysticism was the avenue through which the subtle dark speculations of an Albertus Magnus and a Thomas Aquinas had necessarily to pass in order to prepare coming ages for the light of a Newton, a Kant, and a Darwin. Hence must modern science come down from the pedestal of her pomp and glory, and bow her acknowledgments to the services of many a humble Christian mystic.

Jewish mysticism has a similar act of homage to receive at the hands of every lover of Jewish scholarship. In the 13th century Judaism was in danger of becoming devitalised through the theology of Moses Maimonides--the great Spanish-Jewish theologian and author of the famous *Guide of the Perplexed*--who looked upon reason as the final arbiter of the rightness or wrongness of any Jewish dogma. Judaism for him was a cult of the intellect and the intellect only. The sole representative of the intellect was Aristotle. Nearly everything in Judaism had by hook or by crook to be harmonised with the tenets of Aristotelianism. Thus, Jewish morality must, to have validity, be shown to be in consonance with Aristotle's four faculties of the soul and with his theories of 'the mean.' Judaism's teachings on the unity of God must be brought into line with the Aristotelian indivisible God, who is the principal of all essences, the disposer of the world. Just as intellectual perfection is, to the Greek philosopher, the highest aim of man, so must the teachings of Judaism be interpreted in such a way as to show that, according to the Torah, the life of the saint is a life of the highest intellectuality. Revelation--which is one of the cornerstones of the Jewish faith--must be in accordance with reason. All the truths enunciated by Plato and Aristotle are anticipated in the writings of the Prophets and of some of the Talmudic sages. The prophets, according to Maimonides, were the recipients, orally, of a set of philosophical doctrines which were handed on orally from father to son, from generation to generation, until the age of the Talmud. Philosophy is an echo of them. What a fossilising, deteriorating effect the spread of these teachings must have wielded upon Judaism had they been allowed to go on without check!

The check came in the shape of mysticism. It corrected the balance. It showed that Judaism was a religion of the *feelings* as well as of the intellect. It showed that the Jew's eternal quest was not to be right with Aristotle but to be right with God. It showed that Judaism has a place not only for Reason but for Love too. It showed that the ideal life of the Jew was, not a life of outward harmony with rules and prescriptions, but a life of inward attachment to a Divine Life which is immanent everywhere, and that the crown and consummation of all effort consists in finding a direct way to the actual presence of God.

SOME EARLY ELEMENTS: ESSENISM

THE Old Testament is the fountain-head of Judaism. Hence if it is true, as is contended in a previous page, that the Old Testament contains mystical elements, then the starting-point in any treatment of Jewish mysticism on historical, or even semi-historical, lines must be the Old Testament. But this course will not be adopted here. The Old Testament will be omitted. And for a reason which has already been hinted. The mysticism of the Old Testament is of an elementary, naïve, and unconscious kind, whereas what this book is intended to show is the consciously-elaborated, professional mysticism of the Jews. What we get in the Old Testament are the groundwork and the scaffolding, the indispensable beginnings of the edifice; but not the edifice itself.

Thus it has much to say about the Fatherhood of God. Here we have a basic conception of all mysticism; for the latter in all its phases and stages assumes the possibility of communion with some one who, while greater and more powerful than ourselves, is at the same time loving, and benevolent, and personally interested in us. You can only pray to one who hears; you can only feel love towards one who, you know, has loved you first. The Old Testament scintillates with sublime examples of men whose communion with God was a thing of intensest reality to them, and whose conviction of the 'nearness' of the Divine was beyond the slightest cavil. The sudden and unexpected inrushes of Divine inspiration which seized the Old Testament prophets; Isaiah's vision of a God 'whose train filled the Temple'--an emblem of the All-inclusiveness of Deity, of the presence and the working of an all-embracing Spirit of Life; the ecstasy of an Ezekiel lifted from off his feet by the Spirit and removed from one place to another; the fact of prophecy itself--the possession of a spiritual endowment not vouchsafed to ordinary men, the endowment of a higher insight into the will of God;--all these represent a stage of first-hand, living religion to which the name of mysticism is rightly and properly applied. But they are no more than the preamble to the explicit, conscious, and pronouncedly personal type of Jewish mysticism which is the subject of the present book.

The earliest beginnings of this mysticism are usually accredited, by modern Jewish scholars, to the Essenes. To say this, is to put back Jewish mysticism to a very early date, for according to the theory of Wellhausen (*Israëlitische and jüdische Geschichte*, 1894, p. 261), the Essenes as well as the Pharisees were offshoots of the Ḥasidim (חסידים = 'pious ones') of the pre-Maccabean age. But it is only a theory, and not an established historical fact, seeing that the religious tenets of the Jews during the three centuries immediately preceding the birth of Christianity are veiled in considerable obscurity, and seeing also that the real meaning of the name 'Essenes' as well as their exact relations with the Pharisees are points upon which there is anything but certainty. 'What is certain, however, is that three out-standing literary sources belonging to the first two or three Christian centuries--*viz.* (*a*) Philo, (*b*) Josephus, (*c*) some older portions of the Babylonian and Palestinian Talmuds--all have stray allusions, couched in varying phraseology, to certain sects or parties who differed in their mode of life from the general body of the Jews, and who were in possession of certain esoteric teachings of which those outside their ranks were uninformed.

Thus Philo (*Quod omnis probes liber*, 12) writes of them that they were "eminently worshippers of God (θεραπευταὶ θεοῦ), not in the sense that they sacrifice living animals (like the priests in the Temple), but that they are anxious to keep their minds in a priestly state of holiness. They prefer to live in villages, and avoid cities on account of the habitual wickedness of those who in-habit them, knowing, as they do, that just as foul air breeds disease, so there is danger of contracting an incurable disease of the soul from such bad associations."

Again, in another of his works (*De Vita contemplativa*, ed. Conybeare, pp. 53, 206), Philo says: "Of natural philosophy . . they study only that which pertains to the existence of God and the beginning of all things, otherwise they devote all their attention to ethics, using as instructors the laws of their fathers, which, without the outpouring of the Divine Spirit, the human mind could not have devised . . . for, following their ancient traditions, they obtain their philosophy by means of allegorical interpretations. . . . Of the love of God they exhibit myriads of examples, inasmuch as they strive for a continued uninterrupted life of purity and holiness; they avoid swearing and falsehood, and they declare that God causes only good and no evil whatsoever. . . No one possesses a house absolutely as his own, one which does not at the same time belong to all; for, in addition to living together in companies, their houses are open also to their adherents coming from other quarters. They have one storehouse for all, and the same diet; their garments belong to all in common, and their meals are taken in common."

Josephus speaks of the Essenes in similar terms (see *Antiquities*, XVIII. i. 2-6; also *De Bello Judaico*, II. viii. 2-13).

The points to be noted in both the fore-mentioned authors are: (*a*) the great stress laid on fellowship, amounting to a kind of communism; (*b*) their removal from the general people by reason of their higher sanctity; (*c*) their devotion to the knowledge of the existence of God and the beginning of all things; (*d*) their love of allegorical interpretation.

Although it is exceedingly difficult to know what the Rabbinic term equivalent to 'Essene' is, it is not hard to deduce, from names and phrases scattered throughout the Rabbinic records, a theory that there existed as early as the first Christian centuries either a distinct sect of Jews, or individual Jews here and there, who combined mystical speculation with an ascetic mode of life.

A similar phenomenon is observable in the history of the early Christian Church. There was a life of primitive and austere fellowship. A group here, a group there, gathered together with no other motive than that of gaining a greater hold on the spiritual life than was prevalent in the ordinary circles of the people: "And the multitude of them that believed were of one heart and soul; and not one of them said that aught of the things which he possessed was his own; but they had all things common. . . . For neither were there among them any that lacked: for as many as were possessors of lands or houses sold them . . . and distribution was made unto each according as any one had need" (*Acts*, iv. 32--35).

They seem to have lived on the borderland of an unusual ecstasy, experiencing extraordinary invasions of the Divine, hearing mystic sounds and seeing mystic visions which, to them, were the direct and immediate revelations of the deepest and most sacred truths.

Illustrations of similar experiences in the bosom of the early synagogue, as presented in the Rabbinic records, are the following:

There are several heterogeneous passages which speak of the existence within the ancient Temple at Jerusalem of a special apartment, called the *lishkât ḥashāīm* ('chamber of the silent [or secret] ones'). According to the statement of *Tosefta Shekalim*, ii. 16, there were to be found in some cities of Palestine and Babylon men known as *Ḥashāīm*, who reserved a special room in their house for depositing in it a charity-box into which money for the poor could be put and withdrawn with the utmost silence. It was collected and distributed by men appointed for the purpose by the *Ḥashāīm*, and, as it was all done with the strictest secrecy, it looks as though there was a kind of communism among the members of the order. The special chamber in the Temple, as mentioned above, was also a place where gifts for the poor were deposited in secret and withdrawn for distribution in secret.

Two facts seem to demonstrate that these *Ḥashāīm* were a small mystical sect.

Firstly, they are given the special appellation of *yirē-ḥēt*, i.e. 'fearers of sin.' They were thus marked off by an extra sanctity from the body of the people--and the student of the Rabbinic literature knows that whenever a special title is accorded to a group or sect on the grounds of special holiness, this holiness is always of an exceptionally high order. It is the holiness of men in touch with the Divine. And, as has just been remarked, their enthusiasm for doing good seems to have been grounded on a kind of austere fellowship that reigned among them, impelling them to do their work unseen by the madding crowd.

Secondly, the idea of silence or secrecy was frequently employed by the early Rabbis in their mystical exegesis of Scripture. A typical illustration is the following passage from the *Midrash Rabba* on *Genesis* iii.: "R. Simeon son of Jehozedek asked R. Samuel son of Naḥman (two Palestinian teachers of the beginning of the 3rd century A.D.) and said unto him, Seeing that I have heard concerning thee that thou art an adept in the Haggadah[1], tell me whence the light was created. He replied, It [*i.e.* the Haggadah] tells us that the Holy One (blessed be He) enwrapped Himself in a garment, and the brightness of His splendour lit up the universe from end to end. He [*i.e.* the sage who just replied] said this in a whisper, upon which the other sage retorted, Why dost thou tell this in a whisper, seeing that it is taught clearly in a scriptural verse--'who coverest thyself with light as with a garment'? (*Psalm*, civ. 2). Just as I have myself had it whispered unto me, replied he, even so have I whispered it unto thee."

Another instance of what looks like a sect of esoteric teachers among the Jews of the first centuries is the *Vatīkīn*, *i.e.* 'men of firm principles.' Their mysticism seems to have clustered mostly round the sentiments and outward conduct governing prayer. Indeed, throughout Rabbinical literature the true supplicant before God is in many cases a mystic. Only the mystic mood is the true prayerful mood. There is a discussion in the Mishna of *Berachoth*, i. 2, as to what is the earliest moment in the dawn at which the Shema' (the technical name for *Deuteronomy*, vi. 4-9) may be read. Upon this the comment is made, in *T.B. Berachoth*, 9b, that "the *Vatīkīn* arranged the time for prayer in such a way as to enable them to finish the reading of the Shema' at the exact moment of sunrise." According to the great Rabbinic commentator R. Solomon b. Isaac (11th century), the *Vatīkīn* were "men who were meek and carried out the commandment from pure love." It must be borne in mind that throughout Jewish theology, 'meekness' (*'anavah*) stands for something immensely higher than the moral connotation which we customarily attribute to the virtue. It signifies a level of religious devoutness which it is not given to every one to reach. To carry out a commandment from pure love, means, in Jewish theology of all ages, to attain a high stage of mystic elation which can only be arrived at as the result of a long preliminary series of arduous efforts in the upward path. To recite the Shema' is, as the Rabbis frequently say, "to take upon one's self the yoke of the Kingdom of Heaven," and the phrase 'Kingdom of Heaven' has decidedly mystical associations, as we shall see later. Hence one may plausibly conclude that the *Vatīkīn* were a brotherhood whose dominant feature was a simplicity of living combined with a degree of earnest scrupulousness in prayer amounting to an adoration, a love, of the Divine such as is experienced by the mystics of all nations and all times.

And a similar description might be applied to the members of what apparently was another esoteric order of those days--the *Zenūim, i.e.* 'lowly, chaste ones.' As a matter of fact the Rabbinic records are too vague and disconnected to enable scholars to say with any certainty whether these *Zenūim* were an independent sect or whether the word is merely another term denoting either or both of the other fellowships already alluded to. They bear the hall-mark of all ancient and mediæval Jewish mysticism in respect of the emphasis laid by them on the importance of the letters comprising the Divine Name in Hebrew as well as upon certain manipulations of the Hebrew alphabet generally. The following passage occurs in *T.B. Kiddushin*, 71a:

"R. Judah said in the name of Rab [*i.e.* R. Abba Arika, a Babylonian teacher of the 3rd century A.D.] the Name of forty-two letters can only be entrusted by us to him who is modest [*i.e.* zenūa'] and meek, in the midway of life, not easily provoked to anger, temperate, and free from vengeful feelings. He who understands it, is cautious with it and keeps it in purity, is loved above and is liked here below. He is revered by his fellow-men; he is heir to two worlds--this world and the world to come."

It is interesting to quote here the comment on this Rabbinic passage made by the Spanish-Hebrew philosopher Moses Maimonides (1135-1204) in his great work *The Guide of the Perplexed*. He says (part i. ch. lxii. Eng. Trans. by M. Friedlander, Routledge, 1906):

"There was also a name of forty-two letters known among them. Every intelligent person knows that one word of forty-two letters is impossible. But it was a phrase of several words which had together forty-two letters. There is no doubt that the words had such a meaning as to convey a correct notion of the essence of God, in the way we have stated. . . . Many believe that the forty-two letters are merely to be pronounced mechanically; that by the knowledge of these, without any further interpretation, they can attain to those exalted ends. . . . On the contrary it is evident that all this exalted preparation aims at a knowledge of metaphysics and includes ideas which constitute 'the secrets of the Law' as we have explained."

Maimonides, it should be remembered, was a rationalist and antimystic; and much of the old Rabbinic cosmological mysticism which was looked upon as serious mystical speculation by many of his literary contemporaries, was dubbed by him as metaphysics or physics.

But, to return to our subject, the best insight into the origin and implication of these forty-two letters is afforded us by the Talmudic passage last' quoted (*T.B. Ḳiddushin*, 71a), where we are told that in the last days of the Temple the decadent priests were deemed unworthy to pronounce the Divine Name in their official benedictions, and a name consisting of twelve letters was substituted. What this name was is nowhere given in the Rabbinic records. As time went on, it was deemed inadvisable to entrust even this twelve-lettered name to every priest. It was taught only to an elect set among them, who, when chanting the benedictions in the general company of all the priests, used to 'swallow' its pronunciation (*i.e.* make it inaudible) in order not to divulge it. The forty-two-lettered name probably arose in similar circumstances, but whether the secrets of it were confided to a greater or a smaller circle than that in which the twelve-lettered name was known, is by no means apparent. Let it only be said here--as it is a subject to which we shall return later on that in the elaborated systems of the mediæval Kabbalists these many-lettered names of God (not only forty-two, but also forty-five and seventy-two letters) are the pivots on which huge masses of most curious mystical lore turn. The Ten Sefirot have close connections with these doctrines of letters-- secret doctrines about the Divine nature, about creation, about the relations subsisting between God and the universe.

Reference must here be made to what appears to be another order of Jewish mystics in the opening centuries of the Christian era. The Mishna (Tractate *Sukkah*, v. 2) speaks of 'the Ḥasidim and Anshé Ma'aseh' (*i.e.* saints and miracle-workers) who, at the joyous feast of the water-drawing at the Temple during Tabernacles, used to dance and perform certain acrobatic feats with lighted torches. The allusions are very vaguely worded, and it is hazardous to deduce any hard-and-fast theories. But so much may be said, *viz.* that being mentioned together in the same Mishna passage just quoted, and being mentioned in close succession in another old passage of the Mishna (Tractate *Soṭah,* ix. 15), it is more than probable that they belonged to one and the same sect. Again the phrase 'Anshé Ma'aseh' (as well as the singular form of the first word) is frequently used in Rabbinic to mean 'miracle-worker,' although in the Biblical Hebrew it would signify 'man of action.' There is a passage in *T.B. Berachoth,* 18b, which gives a weird description of the experience of a 'Ḥasid' who heard 'from behind the curtain' certain secrets hidden from ordinary men. And the student of Rabbinics knows how many a Rabbi of these early centuries, gifted with the mystic temperament, wielded a semi-miraculous power of foretelling the future or of creating something out of nothing (see on this, Volz's *Der Geist Gottes,* Tübingen, 1910, pp. 115-118). The vast literature of Rabbinic angelology and demonology shows the same features--upon which Conybeare (in *The Jewish Quarterly Review,* xi. 1-45) has thrown considerable light in his translation of *The Testament of Solomon.*

It is a moot point as to whether these Ḥasidim are the lineal descendants of the saintly party known by that name in the Maccabean epoch. The point, however, which clearly emerges is, that a certain esoteric wisdom and capacity for doing things, unknown to the multitudes, was vouchsafed to certain bodies of men, who by the superior purity of their living, by their unabated devotion to the things of the spirit, and by their cultivation of a kind of brotherhood in which simplicity, single-mindedness, and charity were the reigning virtues, were enabled to enjoy a living in the world of the unseen.

One further matter, in conclusion. The interests of historical accuracy demand that, as has been already pointed out, the student should be in no hurry to say that these esoteric sects whose beliefs are so vaguely and fragmentarily described in the Rabbinic literature, are to be identified with the Essenes described in the writings of Philo and Josephus. Resemblances there certainly are, but there are differences too; and the Rabbinic allusions are too disjointed to enable one to form an impression--even an inexact impression, leave alone an exact one--of the lives and thoughts of these mystic gatherings. Philo and Josephus paint a complete picture. The Talmud and Midrashim give but stray and elusive hints. For one thing, the Essenes practised celibacy; marriage must necessarily dissolve the fellowship characterising the order. The Rabbinic records give no hint of the duty of celibacy. On the contrary, marriage was held to promote a far higher sanctity than celibacy. But the Rabbis tolerated some exceptional cases of celibacy; so that it is difficult to speak categorically. Again, the centre of gravity of Essenic religion seems to have been the cultivation of the highest ethics. They stressed *inward* religion as demanded by the Mosaic code, but, with the exception of a reverence for the holiness of the Sabbath, they were comparatively unconcerned with the *outward* religious duties incumbent upon the Jews of that time. Thus, they made little or nothing of the sacrifices--doubtless a corollary of their emphasis on the allegorical interpretation of Scripture. But it was otherwise with the early mystics of the Rabbinic literature. Although living in an atmosphere of mystery and looking to the Divine secret to unroll itself at any moment, they yet never overlooked the claims of institutional religion; they never flouted the ceremonial side of Judaism; they were inflexible upholders of the Law and its associated traditions. The same phenomenon is, of course, seen in the history of Christian mysticism where the first-hand, inward, individualised experiences of the ground-truths of religion are conformed to the prevailing and accredited dogmas of Christianity.

There were mystics among the Pharisees as well as among the Essenes, and yet we are told that the most spiritually-gifted among the former (who constituted a *habūrah*, *i.e.* 'fellowship') were they who were most scrupulous about the giving of the priestly dues--a purely external religious duty based on the legalism of the Pentateuch. Indeed this blending of legalism with spirituality, this consistent (and successful) interweaving of the formalism of tradition with the mysticism of the individual, is an arresting feature of Jewish theology in all ages.

In fine, as must be apparent from the general trend and contents of this book, the whole of Jewish mysticism is really nothing but a commentary on the Jewish Bible, an attempt to pierce through to its most intimate and truest meaning; and what is the Bible to the Jew but the admonisher to be loyal to the traditions of his fathers? Only then will he find God when he is convinced that He was found of those of his race who sought Him in an earlier day.

---

1. Haggadah is the general name for the narrative or fabular or philosophical sections of the Rabbinic literature.

THE MERKABAH (CHARIOT) MYSTICISM

THE first chapter of Ezekiel has played a most fruitful part in the mystical speculations of the Jews. The lore of the heavenly Throne-chariot in some one or other of its multitudinous implications is everywhere to be met with. Whence Ezekiel derived these baffling conceptions of the Deity, and what historical or theological truths he meant to portray by means of them, are themes with which the scholars of the Old Testament have ever busied themselves. But the Jewish mystic sought no rationalistic explanation of them. He took them as they were, in all their mystery, in all their strange and inexplicable fantasy, in all their weird aloofness from the things and ideas of the everyday life. He sought no explanation of them because he was assured that they stood for something which did not need explaining. He *felt* instinctively that the Merkabah typified the human longing for the sight of the Divine Presence and companionship with it. To attain this end was, to him, the acme of all spiritual life.

Ezekiel's image of Yahve riding upon the chariot of the 'living creatures,' accompanied by sights and voices, movements and upheavals in earth and heaven, lying outside the range of the deepest ecstatic experiences of all other Old Testament personages, was for the Jewish mystic a real opening, an unveiling, of the innermost and impenetrable secrets locked up in the interrelation of the human and the divine. It was interpreted as a sort of Divine self-opening, self-condescension to man. The door is flung wide open so that man, at the direct invitation of God, can come to the secret for which he longs and seeks. This idea is a supreme factor in the mystic life of all religions. The soul is urged on to seek union with God, only because it feels that God has first gone out, on His own initiative and uninvited, to seek union with it. The human movement from within is but a response to a larger Divine movement from without. The call has come; the answer must come.

The Chariot (Merkabah) was thus a kind of 'mystic way' leading up to the final goal of the soul. Or, more precisely, it was the mystic 'instrument,' the vehicle by which one was carried direct into the 'halls' of the unseen. It was the aim of the mystic to be a 'Merkabah-rider,' so that he might be enabled, while still in the trammels of the flesh, to mount up to his spiritual Eldorado. Whether, as has been suggested, the uncanny imagery of the Merkabah lore is to be sought, for its origin, in the teachings of Mithraism, or, as has also been suggested, in certain branches of Mohammedan mysticism, one can see quite clearly how its governing idea is based on a conception general to all the mystics, *viz.* that the quest for the ultimate Reality is a kind of pilgrimage, and the seeker is a traveller towards his home in God.

It was remarked, on a previous page, that the mystic neither asked, nor waited, for any rationalistic explanation of the Merkabah mysteries. He felt that they summarised for him the highest pinnacle of being towards the realisation of which he must bend his energies without stint. But yet, from certain stray and scattered Rabbinic remarks, one takes leave to infer that there existed in the early Christian centuries a small sect of Jewish mystics--the elect of the elect--to whom certain measures of instruction were given in these recondite themes. There was an esoteric science of the Merkabah. What its content was we can only dimly guess--from the Rabbinic sources. It appears to have been a confused angelology, one famous angel Metatron playing a conspicuous part. Much more is to be found in the early Enoch-literature as well as--from quite other points of view--in the mediæval Kabbalah. Let us give some illustrative sayings from the Rabbinic literature.

In the Mishna, *Ḥaggigah*, ii. 1, it is said: "It is forbidden to explain the first chapters of Genesis to *two* persons, but it is only to be explained to *one* by himself. It is forbidden to explain the Merkabah even to *one* by himself unless he be a sage and of an original turn of mind." In a passage in *T.B. Ḥaggigah*, 13a, the words are added: "but it is permitted to divulge to him [*i.e.* to one in the case of the first chapters of *Genesis*] the first words of the chapters." In the same passage another Rabbi (Ze'era) of the 3rd century A.D. remarks, with a greater stringency: "We may not divulge even the first words of the chapters [neither of Genesis nor Ezekiel] unless it be to a 'chief of the Beth Din'[1] or to one whose heart is tempered by age or responsibility."

Yet another teacher of the same century declares in the same connection: "We may not divulge the secrets of the Torah to any but to him to whom the verse in *Isaiah*, iii. 3, applies, *viz.* the captain of fifty and the honourable man, and the counsellor and the cunning artificer and the eloquent orator." (The Rabbis understood these terms to mean distinction in a knowledge and practice of the Torah.)

This insistence upon a high level of moral and religious fitness as the indispensable prelude to a knowledge of the Merkabah has its counterpart in the mysticism of all religions. The organic life, the self, conscious and unconscious, must be moulded and developed in certain ways; there must be an education, moral, physical, emotional; a psychological adjustment, by stages, of the mental states which go to the make-up of the full mystic consciousness. As Evelyn Underhill (*Mysticism*, p. 107) says: "Mysticism shows itself not merely as an attitude of mind and heart, but as a form of organic life. . . . It is a remaking of the whole character on high levels in the interests of the transcendental life."

That the Rabbis were fully alive to the importance of this self-discipline is seen by a remark of theirs in *T.B. Ḥaggigah*, 13a, as follows: "A certain youth was once explaining the Ḥashmal (*Ezekiel*, i. 27, translated 'amber' in the A.V.) when fire came forth and consumed him." When the question is asked, Why was this? the answer is: "His time had not yet come" (*lāv māti zimnēh*). This cannot but mean that his youthful age had not given him the opportunities for the mature self-culture necessary to the mystic apprehension. The Ḥashmal, by the way, was interpreted by the Rabbis as: (*a*) a shortened form of the full phrase *ḥāyot ĕsh mē-māl-lē-loth*, *i.e.* 'the living creatures of fire, speaking'; or (*b*) a shortened form of *'ittim ḥāshoth ve-'ittim mĕ-măllē-lōth*, *i.e.* 'they who at times were silent and at times speaking.' In the literature of the mediæval Kabbalah, the Ḥashmal belongs to the 'Yetsiratic' world (*i.e.* the abode of the angels, presided over by Metatron who was changed into fire; and the spirits of men are there too).[2] According to a modern Bible commentator (the celebrated Russian Hebraist, M. L. Malbim, 1809-1879) the word signifies "the Ḥayot [*i.e.* 'living creatures' of *Ezekiel*, i.] which are the abode [or camp] of the Shechinah [*i.e.* Divine Presence] where there is the 'still small voice.' It is they [*i.e.* the Ḥayot] who receive the Divine effluence from above and disseminate it to the Ḥayot who are the movers of the 'wheels' [of Ezekiel's Chariot]."

Many more passages of a like kind might be quoted in support of the view that the attainment of a knowledge of the Merkabah was a hard quest beset with ever so many impediments; that it pre-supposed, on the one hand, an exceptional measure of self-development, and, on the other, an extraordinary amount of self-repression and self-renouncement.

But the mention of *fire* in the preceding paragraph leads us to the consideration of an aspect of the Merkabah which brings the latter very much into line with the description of mystical phenomena in literature generally. Every one knows how the image of fire dominates so much of the mysticism of Dante. The mediæval Christian mystics--Ruysbroeck, Catherine of Genoa, Jacob Boehme, and others--appeal constantly to the same figure for the expression of their deepest thoughts on the relations between man and the Godhead. The choice of the metaphor probably rests on the fact that 'fire' can be adapted to symbolise either or both of the following truths: (*a*) the brightness, illumination which comes when the goal has been reached, when the quest for the ultimate reality has at last been satisfied; (*b*) the all-penetrating, all-encompassing, self-diffusing force of fire is such a telling picture of the mystic union of the soul and God. The two are interpenetrated, fused into one state of being. The soul is red-hot with God, who at the same time, like fire, holds the soul in his grip, dwells in it.

Examples are the following: In the *Midrash Rabba* on *Canticles*, i. 12, it is said: "Ben 'Azzai [a famous Rabbi of the 2nd century A.D.] was once sitting expounding the Torah. *Fire surrounded him.* They went and told R. 'Akiba, saying, 'Oh! Rabbi! Ben 'Azzai is sitting expounding the Torah, and *fire is lighting him up on all sides.*' Upon this, R. 'Akiba went to Ben 'Azzai and said unto him, 'I hear that thou wert sitting expounding the Torah, with the *fire playing round about thee*.' 'Yes, that is so,' replied he. 'Wert thou then,' retorted 'Akiba, 'engaged in unravelling the secret chambers of the Merkabah?' 'No,' replied he." It is not germane here to go into what the sage said he really was engaged in doing. The quotation sufficiently shows how in the 2nd century A.D. the imagery of fire was traditionally associated with esoteric culture.

Here is another instance, in *T.B. Succah*, 28a. Hillel the Elder (30 B.C.-10 A.D.) had eighty disciples. Thirty of them were worthy enough for the Shechinah to rest upon them. Thirty of them were worthy enough for the sun to stand still at their bidding. The other twenty were of average character. The greatest among them all was Jonathan son of Uziel (1st century A.D.); the smallest among them all was Joḥanan son of Zaccai (end of 1st century A.D.). The latter, smallest though he was, was acquainted with every conceivable branch of both exoteric and esoteric lore. He knew 'the talk of the ministering angels and the talk of the demons and the talk of the palm-trees (*děkālim*).' He knew also the lore of the Merkabah. Such being the measure of the knowledge possessed by 'the smallest,' how great must have been the measure of the knowledge possessed by 'the greatest,' *viz*. Jonathan son of Uziel! When the latter was sitting and studying the Torah (presumably the esoteric lore of the angels and the Merkabah) every bird that flew above him was burnt by fire. These latter words are the description of the ecstatic state, the moments of exaltation, the indescribable peace and splendour which the soul of the mystic experiences when, disentangling itself from the darkness of illusion, it reaches the Light of Reality, the condition so aptly phrased by the Psalmist who said: "For with thee is the fountain of life; in thy light shall we see light" (*Psalm*, xxxvi. 9). The bird flying in the environment of this unrestrained light, must inevitably be consumed by the fire of it.

The monument which Jonathan son of Uziel has left us in perpetuation of his mystical tendencies, is his usage of the term Memra ('Word') to denote certain phases of Divine activity, in the Aramaic Paraphrase to the Prophets which ancient Jewish tradition assigned to his authorship, but which modern research has shown to be but the foundation on which the extant Aramaic Paraphrase to the Prophets rests.

Another illustration of the mystic vision of light consequent on the rapture created by an initiation into the Merkabah mysteries is related in *T.B. Ḥaggigah*, 14b, as follows:

"R. Joḥanan son of Zaccai was once riding on an ass, and R. Eliezer son of Arach was on an ass behind him. The latter Rabbi said to the former, 'O master! teach me a chapter of the Merkabah mysteries.' 'No!' replied the master, 'Have I not already informed thee that the Merkabah may not be taught to any one man by himself unless he be a sage and of an original turn of mind?

'Very well, then!' replied Eliezer son of Arach. 'Wilt thou give me leave to tell thee a thing which thou hast taught me? 'Yes!' replied Joḥanan son of Zaccai. 'Say it!' Forthwith the master dismounted from his ass, wrapped himself up in a garment, and sat upon a stone beneath an olive tree. 'Why, O master, hast thou dismounted from thy ass?' asked the disciple. 'Is it possible,' replied he, 'that I will ride upon my ass at the moment when thou art expounding the mysteries of the Merkabah, and the Shechinah is with us, and the ministering angels are accompanying us?' Forthwith R. Eliezer son of Arach opened his discourse on the mysteries of the Merkabah, and no sooner had he begun, *than fire came down from heaven* and encompassed all the trees of the field, which, with one accord, burst into song. What song? It was 'Praise the Lord from the earth, ye dragons and all deeps; fruitful trees and all cedars, praise ye the Lord' (*Psalm*, cxlviii. 7, 9). Upon this, an angel cried out from the fire, saying, 'Truly these, even these, are the secrets of the Merkabah.' R. Joḥanan son of Zaccai then arose and kissed his disciple upon the forehead, saying, 'Blessed be the Lord, God of Israel, who hath given unto Abraham our father a son who is able to understand, and search, and discourse upon, the mysteries of the Merkabah.' . . .

"When these things were told to R. Joshua [another disciple of Joḥanan], the latter said one day when walking with R. José the Priest [another disciple of Joḥanan], 'Let us likewise discourse about the Merkabah!' R. Joshua opened the discourse. It was a day in the height of summer. The heavens became a knot of thick clouds, and something like a rainbow was seen in the clouds, and the ministering angels came in companies to listen as men do to hear wedding music. R. José the Priest went and told his master of it, who exclaimed, 'Happy are ye, happy is she that bare you! Blessed are thy eyes that beheld these things! Indeed I saw myself with you in a dream, seated upon Mount Sinai, and I heard a heavenly voice exclaiming, Ascend hither! Ascend hither! large banqueting-halls and fine couches are in readiness for you. You and your disciples, and your disciples' disciples, are destined to be in the third set' [*i.e.* the third of the three classes of angels who, as the Rabbis taught, stand continually before the Shechinah, singing psalms. and anthems]."

There are several points which need making clear in this remarkable passage. The objection to discuss the Merkabah while sitting on the animal's back, and the fact of sitting upon a stone under an olive tree, point to the necessary physical and tempera-mental self-discipline which is the *sine quâ non* of the mystic's equipment in all ages and among all nations. He must not be set high on the ass, lest his heart be lifted up too. He must be cleansed of every vestige of pride, lowly and of contrite spirit. It has been mentioned in the previous chapter how meekness was one of the unfailing qualities of the *Zen'uim*. The proud man, said the Rabbis, "crowds out the feet of the Shechinah." "Whosoever is haughty will finally fall into Gehinnom." Pride, to the Rabbis, was the most terrible pitfall in the path of the religious life. Its opposite, humility, was the starting-point of all the virtues. If such was the premium placed upon meekness in so far as it concerned the life of the ordinary Jew, how enormous must have been its importance for the life of the mystic--for him who aimed at knowing Eternal Truth? Everything that savours of evil, of imperfection, of sin, must vanish. The primary means of this self-purification is the culture of humility.

The remark that 'the Shechinah is with us and the ministering angels are accompanying us' emphasises two salient features of Rabbinic mysticism. Firstly, the Shechinah is the transcendent-immanent God of Israel; Israel's environment was saturated with the Shechinah whose unfailing companionship the Jew enjoyed in all the lands of his dispersion. "Even at the time when they are unclean does the Shechinah dwell with them," runs a passage in *T.B. Yoma*, 57a. How unique, how surpassingly vivid must have been the consciousness of this accompanying Shechinah-Presence to the Merkabah initiates, to those who had raised themselves so high above the level of the ordinary crowd by the pursuit of an ideal standard of self-perfection!

Secondly, the 'ministering angels' play a large part in all the Merkabah lore, as is seen from the following Rabbinic comments.

Ezekiel, i. 15, says, "Now as I beheld the living creatures, behold one wheel upon the earth by the living creatures, with his four faces." R. Eliezer said, "There is one angel who stands upon earth but whose head reaches to the 'living creatures' . . . his name is Sandalphon. He is higher than his neighbour [3] to the extent of a five-hundred years' journey. He stands behind the Merkabah wreathing coronets for his Master" (*T.B. Ḥaggigah*, 13b).

Another passage reads: "Day by day ministering angels are created from the stream of fire. They sing a pæan [to God] and then pass away, as it is said, 'They are new every morning; great is thy faithfulness' (*Lamentations*, iii. 23). . . . From each word that comes forth from the mouth of the Holy One (blessed be He) there is created one angel, as it is said, 'By the word of the Lord were the heavens made and all the host of them by the breath of his mouth'" (*Psalm*, xxxiii. 6).

The Rabbis obviously understood the phrase 'the host of them' to refer, not as we suppose, to the paraphernalia of the heavens, *i.e.* the stars, planets, etc., but to the angelic worlds. The idea of the Word of God becoming transformed into an angel, and hence accomplishing certain tangible tasks among men, here on earth, bears strong resemblances to the Logos of Philo as well as to the Prologue of the Fourth Gospel.

The phrase to 'listen as men do to hear wedding music' (or literally 'the music of bride and bridegroom') is a reminiscence of the large mass of Rabbinic mysticism clustering round the love overtures of bride and bridegroom in the Book of Canticles. The book, on the Rabbinic interpretation, teaches the great truth of a 'spiritual marriage' between the human and the Divine, a betrothal between God and Israel. "In ten places in the Old Testament," says *Canticles Rabba*, iv. 10, "are the Israelites designated as a 'bride,' six here [*i.e.* in the Book of Canticles] and four in the Prophets . . . and in ten corresponding passages is God represented as arrayed in garments [which display the dignity of manhood in the ideal bridegroom]."

To the minds of the Rabbis, the super-abundant imagery of human love and marriage which distinguishes Canticles from all other books of the Old Testament, was the truest symbol of the way in which human Israel and his Divine Father were drawn near to one another. The intimate and secret experiences of the soul of the Jew, the raptures of its intercourse with God in senses which no outsider could understand, were best reflected in the language of that august and indefinable passion which men call love.

The remark 'ascend hither! ascend hither! large banqueting halls and fine couches are in readiness for you,' etc., points to another prominent phase of Rabbinic mysticism. It was strongly believed that the pious could, by means of a life led on the highest plane, free themselves from the trammels that bind the soul to the body and enter, living, into the heavenly paradise. The idea was obviously a development of a branch of Old Testament theology. But the latter gets no further than the conception that heaven may be reached without dying, the persons translated thither having finished their earthly career. The experiences of Enoch (*Genesis*, v. 24) and of Elijah (2 *Kings*, ii. 11) are illustrations. A development of the doctrine is the thought that certain favoured saints of history are, after death and when in heaven, given instruction concerning the doings of men and the general course of events here below. The Apocalyptic literature (see especially *Apocalypse of Baruch*, by Dr. Charles) deals somewhat largely in this idea; and there are traces of it in the Rabbinical literature. But these saints, however true the teachings and revelations vouchsafed to them may eventually have turned out to be, are *dead* as far as the world is concerned.

A further development is seen in the theory that certain pious men may temporarily ascend into the unseen, and, having seen and learnt the deepest mysteries, may return to earth again. These were the mystics who, by training themselves to a life of untarnished holiness, were able to fit themselves for entering a state of ecstasy, to behold visions and hear voices which brought them into direct contact with the Divine Life. They were the students of the Merkabah who, as a result of their peculiar physical and mental make-up, were capable of reaching the goal of their quest. "There were four men," says the Talmud (*Ḥaggigah*, 14b), "who entered Paradise." They were R. 'Akiba (50--130 A.D.), Ben 'Azzai (2nd century A.D.), Ben Zoma (2nd century A.D.), and Elisha b. Abuyah (end of 1st century and beginning of 2nd century A.D.). Although this passage is one of the puzzles of the

Talmud, and is variously interpreted, we may quite feasibly lay it down that the reference here is to one of those waking visits to the invisible world which fall within the experiences of all mystics in all ages.

Fragments of what was a large mystic literature of the later Rabbinical epoch (*i.e.* from about the 7th to the 11th century, usually known as the Gaonic epoch) have descended to us. Of these, one branch is the *Hekalot* (*i.e.* 'halls'), which are supposed to have originated with the mystics of the fore-mentioned period who called themselves *Yŏrĕdē Merkabah* (*i.e.* Riders in the Chariot). As Dr. Louis Ginzberg says (see art 'Ascension' in *Jewish Encyc.* vol. ii.), "these mystics were able, by various manipulations, to enter into a state of autohypnosis, in which they declared they saw heaven open before them, and beheld its mysteries. It was believed that he only could undertake this Merkabah-ride, who was in possession of all religious knowledge, observed all the commandments and precepts and was almost superhuman in the purity of his life. This, however, was regarded usually as a matter of theory; and less perfect men also attempted, by fasting and prayer, to free their senses from the impressions of the outer world and succeeded in entering into a state of ecstasy in which they recounted their heavenly visions."

Much of this belief survives in modern Jewish mysticism, whose chief representatives known as Ḥasidim are to be found in Russia, Poland, Galicia, and Hungary.

Although it was stated above that the large volume of this phase of mystic literature originated in the period from the 7th to the 11th century, modern research has clearly proved that its roots go back to a very much earlier date. In fact, it is very doubtful whether its origin is to be looked for at all in the bosom of early Judaism. Mithra-worship is now taken by scholars to account for much of it. But it is hazardous to venture any final opinion. It must never be forgotten that the first chapter of Ezekiel worked wonders on the old Hebrew imagination. Commentaries on almost every word in the chapter were composed whole-sale. In all likelihood, the mysticism of the Merkabah-riders is a syncretism. Mithraic conceptions in vogue were foisted on to the original Jewish interpretations; and, in combination with Neo-Platonism, there was evolved this branch of Jewish mysticism which, though by no means abundant in the Talmud and the Midrashim, occupies a considerable place in the ideas of the mediæval Kabbalah, as well as in the tenets of the modern Ḥasidim.

---

1. Literally 'House of Judgment,' the technical name for a Jewish Court of Law.
2. There were four such 'worlds' in the mediæval Kabbalah. They will be alluded to further on.
3. Sandalphon = Greek συνάδελφος = co-brother.

PHILO: METATRON: WISDOM

SOMETHING must now be said about the mystical elements in the Hellenistic, as distinguished from the Palestinian, branch of early Judaism. The Palestinian (which includes the Babylonian) is, by a long way, the more voluminous; and its significance for the development of the later Judaism totally eclipses that of Jewish Hellenism which really wielded its influence over Christianity rather than over Judaism. Still there are a few outstanding features in Jewish Hellenism which are germane to our subject. Moreover, modern research has shown that there was a certain degree of intercourse, in the opening centuries of the Christian era, between Jewish scholars of Palestine and Babylonia on the one hand, and Jewish scholars of Alexandria on the other, Alexandria being the great centre of the Hellenistic culture then predominant. This must have resulted in an interchange and interaction of ideas and doctrines which found their way into the literatures of both branches.

A noteworthy example of this fusion of ideas is the famous Philo Judæus of Alexandria. Platonic, Stoic and Rabbinic strata make up the philosophy of Philo. They are intermingled not always harmoniously. But what tells hard upon the student of Philo's presentation of Hebrew thought is the difficulty of knowing whether certain parallel ideas in his writings and the writings of the Palestinian Rabbis originated with him or with the Rabbis. It has, however, been shown, with a fair approach to conclusiveness, that where there is a resemblance in *Halachic* interpretation, Philo is the borrower; whereas the *Haggadic* parallels emanate from the Rabbis.

To attempt an examination of Philo's mysticism as a whole lies quite outside the scope of this book. All that can be dealt with--and this very fragmentarily and in-adequately--are certain points in the mysticism of his Logos idea which, by reason of their affinity with the Haggadah, are important to an understanding of Jewish mysticism. How to bridge the chasm between God and the world, how at the first creation of man it was possible for God who is the all-holy and all-perfect, to come into contact with imperfect man, is an oft-recurring subject of speculation in the Talmud and Midrashim. The cosmogony of Genesis comes in for an exceptionally elaborate treatment. In this connection it is only to be expected that angelology should figure largely. Theologians are quite wrong when they say that post-Biblical Judaism removed the Deity further and further away from the world, and then tried to bring Him nearer again by the medium of the angel. The truth is that God was in many senses brought very near, and the angel was but an aspect of this 'nearness.' God was immanent as well as transcendent, and the angel was a sort of emanation of the Divine, an off-shoot of Deity, holding intimate converse with the affairs of the world. It was on these lines that the Rabbis solved their problem of reconciling the idea of a pure God with an impure world. God did not really come into contact with the world, but His angels did--and His angels are really part and parcel of His own being, emanations of His own substance. This was, of course, far from being a logical solution, but the Rabbis, like many other religious thinkers of those early centuries, were not masters of logic.

Philo's ideas run in what seems a similar groove. All matter is to him evil; hence God must be placed outside the world. But though this was his philosophy, his religion--Judaism--taught him otherwise. Obliged to find some way out of the difficulty, he hit upon the idea of the Logoi, *i.e.* divine agencies, which, while being in some senses inherent in God, are, in other ways and at various times, exterior to Him. It would be incorrect to say that he derived this theology from the Rabbinic sources. Platonic and Stoic teachings are largely responsible for them. But Philo endeavoured to bring them into line with Rabbinic modes of Biblical interpretation. He felt that he ought to give them a Jewish dress--with the result that much of what he says about Divine powers, agencies, attributes operating in the world, independently of the Deity and yet as part and parcel of Him, bears a close resemblance to much of Rabbinic angelology and Rabbinic teaching about the Divine attributes. Thus, to give some examples.

The Rabbis (in *Genesis Rabba*, viii. 3, 4, and in many other places) are at pains to justify the usage of the grammatical plural in the words: "And God said, Let us make man" (*Gen.* i. 26). Various opinions are thrown out. But the finally accepted view is that "at the time when God was about to create the first man, He took counsel with the ministering angels." What this interpretation aims at, is to relieve the Deity of the blame for the evil in man, and to place it upon some other shoulders. But what it really does is to show that the earth is the scene and centre of Divine agencies. Angels are emanations of the Divine working here below. Man is in a *double* sense *made* by them. It was they who had a hand in his creation. It is they who fill his environment, and make him realise that he is ever in the grip of a Presence from which there is no escaping. The Talmud and Midrashim overflow with the descriptions of vast hierarchies of spiritual intelligences--angels--who guide the will of man and the course of nature, surrounding man on all sides and at all moments, shielding him and lifting him up to higher planes of thought and feeling. They protect the pious and help them in their transactions. Every angelic host consists of a thousand times a thousand. The angels give instruction in certain matters. Every man has a special guardian angel. All this literature of angelology can have no possible meaning at all unless it is interpreted to mean that God is present and active in the world, a Power behind phenomena, a directing Mind, a controlling Will, an Immanent God.

Philo's doctrine is similar. Thus he says: "For God, not condescending to come down to the external senses, sends His own words (*logoi*) or angels for the sake of giving assistance to those who love virtue. But they attend like physicians to the diseases of the soul, and apply themselves to heal them, offering sacred recommendations like sacred laws, and inviting men to practise the duties inculcated by them, and, like the trainers of wrestlers, implanting in their pupils strength and power and irresistible vigour. Very properly, therefore, when he [*i.e.* Jacob] has arrived at the external sense, he is represented no longer as meeting God, but only the Divine word, just as his grandfather Abraham, the model of wisdom did" (*On Dreams*, i. 12).

In another passage in the fore-mentioned section, he speaks of "the immortal words (*logoi*) which it is customary to call angels" (*ibid.* i. 19). Again, take the following:

"But these men pray to be nourished by the word (*logos*) of God. But Jacob, raising his head above the word, says that he is nourished by God Himself, and his words are as follows: The God in whom my father Abraham and Isaac were well pleased; the God who has nourished me from my youth upwards to this day; the angel who has delivered me from all my evils, bless these children. This now, being a symbol of a perfect disposition, thinks God Himself his nourisher, and not the word; and he speaks of the angel, which is the word, as the physician of his evils, in this speaking most naturally. For the good things which he has previously mentioned are pleasing to him, inasmuch as the living and true God has given them to him face to face, but the secondary good things have been given to him by the angels and by the word of God. On this account I think it is that God gives men pure good health which is not preceded by any disease in the body, by Himself alone, but that health which is an escape from disease, He gives through the medium of skill and medical science, attributing it to science, and to him who can apply it skilfully, though in truth it is God Himself who heals both by these means, and without these means. And the same is the case with regard to the soul. The good things, namely, food, He gives to men by His power alone; but those which contain in them a deliverance from evil, he gives by means of His angels and His word" (*Allegories of the Sacred Laws*, iii. 62).

The intermingling of Greek and Hebraic elements in these passages is curious. But the two sets are easily distinguishable. Two things are clear from these quotations. Firstly, the angel is a kind of representative of the Deity among mortals. It is a sort of God in action. God is very near man and not transcendent. Secondly, the angel and the Logos (Word) or Logoi (Words) have very much the same nature and fulfil very much the same function. The Rabbinic mysticism clustering round angels as well as the Rabbinic doctrine of the Shechinah--which will be dealt with later--have likewise many points in common. Angels encompass the worthy Israelite; the Shechinah likewise accompanies Israel, nay, even dwells in the midst of impure Israelites, as a famous passage in the Talmud says. But there are aspects of Philo's angelology which are strange to Rabbinic modes of thought. One of the most interesting of these is his designation of angels as 'incorporeal intelligences' and as 'immortal souls' (*On Dreams*, i. 20). The Rabbis obviously thought of angels as material beings. They even at times materialised the Shechinah, as will be mentioned in the following chapter. The sight of an angel was a physical phenomenon. Philo's exegesis took quite a different turn.

Thus, in a lengthy comment on *Genesis*, xxviii. 12 ("And he dreamed a dream and behold a ladder was planted firmly on the ground, the head of which reached to heaven, and the angels of God were ascending and descending upon it") he goes on to say: "This air is the abode of incorporeal souls, since it seemed good to the Creator of the universe to fill all parts of the world with living creatures. . . . For the Creator of the universe formed the air so that it should be the habit of those bodies which are immovable, and the nature of those which are moved in an invisible manner, and the soul of such as are able to exert an impetus and visible sense of their own. . . . Therefore, let no one deprive the most excellent nature of living creatures of the most excellent of those elements which surround the earth; that is to say, of the air. For not only is it not alone deserted by all things besides, but rather like a populous city, it is full of imperishable and immortal citizens, souls equal in number to the stars. Now, of these souls some descend upon the earth with a view to being bound up in mortal bodies. . . . But some soar upwards. . . . But others, condemning the body of great folly and trifling, have pronounced it a prison and a grave, and, flying from it as from a house of correction or a tomb, have raised themselves aloft on light wings towards the æther, and have devoted their whole lives to sublime speculations. There are others again, the purest and most excellent of all, which have received greater and more divine intellects, never by any chance desiring any earthly thing whatever, but being, as it were, lieutenants of the Ruler of the universe, as though they were the eyes and ears of the great king, beholding and listening to everything. Now philosophers in general are wont to call these demons, but the sacred scriptures call them angels, using a name more in accord with nature. For indeed they do report (διαγγέλλουσι) the injunctions of the father to his children and the necessities of the children to the father" (*On Dreams*, i. 22).

From this passage the following deductions seem to be obvious: Firstly, one large department of the Philonic angelology is utterly strange to Talmudic and Midrashic exegesis. An angel as an 'incorporeal soul' is more akin to the Aristotelian doctrine of 'intelligences,' the intermediate beings between the Prime Cause and existing things. The general level of the Rabbinic conception of the angel is well characterised by the following passage:

"When Samael saw that no sin was found amongst them [the Jews] on the Day of Atonement, he exclaimed before God, 'O Thou Sovereign of the Universe, Thou hast one nation on earth resembling the ministering angels in heaven. Just as the latter are bare-footed, so are the Israelites bare-footed on the Day of Atonement. Just as the angels neither eat nor drink, so do the Israelites not eat or drink on the Day of Atonement. Just as the angels do not skip about, so do the Israelites stand, unmoved, upon their feet the whole Day of Atonement. Just as peace reigns in the midst of the angels, so does peace reign in the midst of Israel on the Day of Atonement. Just as the angels are free from all sin, so are the Israelites free from sin on the Day of Atonement.' God hearkens to the advocacy of Israel from the mouth of their arch-accuser, and He grants His atonement for the altar, for the sanctuary, and for the priests and for all the people of the congregation."

This quotation is from the *Pirké-de-Rabbi-Eliezer*, a curious Midrashic work belonging to the 9th century A.D. It seems to summarise all the best points in the angelic lore of the Jews in the preceding nine centuries. The *naïveté* of the whole Rabbinic outlook is here very apparent and is ever so far removed from Philo's 'incorporeal soul.' In fact Philo's systematic division of angels into higher and lower grades is foreign to the Rabbinic speculations which are largely without any system whatsoever. Foreign also is his view of angels as 'souls descending upon the earth with a view to being bound up in mortal bodies.' The angel, in Rabbinic thought, is never *inside* any one.

But, in the second place, it is obvious to the student of *mediaeval* as distinct from the *Talmudic* and *Midrashic* mysticism that there is an affinity between the Philonic treatment of angels and the treatment of the subject by such famous Jewish theologians as Sa'adia b. Joseph (892-942), Judah Ha-Levi (1085-1140), Solomon Ibn Gabirol (1021-1058), Abraham b. David (1100-1180), and Moses Maimonides (1135-1204). They, too, like Philo, were influenced by Greek thought they were either Aristotelians, Platonists, or Neo-Platonists; so that what amount of influence came to them *directly* from the works of Philo is a matter that calls for deep research. To the first-named theologian--Sa'adiah--there is, like to Philo, something immaterial, something ethereal, unearthly, about the angel. While being *external* to man, it is, in a sense, *internal* too, Sa'adiah being of opinion that they were visions seen during prophetic ecstasy rather than outward realities. See his philosophical work *Emunot we-De'ot* ('Faith and Knowledge'), ii. 8, iv. 6.

That Ibn Gabirol should develop a more mystical line of thought than this, is not surprising seeing he is dependent, in many of his essential teachings, upon the *Enneads* of Plotinus. The words of Judah Ha-Levi are worth quoting here. He says (*Cusari*, iv. 3):

"As for the angels, some are created for the time being, out of the subtle elements of matter [as air or fire]. Some are eternal angels [*i.e.* existing from everlasting to everlasting], and perhaps they are the spiritual intelligences of which the philosophers speak. We must neither accept nor reject their words [*i.e.* the words of these philosophers]. It is doubtful whether the angels seen by Isaiah, Ezekiel, and Daniel were of the class of those created for the time being or of the class of spiritual essences which are eternal. 'The glory of God' is a thin subtle body (*goof dâk*) produced by the will of God, and which forms itself in the prophet's imagination in the way that the Divine will directs. This is according to the first [*i.e.* simpler explanation]. But according to a second [*i.e.* more complex] explanation, the 'glory of God' denotes the whole class of angels together with the spiritual instruments (*kĕlīm hāruḥniim*), viz. the Throne, the Chariot (*Merkabah*), the Firmament, the Ophanim and the Spheres (*Gālgālim*), and others besides which belong to the things which are eternal. All this is implied in the term 'glory of God.'

Further on, in the same paragraph, Judah Ha-Levi brackets together as having one meaning, the phrases 'Glory of God,' 'Kingdom of God,' and 'Shechinah of God.' Maimonides speaks on the subject thus (*Guide of the Perplexed*, ii. 6):

"The angels are not corporeal; this is what Aristotle also said; only there is a difference of name; he calls them 'separate intelligences' (*sichlim nifrādīm*), whereas we designate them angels. Moreover, when he says that these 'separate intelligences' are also intermediaries between the Creator and existing things, and that through their means the spheres are moved--the motion of the spheres being the prime cause of all being--this also is written in all books, because you will not find that God does any deed except by means of an angel. . . . The movement of Balaam's ass was done by means of an angel . . . even the elements are called angels. . . . The term angel is applied to a messenger of men, as, *e.g.*, in the phrase 'and Jacob sent messengers' (*mălākīm*), in *Genesis*, xxxii. 3. It is applied to a prophet, as, *e.g.*, in the phrase 'and an angel of the Lord went up from Gilgal to Bochim,' in *Judges*, ii. 1. It is the term used of the 'separate intelligences' which are seen by the prophets in the prophetic vision. It is the designation also of the vital powers as we shall explain."

Maimonides takes a Rabbinic apothegm such as "God does nothing without previously consulting his heavenly [or upper] host," or "God and his Court of Justice have taken counsel together over every limb in the human body, and have put each in its rightful place," and is at pains to show how these statements must not be taken literally to mean that the Deity asks advice or seeks help, but that what they convey is that the term 'angel' stands for the powers embodied in all earthly phenomena, the world-forces which are outflowings of God and represent the aspect of the Divine activity in the universe. Paradoxically enough, Maimonides is rationalist and mystic at one and the same time. While striving to strip the Hebrew scriptures of the supernatural and the miraculous, he exhibits his strong belief in a world impregnated with traces and symptoms of a Divine Life.

But let it not be thought that Philo's Logos and Logoi and his angelology are nothing but symbols of abstract thinking on the ways in which the Deity participates in the affairs of men and of the world. It has been mentioned a little above, that the Rabbis often materialised the Shechinah and gave strongly definite personality to their 'angels.' There is one respect in which Philo followed a similar line of exposition. He too gave personality to his Logos--personality as understood in Philo's time, and very different from our modern ideas of personality. Not alone does he speak of the Logos as the being who guided the patriarchs, as the angel who appeared to Hagar, as the cloud at the Red Sea, as the Divine form who changed the name of Jacob to Israel, but he also describes him as "a suppliant to the immortal God on behalf of the mortal race which is exposed to affliction and misery; and is also the ambassador sent by the Ruler of all to the subject race" (*Who is Heir to the Divine Things*, xlii.). He is "an attendant on the one Supreme Being" (*ibid*. xlviii.). He is a paraclete. "For it was indispensable that the man who was consecrated to the Father of the world, should have, as a paraclete, his son, the being most perfect in virtue, to procure forgiveness of sins, and a supply of unlimited blessings" (*Life of Moses*, iii. 14).

The resemblances between these teachings and much of the mysticism of Paul, as well as of the author of the Fourth Gospel, are unmistakable; and whether they show borrowing or are explicable as belonging to the modes of thinking current in that age, is a moot point. But what strongly concerns our presentation of this subject, is the fact that this branch of Philonic theology is mirrored in the early Jewish, as well as in the early Christian, teaching about God. But with this considerable difference--that whereas some of the cardinal doctrines of Christianity are embedded in these ideas, their significance for Judaism was, at no epoch, vital. They belong to the *literature*, not to the *faith*, of the Jew. They were ever for the few rather than for the many.

It is to the figure of Metatron that we must turn for the counterpart in Rabbinic mysticism to the personified Logos of Philo. "Behold I send an angel before thee, to keep thee in the way and to bring thee into the place which I have prepared. Beware of him and obey his voice, provoke him not; for he will not pardon your transgressions; *for my name is in him*" (*Exodus*, xxiii. 20, 21). This angel in whom God's name exists is, said the Rabbis, Metatron. And why so? Because, said they, the numerical value of the Hebrew letters composing the name Metatron (314) corresponds with those comprising the word Shaddai (= Almighty, one of the Divine appellations).

This is a typical illustration of the Rabbinic mysticism clustering round (i.) arithmetical numbers, and (ii.) the Divine Name. 'My name is in him,' *i.e.* the name 'Almighty' is comprehended in the name 'Metatron.' And the Divine Name is not merely a grammatical part of speech. It is a kind of essence of the Deity Himself. Hence, the essence of the Deity exists in Metatron. He is God's lieutenant. He represents the active phase of Deity as manifested in the universe.

The command to 'beware of him and obey his voice,' failing which 'he will not pardon your transgressions,' forcibly brings out the intercessory powers of Metatron. In the Midrash *Tanḥuma* (on portion *Wa'-ethḥanan*) it is graphically related how Moses, when he knew that he must die, implored all the different parts of creation-- the sea, the dry land, the mountains and the hills--to pray that he might live. But they all refuse. He finally betakes himself to Metatron and says to him: "Seek mercy for me that I may not die." But Metatron replies: "O Moses, my master, why troublest thou thyself thus? I have heard behind the veil that thy prayer for life will not be heard." Metatron confesses that his intercession would be vain, but yet--and here is a great point--the Midrashic passage in question states that immediately after "the anger of the Holy Spirit grew cool." Metatron did not succeed in securing a prolongation of life for Moses, but he managed to turn away Divine wrath from him.

The title 'Prince of the Presence' (*Sār Hā-Pānim*) as well as 'Prince of the World' (*Sar Ha-'Ōlam*) is often applied to Metatron. A striking passage again depicting Metatron, not alone as pleader for Israel, but as taking upon himself the sorrow for Israel's sins, is as follows (*Introduction to Lamentations Rabba*, xxiv.):

"No sooner was the Temple burnt than the Holy One (blessed be He) said: Now will I withdraw my Shechinah from it and I will go up to my former habitation, as it is said (*Hosea*, v. 15), 'I will go and return to my place, till they acknowledge their offence and seek my face.' At that hour the Holy One (blessed be He) wept, saying: Woe is me! What have I done! I caused my Shechinah to abide below for the sake of Israel, but now that Israel has sinned I have returned to my original dwelling-place. Far be it from me that I should be a derision to the nations and a mocking to all creatures! Forthwith *Metatron fell upon his face*, exclaiming: O Sovereign of the Universe, let me weep, but weep thou not! "

The title 'Prince of the Presence' or 'Prince of the World' denotes

Metatron's active interference with the happenings of the universe. *T.B. Yebamoth*, 16b, has the following extraordinary saying:

"No one but the 'Prince of the World' could have uttered verse 25 of *Psalm*, xxxvii, 'I have been young and now am old; yet have I not seen the righteous forsaken, nor his seed begging bread.' Who else could have said this? Could God have said it? Does old age apply to God? Could David have said it? Was he advanced in years [when he composed this *Psalm*]? No one else but the 'Prince of the World' could have said it."

Two important ideas are enshrined here. Firstly, Metatron's existence is made to date from the Creation. A kind of pre-existence is accorded him--and the doctrine of pre-existence, or rather pre-existences, is a ubiquitous element in the old Rabbinic treatment of cosmogony. "Seven things preceded the Creation of the world, *viz.*: (*a*) the Torah, (*b*) the Divine Throne, (*c*) the Temple, (*d*) the Name of the Messiah, (*e*) Paradise, (*f*) Hell, (*g*) Repentance." Whether Metatron ought to be an eighth, or is to be identified with one among these seven, is a point for further research.

Secondly, Metatron speaks words of worldly wisdom garnered from an intimate experience of contact with the multitudinous facts and phases of earthly existence. He knows men as no one else could know them. He resembles, in this respect, the strongly-personified 'Wisdom' of the Jewish-Alexandrian literature. Like it, he is given a sort of prime part in the cosmic process.

The Aramaic commentary (Targum) on *Genesis*, v. 24 ("And Enoch walked with God; and he was not, for God took him") renders the name 'Enoch' by 'Metatron.' And just as Enoch in the Apocrypha (*Book of Jubilees*, iv. 23; 2 *Enoch*, liii. 2) appears as the heavenly scribe, so Metatron is often described in the Talmud and Midrash (see *TB Ḥaggigah*, 15a).

The idea fundamental to both these branches of literature is probably the same; *viz.* that Metatron is a link uniting the human with the Divine, the bridge over which the knowledge of what is passing here below is brought to the realms above, and over which, in return, the Divine concern for men and the world passes down to the scenes of earth. A truly poetic rendering of this Divine concern is given in the Talmud (*Abodah Zarah*, 3b), where God is described as giving instruction a certain number of hours every day, to prematurely-deceased children. "Who instructed them in the period previous to their death?" So the question runs. And the answer is "Metatron! " On this understanding, Metatron is the helper to the Deity; he, as it were, takes up the Divine work at points where its omnipotence cannot, if one may so speak, reach; not even the smallest, meanest child need be forgotten, forsaken of God, so long as Metatron is its guide and instructor.

Metatron has been identified with the Zoroastrian Mithra. It certainly possesses features resembling Philo's Logos. It has also much in common with the theology of the early Gnostics. In all probability it is the result of a fusion of all these systems of thought. The same can be predicted of more than one other branch of Rabbinic angelology. Noteworthy, however, is the fact that though the Jews could get so far as to bring themselves to look at Metatron in the light of a heavenly co-worker with God, a kind of semi-divinity having an access to the Deity in a measure utterly unique, yet so extraordinarily uncompromising were their notions of the *Divine Unity* that, as far as the religion of their daily life was concerned, God alone was God, and Metatron was ignored. His name figures somewhat in certain departments of the Jewish liturgy. He plays a *rôle* in mediæval Jewish mysticism. But the stringent, inelastic emphasis on the idea of safeguarding the Divine Unity--an emphasis rarely appreciated by the non-Jew--could brook no recognition of Metatron in the sphere of the Jew's most intimate religious concerns.

One other dominating characteristic of the Jewish-Hellenistic mysticism is to be found in the functions assigned to the idea of Wisdom. The grand preliminary to this branch of doctrine is to be found in the Old Testament (*Proverbs*, viii. 22-31):

The Lord possessed me in the beginning of his way, before his works of old.

I was set up from everlasting, from the beginning, or ever the earth was.

When there were no depths, I was brought forth;
When there were no fountains abounding with water.

Before the mountains were settled, before the hills, was I brought forth:
While as yet he had not made the earth, nor the fields, nor the highest part of the dust of the world.
When he prepared the heavens, I was there:
When he set a compass upon the face of the depth:
When he established the clouds above:
When he strengthened the foundations of the deep:
When he gave to the sea his decree
That the waters should not pass his commandment:
When he appointed the foundations of the earth:
Then I was by him, as one brought up with him:
And I was daily his delight,
Rejoicing always before him;
Rejoicing in the habitable part of his earth,
And my delights were with the sons of men.

Wisdom is the quality through which God acts in the world, and by the instrumentality of which the Deity is known to man. It is, in the passage just quoted, personified and objectified. It dwells among the sons of men and finds its special delight in intercourse with them. It resembles the Divine Pneuma or Spirit of the Stoic philosophy which, too, is given a prime part in the cosmic process.

The Rabbis, it is interesting to notice, made much of the phrase 'as one brought up with him.' The phrase is represented in the original Hebrew by one word '*Amun*.' By slight alterations in the vowelling they extracted three meanings from it: *viz*. (i.) pedagogue, (ii.) pupil, (iii.) workman. Thus (i.) Wisdom (which they identified with the Torah or Law) was the school-master, tutor in the Divine household, giving guidance to his Divine Master in his plans for the creation of the universe. (ii.) Wisdom was the pupil or child of the Divine (according to Rabbinic teaching a pupil stood to his master in the position of child to a father), hidden away by reason of its preciousness in the lap of the Father, until the time when it became a gift to a newly-launched universe. (iii.) Wisdom was God's workman, or servant, in the work and administration of the universe.

And yet, in spite of all this obvious and strong personification, Wisdom is but "a quality belonging to God, one of His attributes by which He makes Himself known and felt in the world of men and in the human heart, one of the elements in the Divine nature which is most in sympathy with the innate tendency in man to go on striving ever upward and onward." [1]

It is, after all, only God's Wisdom, no matter how near an approach to personality there may be in the various descriptions of the term. It is a potency wholly in God, and yet at one and the same time wholly out of God. It is an embodiment, a revealer of one aspect of Divine Spirit. As has already been remarked, the Jew always vindicated the *Unity of God* no matter into what dubious fields his theological speculations otherwise led him.

The apocryphal *Wisdom of Solomon* shows forth similar mystical elements. "For wisdom is more mobile than any motion; yea, she pervadeth and penetrateth all things by reason of her pureness" (vii. 24). This is the Stoic conception of the immanent Pneuma. Again:

For she is a breath of the power of God,
   And a clear effluence of the glory of the Almighty.
   . . . .
   For she is an effulgence from everlasting light,
   And an unspotted mirror of the working of God.

(vii. 25, 26.)

This seems to be rather the language of Platonism. So is the following pronouncement on the soul's pre-existence:

For I was a witty child
   And had a good spirit,
   Yea, rather, being good, I came into a body undefiled.

(viii. 19, 20.)

Platonic, too, is the notion of earth and matter pressing down the soul:

For the corruptible body presseth down the soul,
    And the earthly tabernacle weigheth down
    The mind that museth upon many things.

(ix. 15.)

Wisdom is man's anchorage in time of trouble. It is the immanent protector and redeemer of mankind. The whole of chapter x. is given over to this theme. In xviii. 14-16, Wisdom becomes a personality. It is identified with the 'Word' which dominates the Prologue of the Fourth Gospel, and which in very similar senses appears in the Rabbinic mysticism as 'Dibbur,' 'Mā-amār' or 'Memra.'

For while peaceful silence enwrapped all things,
    And night in her own swiftness was in mid-course,
    Thine all-powerful Word leaped from heaven out of the Royal Throne,
    A stern warrior into the midst of the doomed land,
    Bearing as a sharp sword thine unfeigned commandment;
    And standing, it filled all things with death;
    And while it touched the heaven, it trode upon the earth.

The Word in this extraordinary pronouncement holds the idea of the Divine *Energy* (as distinguished from the Divine *Love*) which is operative in all things and which "links the Transcendent Godhead with His creative spirit, creature with Creator, and man with man" (Evelyn Underhill, *The Mystic Way*, p. 223). Truly enough, the passage breathes what seems an unedifying spirit of revenge and bloodthirstiness, but it is explicable as an echo of the Old Testament idea of the God of righteousness who hates wickedness and slays the wicked. Divine Justice energises in the world, it is embedded in the scheme of the cosmos, it brooks no evil, it recognises nothing but uprightness and truth. This idea of an antagonism between an immanent God and sin is, as will be seen in our next chapter, a feature of the Rabbinic conception of the Shechinah. In *Exodus Rabba*, xxviii. and xxix., the Divine Voice at the revelation on Sinai deals out death to the idolaters. Similarly, the Targum (Aramaic paraphrase on the Old Testament) renders the Hebrew for "And my soul shall abhor you" (*Leviticus*, xxvi. 30), by "And my Memra [2] shall remove you afar." The Memra here is the avenger of the wayward Israelites. The Jewish-Hellenistic 'Wisdom,' the 'Word' of the Fourth Gospel, the 'Memra' of Targumic literature, the 'Shechinah' of the Talmud and Midrashim--all point--though in somewhat different ways and degrees--to the great fact that the world of matter and of spirit is the scene of the immanent manifestation of Divine Wisdom, Divine Power, Divine Love, Divine Justice.

---

1. For a fuller treatment of this point see the author's work, *The Immanence of God in Rabbinical Literature*, pp. 198-201 (Macmillan & Co., 1912).
2. 'Memra' is the Aramaic for 'word.' For the full theological significance of the 'Memra' see the author's *Immanence of God in Rabbinical Literature*, pp. 146-173.

KINGDOM OF HEAVEN: FELLOWSHIP: SHECHINAH

THE Old Testament, which alone is, and ever was, the Bible of the Jew, contains two oft-recurring ideas which rank among the principal elements of its theological teaching. These ideas are: (*a*) God as Father; (*b*) God as King. To give illustrations from the Old Testament is unnecessary, as the present work is not concerned with the theology of the Bible. It is our business to see in what ways they were developed by the Rabbis of the Talmud and Midrash, and adapted to their systems of thought about the relations between the Divine and the human. The fatherhood of God necessarily involves the sonship of man. The Rabbis living under the rule of foreign masters-- the yoke of Rome and the memories of other yokes all equally galling-- were loth to think that the oppressors of Israel could possibly enjoy so incomparably sublime a privilege as the Divine Fatherhood. It seemed a glaring contradiction that nations who did not hold themselves bound by the Mosaic code, should fall into the category of 'sonship' in relation to the Father. Hence Fatherhood and Sonship became limited to the Jew--although it should be said, for the sake of historical accuracy, that gleams of a far more comprehensive outlook occasionally peep through the pages of Rabbinic literature.

God's Fatherhood to the Jew is evidenced by the outflow of His love towards him. This love, which is ceaseless and rapturous, is described by the Rabbis in numberless ways--in parables, proverbs and similes of a highly picturesque kind. The Jew is possessed by the power of a Spirit of Love which encircles him, holds him in its grip, assures him that forgiveness, protection from enemies, safety from mischief, every coveted thing in heaven and earth, are his.

"Beloved are the Israelites," said R. 'Akiba (50-130 A.D.), "inasmuch as they are called sons of God; especially did that love manifest itself in making known to them that they are sons of God" (*Aboth*, iii. 15). The same Rabbi declared the Book of Canticles to be 'the holiest of all holy books' inasmuch as it symbolises the bond of loving union in which Israel is joined to God (*Canticles Rabba*, Introduction).

In a comment on *Deuteronomy*, xiv. i. ("Ye are children unto the Lord your God") the *Sifri* states the conflicting opinions of two Rabbis. One of them asserts that the verse implies that the Israelites are only called children of God when they conduct themselves as children should, *i.e.* in the right way. The other maintains that the high privilege belongs to them even when they are wayward and sinful. The Father's love is with them no matter how little deserving they may be of it.

Strikingly poetical is the view given in the *Mechilta* (p. 30, Friedmann's ed.). Commenting on *Exodus*, xiv. 19 ("And the angel of the Lord which went before the camp of Israel, removed and went behind them"), it says: "Unto what may it be likened? It may be likened unto a man who was walking by the way and leading his son before him. Robbers came to snatch the son away from him. Seeing this, the father removed the son from before him and placed him behind him. Then came a wolf behind him to steal the son away. So the father removed him from before him and placed him once again behind him. Then came the robbers from before him and the wolf from behind him in order to take the son away. What did the father do? He took the son and placed him upon his arms. But the son thereupon began to feel the pain of the sun's heat upon him. So the father spread his mantle over him; and when he felt hungry he gave him food to eat, and when he felt thirsty he gave him water. Likewise did the Holy One (blessed be He) for Israel, as it is said, 'And I taught Ephraim to go, I took them on my arms; but they knew not that I healed them' (*Hosea*, xi. 3). When the son [Israel] felt the pain of the sun's heat, He [the Father] spread his mantle over him, as it is said, 'He spread a cloud for a covering; and fire to give light in the night' (*Psalm*, cv. 39). When he began to feel hunger, He gave him food, as it is said, 'Behold, I will rain bread from heaven for you' (*Exodus*, xvi. 4). When he began to feel thirst, He gave him to drink, as it is said, 'And he brought forth streams out of the rock' (*Psalm*, lxxviii. 16)."

The truth enshrined in this parable--a parable which has its counterparts in all branches of the Rabbinic literature--is that the closest and most loving of relationships subsists between Israel and God. The love of the Father forms an environment for Israel. The atmosphere the latter breathes is saturated with that love. His whole life is, as it were, a response to it, infected with it, absorbed in it. It gives him the sense of a companionship with a greater and far more real Life than himself. He is ever-lastingly conscious of an intimate union with a Power who can work all things for him, because the governing motive of that Power is Love. Israel and the Father are one.

The Rabbis summarised all the far-reaching implications of this deeply mystical thought of Fatherhood by the usage of the term 'Shechinah.'

But the roots of the teaching about the Shechinah lie in something more than this Fatherhood idea. The Kingdom idea must be reckoned with--the Kingdom of Heaven, as it is familiarly designated both in the Rabbinic literature and in the Prayer-book of the Synagogue. As in the case of the Fatherhood, so here, too, we must seek the origin of the Kingdom in the compass of the Old Testament. In the latter, the kingship of God is sometimes pictured as an event consummated in the present and sometimes as some 'far-off divine event' in the remote future. Thus *Psalm*, cxlv. 13, says: "Thy kingdom is an everlasting kingdom, and thy dominion endureth throughout all generations." This is clearly a *present* kingship. Zechariah, xiv. 9, says: "And the Lord shall be king over the whole earth, on that day shall he be one and his name one." This is obviously a future kingship.

The student of Apocryphal and Apocalyptic literature will find it bearing the same duality of meaning there too. In the Rabbinic literature it is further amplified. The favourite expression there is 'the taking upon one's self [or the receiving] of the yoke of the Kingdom of Heaven.' An examination of several of the contexts in which the phrase is embedded, proves that it stands for a conglomeration of doctrines, such as that: (*a*) The Jew must abandon idolatry (*i.e.* servitude to man or the work of man's hands). (*b*) He must desire and work for the universal recognition of the Jewish God. (*c*) He must acknowledge and feel the 'nearness' of God to him, the Divine companionship ever enshrouding him and his race, the direct revelation of a living and loving God in all fields of his activity and hope. (*d*) The Jew must acknowledge himself as one of a band, and not as an isolated unit--a band held and welded together by the feeling that it is a kingdom within a Kingdom--a greater Kingdom, the Kingdom of Heaven. The so-called 'clannishness' of the Jews, their tendency for herding together, a fault for which they are continuously scolded, abused or, at best, derided, is thus seen to be based upon a motive which is by no means as undesirable as it is generally pictured to be. The Jewish flock must be one because the 'kingdom' of the Jews must be one--and the latter 'kingdom' must be one because the 'Kingdom of Heaven' in which it is comprised and which thrills it through and informs it, is one. "God is king in Jeshurun," say the sages (in allusion to their particular interpretation of *Deuteronomy*, xxxiii. 5), only when "the heads of the people are assembled, and the tribes of Israel are together." In other words, the earthly kingdom is the *fons et origo* of the Heavenly. Remove the earthly kingdom and you remove the Divine Revelation of God in the midst of Israel. The Heavenly Kingdom is broken up and vanishes. Its *raison d'être* is completely gone.

For the individual Jew there are two avenues along which the Kingdom of Heaven can be brought in and consolidated. These are: (*a*) as already said, by his harbouring an intense sense of the solidarity of his race; (*b*) by prayer. A remarkable passage, in *T.B. Berachoth*, 10b, runs thus: "Whosoever eats and drinks previous to praying, of him it is said, 'And me hast thou cast behind thy back' (1 *Kings*, xiv. 9). Do not read 'thy back' (*gey-vě-kāh*) but read 'thy pride' (*gey-ě-kāh*), *i.e.* after priding himself (with food and drink) this man thinks to take upon himself the Kingdom of Heaven."

These two conceptions already described, *viz.* (*a*) the abounding, manifested love involved in Fatherhood, combined with (*b*) the incorporation of a Heavenly Kingdom within the folds of an Israel welded in strictest fellowship, these two conceptions lie at the root of the mysticism of the Shechinah.

'Shechinah' comes from *shachan* = to dwell. The whole edifice of thought about the Shechinah is based upon such passages in the Old Testament as "And let them make me a sanctuary that I may dwell among them" (*Exodus*, xxv. 8). "Defile ye not therefore the land which ye shall inhabit, wherein I dwell: for I the Lord dwell among the children of Israel" (*Numbers*, xxxv. 34). "And I will set my tabernacle among you and my soul shall not abhor you. And I will walk among you and will be your God, and ye shall be my people" (*Leviticus*, xxvi. 11, 12).

The Israelites were one compact fellowship, an indivisible organism, and not a series of separate units. God's dwelling among them, or placing His Tabernacle among them in Old Testament times, was interpreted by the Rabbis of the Talmud and Midrashim as implying that there is a permanent presence of the Divine Spirit in the midst of the people of Israel; and that this Divine Spirit not only accompanies them without ceasing, but that it also imparts itself, communicates itself, to every member of Israel whenever he orders his life in such a way as to be capable of realising it. It is a perpetual incoming of the Divine Life into the human life of the Jew. It is a "Divine-human fellowship which only fails when the human partner [the people of Israel] is in sin." Israel is bathed in a Divine environment. As the great mystic theologian among the Jews of the middle ages (Moses Naḥmanides, born in Spain 1194, died in Palestine about 1270) says, in commenting on *Leviticus*, xxvi. 11: "The Divine soul, of which His dwelling among us is a part, will not thrust us forth [when we work and live aright] as a vessel when heated by hot water thrusts forth its impurities."

All this is meant by the Shechinah. Writers on mysticism, no matter to what school of religious thought they may happen to belong, familiarise us with the great fact that the mystic, by reason of the high levels of spiritual intensity on which his life is lived, experiences certain physical sensations which enable him to *see* or to *hear* something of the mystery of the Divine Presence. Christian mysticism invariably quotes the experiences of Paul in this connection--Paul who was so deeply struck by the brilliant light about him that he "was three days without sight and neither did eat nor drink" (*Acts*, ix. 9). Evelyn Underhill says of a certain mediæval German mystic, Rulman Merswin, that "a brilliant light shone around him; he heard in his ears a Divine voice of adorable sweetness; he felt as if he were lifted from the ground, and carried several times round the garden" (*The Mystic Way*, p. 162).

Phenomena of a similar type cluster round the Shechinah mysticism. Thus, a passage in *Leviticus Rabba*, xx. 10, commenting on *Exodus*, xxiv. ("And upon the nobles of the children of Israel he laid not his hand; also they saw God, and did eat and drink"), runs thus: "R. Tanḥuma said that this verse teaches us that they [*i.e.* the nobles of Israel] uncovered their heads and made their hearts swell with pride and feasted their eyes on the Shechinah. . . . But Moses did not feast his eyes on the Shechinah, and yet he gained a benefit from the Shechinah [*viz.* that 'the skin of his face shone' (*Exodus*, xxxiv. 35)1."

Three points are noteworthy here. Firstly, the *strongly materialised* characterisation of the Shechinah. It was actually a physical food to the onlookers. Secondly, the physical impressions created by the sight of it. The uncovering of the head was no trivial bodily movement. Involving as it did a distinct breach of the oriental mode of showing veneration to a superior, it must have been a highly purposeful act. Thirdly, the contrast between the experience of Moses and that of the nobles is intended to bring out what is a cardinal feature of the Shechinah mysticism, *viz.* that in spite of the fact that the Shechinah is the Presence inseparable from Israel, accompanying him whithersoever he goes, yet the realisation of this Presence by the individual Israelite can only come after a series of spiritual and moral disciplinary acts of the highest order have been gone through by him.

Thus said the Rabbis, the Shechinah says of the proud man: "There is no room for this man and myself in the world." Again: "Whosoever commits a sin in secret acts as though he were pressing against the feet of the Shechinah, as it is said (*Isaiah*, lxvi. 1), 'Thus saith the Lord, the heavens are my throne and the earth is my footstool'" (*T.B. Kiddūshin*, 31a). "Whosoever shows anger regards the Shechinah as though it were a thing of nought" (*T.B. Nedarim*, 22b). "The Shechinah only resides with him who is at once wise, strong and wealthy" (*T.B. Sabbath*, 92a)--'wise' denoting the perfection of spirituality; 'strong' denoting the perfection of the physical faculties; [1] 'wealthy' standing for the perfection of the moral qualities, because, as the Rabbis explained, the man of wealth being independent of the smiles and favours of his fellow-men, will not readily fall a prey to that great perverter of morals--the sin of accepting bribes.

Other instances of the way in which the Shechinah was objectivised and experienced through the channels of the visual or auditory senses are the following: "The Shechinah used to beat before Samson like a bell" (*T.B. Soṭah*, 9b). This is a commentary on Judges, xiii. 25, "And the Spirit of the Lord began to move him" (the Hebrew word for 'to move' is here from the same root as the Hebrew word for a 'bell'). In *Canticles Rabba*, ii., the Shechinah is visible from between the shoulders and fingers of the priests at the time they pronounce upon Israel the priestly benediction of *Numbers*, vi. 24-26: "The Lord bless thee and keep thee; the Lord make his face shine upon thee, and be gracious unto thee; the Lord lift up his countenance upon thee and give thee peace."[2]

In the Midrash *Tanḥuma* on chapter xvi. of *Leviticus*, the Shechinah is associated with the sense of smell--another phenomenon of the mystic life much dwelt upon by modern writers on the subject. Aaron's rod is stated to have 'smelt the Shechinah.' Similarly in the *Yalḵut* on *Canticles*, i., a mystical inference is drawn from the usage of the metaphor of 'a bundle of myrrh' applied to 'my well-beloved,' *i.e.* God.

In *T.B. Megillah*, 29a, it is stated as follows: "The father of Samuel and Levi [Babylonian Rabbis of the 3rd century A.D.] were once sitting in the synagogue of Shef-Ve-Yatib in Nehardea [Babylon]. They suddenly heard a sound of movement. *It was the Shechinah coming*. They at once rose and went out. A fellow-Rabbi by name Shesheth (who was blind) was once sitting in the same synagogue, and when the Shechinah came, he did not go out. Then the ministering angels came and struck terror into him." In the end Shesheth addresses the Shechinah, who advises the angels to cease from vexing him.

It must be borne in mind, in this connection, how intimately conjoined, in the minds of the Rabbis, was the idea 'synagogue' with the idea 'Shechinah.' The blending of the two even went so far as to prompt the Rabbis to say--what is sometimes falsely and foolishly described as 'grotesque'--that God prays and the synagogue is His house of prayer. Hence if it is true, as Evelyn Underhill maintains, that the visionary experience of mystics is 'a picture which the mind constructs . . . from raw materials already at its disposal' (*Mysticism*, p.

325), one can quite see how the consciousness of being inside the synagogue should bring home to the Rabbi, in so particularly drastic a fashion, the reality of the Shechinah's intercourse with men.

Noteworthy also--and this is, as well, one of the distinguishing features of the mystical temperament--is the contrast in the effects which this sudden invasion of a Divine Presence had upon the objects of the visitation. The two Rabbis who left the synagogue did so, most probably, as the result of the fearful weakening and depressing effect of the vision. The Rabbi, however, who stayed on and succeeded in eliciting from the Shechinah a promise that the ministering angels should henceforth cease from troubling him, is the type of the mystic who feels the mental and physical elation, the joy, the rapture, the triumph consequent upon the conviction of his having, at last, reached the goal of his quest--the sight, sound and touch of the Ultimate Reality.

A feature of the Shechinah mysticism which deserves a deeper appreciation than is usually accorded it, is to be found in the reiterated Rabbinic belief that goodness and piety radiate an atmosphere of divinity which infects all who breathe it, with a new impulse towards the good, the beautiful and the true. The good man can bring the Shechinah to his fellows. He can invest earth with the quality which belongs to Heaven. Sight of, or contact with, a saint, is equivalent to an inflowing of the Shechinah. Thus, a striking passage in *Canticles Rabba*, vi., says:

"The original abode of the Shechinah was among the 'taḥtonim,' *i.e.* the lower ones, *i.e.* human beings, earth. When Adam sinned, it ascended away to the first heaven. With Cain's sin, it ascended to the second; with Enoch's, to the third; with the generation of the Flood, to the fourth; with the generation of the Tower of Babel, to the fifth; with the Sodomites, to the sixth. With the sin of the Egyptians in the days of Abraham, it ascended to the seventh. Corresponding to these there arose seven righteous men who brought the Shechinah down back to earth again. These were Abraham, Isaac, Jacob, Kehath, Amram, and Moses."

There is, of course, a strong sprinkling of the 'fellowship' idea which, as was said on a previous page, is a basic factor in Jewish spirituality. The greater the bond of union between the members of the

Jewish brotherhood, the greater the realisation of the Divine Presence in their midst. Add to this the existence of men of conspicuous piety within the bosom of the fellowship, and you have all the essentials for a deeper and stronger infiltration of the Divine stream. The Shechinah is brought back to men by the aid of the better men.

The same train of thought is expressed more pointedly by the following aphorisms:

T.B. Berachoth, 64, says: "Whosoever partakes of a meal at which a 'disciple of the wise' is present, it is as though he enjoyed of the splendour of the Shechinah." Clearly, the presence of the 'disciple of the wise' makes the life of the company about him to be lived on higher levels. He gives it an access to the Divine which it would not otherwise have had. *T.B. Ketuboth*, 105a, says: "Whosoever brings a gift to a 'disciple of the wise' it is as though he brought the first-fruits (*bikkurim*) to the Temple." The 'disciple of the wise' is here a Temple in human form. To approach him is to approach a Holy of Holies. Contact with him is a sanctifying influence. He radiates divinity.

T.B. Ketuboth, 111b, says: "Is it possible for any man to cling to the Shechinah? For is it not said, in *Deuteronomy*, iv. 24, 'For the Lord thy God is a consuming fire'? But the meaning is this: Whosoever marries his daughter to a 'disciple of the wise' or engages in any enterprise with him, or who lets a 'disciple of the wise' enjoy of his worldly possessions, it is counted unto him, by Holy Writ, as though he clung to the Shechinah."

Companionship with the good must be acquired at all costs. It is the dynamic power for opening the door to the spiritual world. The man of virtue is Shechinah-possessed; and to touch only the hem of his garment is to become Shechinah-possessed too.

When Ruth the Moabitess forsakes her ancestral gods in favour of the God of Israel, when Abram, according to the Rabbinic interpretation of *Genesis*, xii. 5 ('And the souls that they had gotten in Harran'), brings the weary and footsore into his home and initiates them into the belief in the God in whom he himself believes, the Rabbis say that the act performed in both cases is 'the entering of the non-Israelite under the wings of the Shechinah.'

The narrow, exclusive nationalist view of the Deity is very apparent in these and many other similar utterances. The Shechinah is for Israel only. The Shechinah is primarily for Israel. God is near to the Jew, far from the non-Jew. These are seemingly natural and correct deductions from the Rabbinic records. If so, is not the term 'mysticism' as applied to the Shechinah a misnomer, seeing that the primal assumption of mysticism is the truth that every soul, notwithstanding race or religion, can have intimate intercourse with the Divine? The answer is this:

The title 'Jew' or 'Israelite' is frequently used by the Rabbis in a more comprehensive sense than they are usually given credit for. Thus *T.B. Ķiddushin*, 40a, says: "Whosoever denies the truth of idolatry becomes a believer in the whole Torah." *T.B. Megillah*, 13a, says: "Whosoever denies idolatry is called a Jew." In the Midrash *Sifra* on *Leviticus*, xvi. there is a comment on *Psalm*, cxxv. 4, "Do good, O Lord, unto those that be good, and to them that are upright in their heart." "The Psalmist," says the *Sifra*, "does *not* say 'Do good to the Priests or to the Levites or to the Israelites.' But he says 'Do good unto those that be good.'" More instances could be quoted did space not forbid.

From the first of the quotations just given, it follows that 'Jew' is a term of the widest scope. From the second one infers that the Jew fills no higher a place in the Divine favour than do the good and worthy of all men and races.

"Yea, He loveth the people," says the Deuteronomist (xxxiii. 3). "Yes," says Rabbi Samuel b. Meir, the great Rabbinic commentator of the 12th century, "God loveth also the nations of the world." Of King Solomon's chariot it is said (*Canticles*, iii. 10) that "the midst thereof is paved with love." "This love in the midst thereof," say the Rabbis, "is the Shechinah." It is certainly not meant in any sectarian sense. The Divine Chariot in Jewish mysticism is, broadly, the idealised universe. And all degrees of creation from amoeba to man hold and reveal the traces of the Divine love which is ever born anew in our hearts and which guarantees the ultimate goodness of the world.

---

1. The Rabbis (in *T.B. Nedarim*, 38a) give some curious illustrations of Moses' wealth, strength and wisdom--all deduced from Old Testament verses.
2. Philo says: "For what life can be better than that which is devoted to speculation, or what can be more closely connected with rational existence? For which reason it is that though the voices of mortal beings are judged of by the faculty of hearing,

nevertheless the Scriptures present to us the words of God to be actually visible to us like light; for in them it is said that, 'All the people *saw* the voice of God' (*Exodus*, xx. 18); they do not say 'heard' it, since what took place was not a beating of the air by means of the organs of the mouth and tongue, but a most exceedingly brilliant ray of virtue not different in any respect from the source of reason, which also in another passage is spoken of in the following manner, 'Ye have seen that I spake unto you from out of heaven' (*ibid*. 22), not 'Ye have heard' for the same reason" (*On the Migration of Abraham*, ix.).

THE BOOK 'YETSIRAH'

THE date and origin of this extraordinary book--the oldest philosophical work in the Hebrew language--are shrouded in obscurity. There is as yet no critical edition of it, although there are several translations of it, both of the whole and of parts, into Latin, German, and French; and the numerous commentaries written on it in Arabic and Hebrew (and the subsequent translations of these into Latin, German, etc.) show, not only the high position which it held in the estimation of Jewish thinkers from the 10th century onward, but also the great influence which it wielded on the general development of Jewish mystical speculation.

The difficulties of fixing its date and origin are illustrated by the fact that whereas the voice of mediæval Jewish scholarship assigned its authorship to the patriarch Abraham (on the grounds of some supposed internal evidence), individual writers here and there credited the book to Rabbi 'Akiba (50-130 A.D.)--'Akiba having been an adept in the mystic lore of numbers; and the Book *Yetsirah* is pervaded with the mystical significances of numbers. Others, again, without touching the question of authorship, give it an origin in the late Talmudic epoch--about the 6th century A.D. This theory is the likeliest of all, because the 6th century marks the beginning of what is known in Jewish history as the Gaonic epoch, when several Rabbinic-mystical works, second in importance only to the Book *Yetsirah*, were composed.

The latest theory is that of Reitzenstein (*Poimandres*, pp. 14, 56, 261, 291) who, arguing from the resemblances between the doctrines of letters and numbers in this book and the miraculous cosmic powers wielded by numbers and letters in the thaumaturgical books current among the Gnostics of the 2nd century B.C., concludes that it is a Hebrew production of the 2nd century B.C. The fatal objection to Reitzenstein's theory, however, seems to lie in the fact that his argument holds good of only one aspect of the work, *viz.* the philological part. The other part--the philosophical--although vitally connected with the philological and deduced from it--contains elements of thought and modes of expression which are many centuries later than the pre-Christian Gnosticism. But Reitzenstein's theory cuts very deeply and cannot be disposed of in a few words.

The clue to the particular nature of the Book *Yetsirah* lies in its two constituent elements which we have a moment ago contrasted. It is a mystical philosophy drawn from the sounds, shapes, relative positions, and numerical values of the letters of the Hebrew alphabet. The nucleus of much of this teaching is to be found in the Talmud, but the Rabbis were certainly not the originators of it. Just as Philo excelled in the art of clothing Grecian philosophy in a Hebraic dress, so did the Rabbis show a considerable capacity for 'naturalising' many an alien product. In the case of the mysticism under consideration they drew from older available sources--Egyptian, Babylonian, Mandæan--and adapted the idea to the framework of their own essential lore.

Thus in *T.B. Berachoth*, 55a, there occurs the remark, "Bezaleel [the architect of the Tabernacle in the desert] knew how to join together (*lĕ-tsa-rĕf*) the letters by means of which the heavens and earth were created." This is because he was "filled with the spirit of God, with wisdom and understanding" (*Exodus*, xxxi. 3), and this wisdom is the same as that of *Proverbs*, iii. 19: "The Lord by wisdom founded the earth." This belief in the magic power of the letters of the alphabet can be traced to Zoroastrianism and ultimately to Chaldea--as Lenormant has shown in his *Chaldean Magic*. It was by means of the combination of letters comprising the Holy Name of God that the disciples of Judah the Prince (c. 135-220 A.D.), who were keen on cosmogony, used to create a three-year-old calf on the eve of every Sabbath and used to eat it on the Sabbath. So says a passage in *T.B. Sanhedrin*, 65b. There is a strong flavour of old Semitic witchcraft here. It is an *exotic* notion introduced for the purpose of intensifying an essentially Jewish belief--the belief in the wonder-working powers bestowed by the Sabbath on those who scrupulously uphold it. The practice of magic and witchcraft was sternly repro-bated by the Old Testament, and the Rabbis were equally severe in its condemnation.

One quotation from the book will suffice to give us a glimpse into the supernatural importance of the forms, sounds, and relative positions of the letters in the Hebrew alphabet. It says: "Twenty-two letters: He drew them, hewed them, combined them, weighed them, interchanged them, and through them produced the whole creation and everything that is destined to come into being" (ii. 2). Each of the actions here mentioned, *viz.* 'drawing,' 'hewing,' 'combining,' 'weighing,' 'interchanging,' is described with a fulness which is as bizarre as it is bewildering; and although the interest is mainly a philological one, it is an indispensable part of the book's philosophy.

As it would be impossible to give the reader any tangible notion of these involved stretches of philological reasoning, without introducing a considerable amount of Hebrew words and Hebrew grammatical terminology, the subject can only be dealt with fragmentarily. The letters of the Hebrew alphabet are pressed into the service of a doctrine which is an element of ancient Semitic theosophy, and which passed thence into Greek philosophy. It is the doctrine of the three primordial substances--water, fire, and air. These three substances underlie all creation, and are the fountain-head of all existence. The three Hebrew letters playing the principal part in connection with these three primal substances are Aleph (א), Mem (מ), and Shin (ש). Why just these letters? For two reasons.

Firstly, these three letters represent three cardinal divisions into which the twenty-two letters of the Hebrew alphabet naturally fall. The divisions are: (*a*) mutes unaccompanied by any sound in producing them (as can be seen by any one who tries the pronunciation of the sound of Mem--it is merely a compression of the lips); (*b*) sibilants, best represented by Shin; (*c*) aspirates, the class to which Aleph belongs--this class being, in the naïve imagination of these theosophists, intermediate to the mutes and the sibilants and, as it were, holding the balance between them. Hence these three letters are called 'mothers' (*ĕm* = mother) because all the other letters are, as it were, born from them. The mediæval Kabbalah, as will be mentioned later on, likewise speaks of 'father' and 'mother' in somewhat similar connections.

Secondly, these three representative 'parent' letters--the mute, the sibilant, the aspirate--symbolise the three basic elements of all existing things, the three primordial substances. Thus water (the first letter of which word in Hebrew is Mem) is symbolised by the mute Mem. Why? Because the chief product of water is fish; and fish are the representatives of the mute creation. Fire (in Hebrew *esh*, most prominent in pronunciation is *sh*) is symbolised by the sibilant Shin. Why? Because the characteristic of fire is its hissing sound; and the equivalent in Hebrew for 'sibilant' is a word which means 'hissing.' Air (the first letter of which word in Hebrew is Aleph) is symbolised by the aspirate Aleph, which has an airy, vacant pronunciation. Just as Aleph holds the balance between the mute letters and the sibilants, so air is, in the natural world, intermediate to the water which always tends in a downward direction, and fire which by its nature always ascends. Of course it needs no hard reasoning here to see how an alien system of very early thought has been mechanically and arbitrarily foisted on to the Hebrew alphabet.

But, as was before mentioned, all the twenty-two letters of the Hebrew alphabet play a dominant *rôle* in the book's philosophy. Thus we read (ii. 2):

"By means of the twenty-two letters, by giving them a form and a shape, by mixing them and combining them in different ways, God made the soul of all that which has been created and of all that which will be. It is upon these same letters that the Holy One (blessed be He) has founded B is high and holy Name."

This remark probably indicates that the existence of these letters and the impress which they leave in every particle of creation are the unfailing source of our knowledge of that supreme Intelligence which, while being immanent in the universe, is its guide and controller and holds all the different parts together. In short, the harmony of the cosmos is due to the Divine wisdom underlying the manipulations of the twenty-two letters.

These twenty-two letters are split up into three divisions. These are: (i.) The three which have just been considered, the three 'mothers' or 'parent' letters (Aleph, Mem, Shin) which symbolise the elements, air, fire, and water, which together make up the cosmos. The year (or time), which is part of the cosmos, also consists of three parts--three seasons, *viz.* summer, which corresponds to the element fire; winter, which corresponds to the element water; spring and autumn, which form a season intermediate to the other two, correspond to. the element air, which also is intermediate to the fire and the water. Again, the human body is likewise a trinity, composed of head, chest, and stomach, and likewise corresponds to the three elements. And the world is a trinity too. Fire is the substance of the heavens, water (condensed) is the basis of earth, air is the dividing medium necessary for preserving the peace between the two.

(ii.) The seven double letters typify the 'contraries' in the cosmos, the forces which serve two mutually opposed ends. Thus, there are seven planets which exercise at times a good and at times a bad influence upon men and things. There are seven days in the week; but there are also seven nights. And so on. It is all arbitrary and highly dubious. The seven 'double' letters are Beth, Gimel, Daleth, Caph, Pĕh, Resh, Tau. They are 'double' because they express two different sounds according as they possess *dagesh* or not. The letter Resh is not usually classed among these by Hebrew grammarians. By deducting these seven and the three 'parent' letters, we get the remaining twelve 'simple' letters.

(iii.) The twelve 'simple' letters are emblematic of the twelve signs of the zodiac, the twelve months of the year, the twelve organs in the human body which perform their work independently of the outside world and are subject to the twelve signs of the zodiac. A strong Gnostic colouring pervades the whole.

Thus the cosmos--embraced ideally in the twenty-two letters--is an expression of the Divine Intelligence. Man, the world, time--these three constitute the cosmos, and out-side them there is but one great existence, the Infinite.

This brings us to two doctrines of Jewish mysticism which appear for the first time in the Book *Yetsirah*, and which were developed subsequently on diverse lines. These are: (*a*) the doctrine of emanation; (*b*) the Ten Sefirot.

In the general literature of mysticism, the doctrine (or rather doctrines) of emanation is usually associated for the first time with the great name of Plotinus (born at Lycopolis, in Egypt, about 205 A.D.). This remark raises a twofold reflection which is of the highest interest. Firstly, it shows how one particularly influential aspect of mysticism, *viz*. emanation, is a feature common to the theologies of both the early Church and the early Synagogue--sundered as these two were from one another by so many other irreconcilable points of disagreement. Secondly, it shows how both Jewish and Christian mysticism are alike indebted to one and the same set of sources, *viz*. Gnosticism and its development--the Alexandrian Neoplatonism. The latter is the pith and core of the emanation doctrines of Plotinus. It is equally the root of the emanation doctrines of the Book *Yetsirah*, the *Zohar*, and, in fact, all branches of the mediæval Kabbalah.

Emanation implies that all existing things are successive outflowings or outgoings of God. God contains within Himself all. He is perfect, incomprehensible, indivisible, de-pendent on nothing, in need of nothing. Everything in the cosmos, all finite creatures animate and inanimate, flow out, radiate, in a successive series, from God, the Perfect One. The *motif* of this teaching is that of explaining the difficulties involved in the inevitable assumption of all religion, *viz*. that there is a bond of relationship between God and His creation. How can there be any connecting link between a Being who is self-sufficient, unchangeable, infinite, perfect, and matter which is finite, changeable, imperfect, etc.? This is the difficulty. All doctrines of emanation answer it in more or less the same way, by saying that God is not really external to any one or anything. Everything is originally comprehended in Him, "with no contrasts of here or there, no oppositions of this and that, no separation into change and variation" (Rufus Jones, *Studies in Mystical Religion*, p. 73). On this understanding there is no necessity for hunting after 'the missing link' between the Divine and the human. The multiplicity that one beholds in the cosmos, the whole panorama of thought, action, goodness, badness, the soul, the mind-- all things that go to make up the pageant of man's life in the universe, are emanations, radiations from the one Unity, manifestations of the God from whom all things flow and to whom they must all finally return because they are ultimately one with the One, just as the flame is one with the candle from which it issues.

In the Book *Yetsirah*, the teaching about emanation is intertwined with the doctrine of the Ten Sefirot. The object of this inter-twining is that of giving a more decidedly *Jewish* colouring to the Neoplatonic conceptions of emanations. The Jewish mystics, however far they may have wandered into other fields for their views about God, always felt that the *Hebrew Bible and God as preached by the Hebrew Bible* must be the core of their message. There, thought they, lies the final Truth. Final Truth, taught they, is but a commentary on the Hebrew Bible.

Where did the idea of the Sefirot originate? In all probability it originated with the Rabbis of the Talmud in the first three centuries of the Christian era. Thus, a passage in *T.B. Ḥaggigah*, 12a, speaks of the "Ten agencies through which God created the world, *viz.* wisdom, insight, cognition, strength, power, inexorableness, justice, right, love, mercy."

There are, as will be shown more fully in a later chapter, some obvious resemblances between these ten creative potentialities of the Talmud, and the Ten Sefirot of our Book and of the mediæval Kabbalah (though the resemblances between those of the Talmud and of the Kabbalah are considerably stronger than the resemblances between those of the Talmud and our Book *Yetsirah*). To these facts must be added also the personification of Wisdom as well as of Torah by the early Rabbis, and their doctrine about the creation of the world by two *Middot* (Attributes), *viz.* the Attribute of Mercy and the Attribute of Justice.

Let us turn to the description of the Ten Sefirot as given by the Book *Yetsirah* (i. 9):

"There are Ten Sefirot--ten, not nine; ten, not eleven. Act in order to understand them in thy wisdom and thy intelligence; so that thy investigations exercise themselves continually upon them; also thy speculations, thy knowledge, thy thought, thy imagination; make things to rest upon their principle and re-establish the Creator upon his foundation."

Again (i. 8):

"The Ten Sefirot are like the fingers of the hand, ten in number, five corresponding to five. But in the middle of them is the knot of the Unity."

There is a tantalising vagueness about these descriptions, and, as modern scholars always hasten to point out, the Sefirot of the Book *Yetsirah* differ from those of the *Zohar* and the mediæval Kabbalah generally in one cardinal respect, *viz.* that whereas in the two latter systems the Sefirot have the fullest possible mystical connotation, in the *Yetsirah* Book they cluster mainly round the mysticism of numbers. Numbers and letters (of the Hebrew alphabet, as we have seen) give the main impetus to the peculiar teaching. Divine action in its relation to the universe is conceived in the form of abstract numbers. But yet the following quotation from the book shows a clear foreshadowing of a real mystical system such as is seen in the *Zohar*.

"The first of the Sefirot, *one*, is the spirit (*Ruah*) of the living God (blessed be His Name, blessed be the Name of Him who inhabits eternity!). The spirit, the voice, and the word, these are the Holy Spirit."

The second of the Sefirot, *two*, is the air which comes from the spirit. On it are hewn and engraven the twenty-two letters which form altogether but one breath.

The third of the Sefirot, *three*, is the water which comes from the air [*i.e.* condensed vapour]. It is in the water that He has dug the darknesses and the chaos, that He has formed the earth and the clay, which was spread out afterwards in the form of a carpet, hewn out like a wall and covered as though by a roof.

The fourth of the Sefirot, *four*, is the fire which comes from the water, and with which He has made the throne of His glory, the heavenly Ophanim (Wheels), the Seraphim, and the ministering angels. With the three together He has built his dwelling, as it is written, "He maketh the winds his messengers, his ministers a flaming fire" (*Psalm*, civ. 4).

The remaining six Sefirot are the six dimensions of space--the four cardinal points of the compass, in addition to height and depth.

The difficulties here are many, and some are insuperable. Are the Sefirot really a piece of Jewish mysticism (as was suggested before) or are they nothing more than echoes of the Gnostic systems of number-manipulations?

What is the relation between the cosmic powers of the twenty-two letters of the Hebrew alphabet and the cosmic powers of the Sefirot?

What bearing has the doctrine of the three primal elements upon the first four Sefirot which seem to contain very much the same thought?

In the answer to the first of these queries lies the clue to the nature of the book. The Book *Yetsirah* is syncretic, and while the emphasised significance of the number 'ten,' as well as the importance of the idea of the world as the scene of Divine Agencies (or *Middot*), is in its native origin Jewish, the teaching about the creative powers of letters and numbers is only Jewish by adoption, and whether the word 'Sefirot' is originally Jewish or alien is a moot point; the notion of the three primal substances is clearly an exotic foisted on to the book to give it the appearance of the philosophic completeness which the age demanded. Viewing the book, therefore, as a mosaic rather than a concrete and continuous whole, it is futile to ask questions about the consistency of its parts. What, however, we can do, and ought to do, is to try to see how the author pieced his mosaic together so as to give to his readers what, in his opinion, was a presentation of the doctrine of emanation as interpreted by the spirit of Judaism.

It will be noticed that the three primal substances, air, fire, water, are identical with the second, third, and fourth of the Sefirot, but whereas each of these is produced from the preceding one, the three primal substances seem to be all independent of one another as regards production. And again, the second, third, and fourth of the Sefirot all emanate originally from the first, *viz.* the *Ruaḥ*--the Spirit of the living God. No such notion attaches to the three primal substances. The object in all this seems to be that of giving an essentially Jewish colouring to cosmogony. Everything was brought forth by the Spirit of God. As the Psalmist says: "By the word of the Lord were the heavens made; and all the host of them by the breath of his mouth" (xxxiii. 6). It is a counterblast to the Aristotelian doctrine of the eternity of matter which to the Jewish mediæval mind was rank blasphemy. To say that everything emanates originally from the Spirit of God is tantamount to the assertion that the prototypes of matter are all of them aspects or modifications of the Divine Spirit. This, again, is to put a more Jewish complexion on the doctrine of emanation, which, when carried out to its logical conclusion in the philosophy of Neoplatonism, leads to pantheism--another pitfall which our author apparently wanted to avoid.

That such a construction is a tenable one is seen from the book's remark, "The last of the Sefirot unites itself to its first just like a flame is joined to the candle, for God is one and there is no second" (i. 5). The offence of recognising 'two Divine powers' (shêté-rĕ-shooyôt) was always a terrible one to the Jewish mind. Again, all the numbers from two to ten are derived from the unit, one. Even so does all the multiplicity and variety of forms, types, etc., in the cosmos find its highest consummation, its ultimate home and goal, in the Unity, *viz.* God. Here, again, we see how an alien system of number-mysticism is drafted into the fold of an essentially Jewish type of mysticism, *viz.* that clustering round the cardinal notion of the Unity of God. This theme, after being elaborated by the Talmudic Rabbis of the opening centuries of Christianity, was again taken up by the mediæval Jewish theologians, and reached the zenith of its mystical development in the pages of the *Zohar* and the mediæval Kabbalah generally.

But what is the relation between the cosmic powers of the twenty-two letters of the Hebrew alphabet and the cosmic parts played by the Ten Sefirot? The answer would seem to lie in the peculiar description which the book itself, in one place, gives to the Sefirot. The latter are, it says, 'Ten Sefirot without anything' (bêlēē mā). In other words 'abstracts.' They are the categories of the universe, the forms or moulds into which all created things were originally cast. They are *form*, as distinguished from matter. Whereas the Sefirot are responsible for the first production of form, so the twenty-two letters are the prime cause of matter. All existence and development are due to the creative powers of the letters, but they are inconceivable apart from the *form* with which the Sefirot has invested them.

The Book *Yetsirah* lands us into the heart of Jewish mysticism and prepares the way for the ramified literature of the *Zohar*. It does this by teaching that God and the world are a unity rather than a dualism. The Sefirot and the twenty-two letters of the alphabet, or, in other words, the forms and essences which make up the visible universe, are all an unfolding of the Divine, all emanations from the Spirit. God is at one and the same time both the matter and form of the universe. But He is something more. He is not identical with the universe. He is greater than it, transcends it. Nothing exists or can exist outside Him. Though immanent, He is also and at the same time transcendent. This insistence upon the Divine transcendence runs like a golden thread throughout all branches of Jewish mysticism, thus enabling it, both as a system of thought and as a phase of practical religion, to do justice at once to the 'legal' and spiritual elements which are inextricably intertwined in Judaism.

But if the Book *Yetsirah* gave the impulse to the great books of mediæval Jewish mysticism, it was eclipsed by them in one great particular. The naïve conception of the mysterious powers of letters and numbers was superseded by the introduction of theological and moral ideas. The object of discussion became not so much the relationship between the Creator and His cosmos as the relationship between God and that inner surging world of thought and emotion which we term man. How man can ascend to God whilst bound in the trammels of the flesh or after having shuffled off this 'muddy vesture of decay,' how God communicates Himself to man, imparting to him the knowledge which has its fountain-head in His own inexhaustible Being and the love which is the seal of His abiding goodness and nearness,--these themes form, roughly speaking, the staple of the *Zohar* mysticism which presents itself for brief consideration in the coming pages.

SOME GENERAL FEATURES OF THE 'ZOHAR' MYSTICISM

THE *Zohar* (lit. = 'Shining' or 'Brightness' from the word in *Daniel*, xii. 3--"And they that be wise shall shine as the brightness of the firmament") is, *par excellence*, the textbook of Jewish mediæval mysticism. Its language is partly Aramaic and partly Hebrew. While purporting to be but a commentary on the Pentateuch, it is, in reality, quite an independent compendium of Kabbalistic theosophy. Its style, its subject-matter, its spirit lead the reader into realms which bear hardly any conceivable resemblance to the manner and substance of the Pentateuch.

The *Zohar* compares well with the Talmud in one respect. They are both painfully unsystematic in the handling of their subject-matter. Both present us with a bizarre medley of ideas and facts, an ill-assorted conglomeration of history and fable, truth and fiction, serious comment which has a value for all time and observations which the march of time asks us to dismiss as outworn and valueless. Both works, too, cover a long stretch of time.

The *Zohar* is a pseudepigraphic work. It is impossible, in the present book, to give the reader even the faintest outlines of the literature written by Jews of many countries and many centuries, on the vexed question of the authorship of the *Zohar*. It pretends to be the record of a direct Divine revelation to Rabbi Simeon ben Yoḥai (born in

Galilee 2nd century A.D.); and it is mainly written in the form of a series of utterances from the mouth of Simeon to his disciples, who believed him to be conveying to them the truths which he had received first-hand from Heaven. Criticism has long ago demonstrated the utter untenability of this view. The *Zohar* made its first appearance in Spain in the 13th century, and its contents show incontestably that not alone must the work, as a whole, be considerably later than the 2nd century (although many an idea and doctrine certainly does go as far back as that, and further too), but that it could not possibly be the production of a single author or a single period of history. It is, like the *Yetsirah* book, a syncretism. Many civilisations, many faiths, and many philosophies went to the making of it. All these were, in some instances, taken in their original state and incorporated in the work, while, in other instances, they found room in it only after they had passed through the crucible of the Jewish mind and had thus become 'judaised' in the process. But that a goodly proportion of it is the development of many a doctrine embodied in the Talmud and Midrashim, there cannot be the least doubt. To ask whether this or that doctrine of Talmudic literature is indigenous to the Talmud or has its source elsewhere, is, of course, quite another matter. But that it reached the *Zohar* from the Talmud and Midrashim and their progeny, *directly*, is certain.

Where the foreign elements are drawn from is a fruitful subject of speculation amongst scholars. There is general admission, however, that Neoplatonism and Gnosticism are responsible for much.

And to this must be added a newer theory, which finds echoes of Persian Sūfism in the *Zohar*. The sūfi mystics were very numerous in Persia from the 8th century onwards, and it is maintained that the Jews of Persia, influenced by Sūfism, transmitted to the Jews of Spain (who were very numerous, very influential, and very distinguished in learning from the 10th to the 15th century) many mystical interpretations of esoteric tenets which in various shapes found an entrance into the *Zohar*.

Be this as it may, we must be on our guard against following the mistaken opinion of a certain set of Jewish theologians who would have us regard the whole of the mediæval Kabbalah (of which the *Zohar* is a conspicuous and representative part) as a sudden and strange importation from without. It is really a continuation of the old stream of Talmudic and Midrashic thought with the admixture of extraneous elements picked up, as was inevitable, by the stream's course through many lands--elements the commingling of which must have, in many ways, transformed the original colour and nature of the stream.

The *Zohar*, as was said above, purports to be but a commentary on the Pentateuch. It is self-explanatory on this point. The following is a. direct quotation:

"Woe unto the man," says Simeon ben Yoḥai," who sees in the Torah nought but simple narratives and ordinary words. For if, in truth, it contained only that, we should have been able, even to-day, also to compose a Torah which would be, in very much another way, worthy of regard. In order to find only simple statements we should only have to betake ourselves to the ordinary legislators, among whom we could find valuable words in even greater quantity. It would suffice us to imitate them and to make a Law after their words and example. But it is not thus. Every word of the Torah contains an elevated sense and a sublime mystery."

Here is a direct intimation of the *Zohar's* emphasis upon the existence of higher truths in the Bible. It continues:

"The narratives (or words) of the Law are the garment of the Law. Woe unto him who takes this garment for the Law itself! It is in this sense that David spake, saying, 'Open thou mine eyes, that I may behold wondrous things out of thy Law' (*Psalm*, cxix. 18). David wished to speak of that which is hidden beneath the garment of the Law. There are fools who, seeing a man covered with a beautiful garment, look no further than that; and yet that which gives a worth to the garment is his body, and what is even more precious than that, his soul. The Law, too, has its body. There are precepts which one might call the body of the Law. The ordinary narratives which are intermingled are the garments with which the body is covered. Simpletons have regard only to the garments or narratives of the Law. . . . The better instructed pay no regard to the garment, but to the body which it encloses. Finally, the wise, the servants of the supreme King, they who inhabit the heights of Sinai, are concerned only with the soul which is the foundation of all else, which is the *real* Law. And in the time to come they will be prepared to gaze at the soul of that soul. which breathes through the Law."

The mystical sense of the Law, then, is its highest and truest sense. What edifice of thought does the *Zohar* erect on this foundation? It posits the cardinal principle that there is an esoteric as well as an exoteric reality in the phenomena of the world. The world is a series of emanations from the Divine. To quote the original:

"He is the beginning as well as the end of all stages (*dargin*); upon Him are stamped (*etrashim*) all the stages. But He can only be called *One*, in order to show that although He possesses many forms, He is nothing other than ONE" (i. fol. 21).

Or, to give a fuller and more striking version of the same thought:

"Before the Holy One (blessed be He) created this world, He went on creating worlds and destroying them. Whatsoever exists in this world, everything that has been in existence throughout all generations, *was in existence in His presence* (*kāmé*) in all their manifold forms" (iii. fol. 61).

In other words, the universe is the outward expression of the inner Divine thought. Everything germinated from the eternal archetypal Divine idea. Or as it is put in another way:

"He made this world of below to correspond with the world of above. Everything which is above has its pattern here below and *all constitutes a unity*" (ii. fol. 20).

What the *Zohar* thus aims at teaching us is, that man, having the privilege to behold everywhere the Divine image--the world being an embodiment of God--can, if he will, make his way to the Invisible Author of all; can have union with the Unseen. "Whatsoever belongs to the domain [literally 'side,' *sitrā*] of the Spirit, thrusts itself forward and is visible" (ii. fol. 20). The universe is Divine Spirit materialised, and it is given to man to have contact with it. The Rabbis of the Talmud and Midrashim had an idea of a sort of image of God which is immanent in the universe. Thus, a passage in the *Tanḥuma* (on *Genesis*, xxiii.) says: "If a mortal king engraves his image upon a tablet, the tablet is greater than the image. But God is great, and yet His image is greater than the whole world."

But it is only fair to add--and it bears out the remark already made about the curious mixture of ingredients which make up the *Zohar*--that in conjunction with this high note of thought there is another note which strikes the modern reader as being of a pitifully inferior nature. The juxtaposition is deplorable. We are presented with an almost unintelligible mass of mediæval astrology. Thus: "In the firmament above which covers all things, signs are engraven in which are fixed hidden things and secrets. These marks are those of the constellations and the planets" (ii. fol. 74). Here is a tiny quotation representative of a huge quantity of the *Zohar's* material. "He who has to set out on a journey in the morning must rise at the break of day and must look towards the east. He will behold letters moving in the heavens, one ascending and another descending. These brilliant forms are those of the letters with which God created the heaven and the earth. They form His mysterious and holy Name" (*Ibid.* 76). This looks very much like a mixture of Pythagorean theories of letters with mediæval astrological notions. "When the spirits and the souls come out of Eden [the *Zohar*, like all the Kabbalah, abundantly teaches the pre-existence of souls] they all possess a certain appearance which, later on, is reflected in the face" (*Ibid.* 73). From this, all sorts of the strangest facts of physiognomy are seriously deduced.

In a work which professes to draw its substance from the secret and esoteric aspect of the Old Testament, and which, as we have said, makes the seen world so much akin to the unseen, it is only to be expected that angelology should fill an important place. The impetus to much of it is directly given by a saying of the Talmud, to the effect that "the righteous are greater than the ministering angels" (*T.B. Sanhedrin*, 93a). This idea is just of a piece with the general drift of the *Zohar*. For, by its theories of emanation, and by its insistence on the idea of the macrocosm or of the world as being an evolution of the image of God and of man as a small copy of the world, a microcosm, it cannot but make man as the centre, the crown and consummation of all creation. Hence man must rank above the angels.

It is important to observe the framework of thought into which the *Zohar* fits its ideas on the relative positions of angels and men in the microcosm. The world as a manifestation of the Divine, as the materialised expression of God's immanent activity, is really made up of four component parts (or 'worlds,' as the Kabbalah always styles them). These are: (*a*) the world of Azilut or emanation; (*b*) the world of Beriah, *i.e.* creative ideas; (c) the world of *Yetsirah* or creative formations; (d) the world of 'Asiyah or creative matter.

The first term, Azilut, is based on the Hebrew verb *azal* in *Numbers*, xi. 17 ("And I will take of the spirit which is upon thee and will put it upon them"). The second, third, and fourth terms are derived from the three Hebrew verbs in *Isaiah*, xliii. 7, 'I have created,' 'I have formed,' 'I have made.' The world of Azilut constitutes the domain of the Ten Sefirot--which will be considered in our next chapter. The world of Beriah holds the Divine throne which emanates from the light of the Sefirot, also the souls of the pious. The world of *Yetsirah* is the scene of the 'divine halls' (*hekalot*)--the seven heavenly halls guarded by angels, into which the ecstatic seekers for the Merkabah (Chariot) strive to gain admission. The angels have their abode there, presided over by Metatron; and there also are the souls of ordinary men (as distinguished from the pious). In the world of 'Asiyah are the lower order of angels--the Ophanim, whose business it is to combat evil and to receive the prayers of men. Thus, seeing that the hierarchy of angels only begins with the 'third world,' whereas the souls of the pious belong to the 'second world,' the position of man in the Divine evolution is superior to that of the angel.

The idea of the active part thus played by angels in the emanation-worlds of Jewish mediæval mysticism is primarily derived from such Old Testament verses as "he maketh his angels winds [A.V. spirits]; his ministers a flaming fire" (*Psalm*, civ. 4), which has already been quoted in a similar connection before. But suppose we attempt to rationalise the old-world allegorical language, what constructions would we place upon these angelic activities in the scheme of man and the universe? Much light is shed on the subject by the fact of the decisive names which are accorded to the angels--names which denote missions. Thus Raḥmiel is the angel of mercy, Tahariel is the angel of purity, Pedāel is the angel of deliverance, Tsadkiel is the angel of justice, Raziel is the angel who guards the Divine secrets. Metatron is the master of all these, and it has been shown in a previous chapter how closely Metatron is allied to the Deity, playing in the world a *rôle* akin to that of the Deity. The inference from all these statements is that every particle of the natural world, every shred of man's organism, is saturated with some manifestation or other of the Divine Will--the Divine Will which is goodness and truth and love and justice made manifest and real. It is this impregnable Force underlying all phenomena that preserves the world in its course and that makes its manifold and variegated parts work in harmonious relations.

But what about the existence of sin and evil? How can their existence be justified in a world such as the Zoharic mysticism implies--a world which is a series of emanations from the Divine, a world wherein God is eternally and intimately present in its every part, because the whole is but a manifestation of Himself? If all things, *i.e.* everything good and everything evil, are similarly and equally phases of the same Divine Life, then the distinction between good and evil becomes meaningless. But to affirm this, is to deny the first principles of both religion and morality. It is the quagmire of pantheism. Does the *Zohar* lead to any pantheistic conclusion? If not, how does it evade the difficulty?

The reply to these queries is that the *Zohar* steers clear of the dangers of pantheism, and that it solves the problem of evil in a way which, while appearing highly unsatisfactory to the modern scientific Western mind, is quite in keeping with the intellectual level of the times in which its writers lived. Evil, sin, and their personifications, the demons, are termed *kĕlīfoth*, *i.e.* the coverings, wrappings, externals of all existing things. Just as the covering (or husk) of anything is not the real thing and far inferior to it, so sin and evil are, as it were, the gross, inferior, imperfect aspects of creation. And as the world is an emanation of the Divine, it follows that whatsoever in the world is evil, and not of the Divine, cannot be real. Hence evil is that which has no being; it is a sort of illusion; it is a state of absence, negation; it is a thing which merely appears to be but is not. It is symbolised, according to the *Zohar*, by the condition of the primæval chaos as described in *Genesis*, i. 2, *viz.* 'without form,' 'void,' 'darkness,' *i.e.* the absence of all visible form, order, life. By means of the creation of the world (which is an emanation of the Divine) the Infinite became, as it were, 'contracted' (*Tsimtsum*) and took on certain attributes of the finite. To this finite belongs the 'darkness' of the first chaos or, in other words, evil. Hence the finite stands at the uttermost extremity of the Divine emanation, *i.e.* the world. And as it is man's duty to strive after union with the Infinite, his pursuit of the finite leads him to that which lies at the extremity of the Divine nature rather than that which lies at the heart of it. This constitutes evil. It is a state of absence, a negation, because man who, like the universe, is but one of the manifestations of the Divine, can only attain the real when he seeks the Real who is his fount, his home.

It is of interest--and vital to an understanding of all Kabbalistic literature--to note some of the favourite technical terms employed, in addition to those already here mentioned in passing. A ubiquitous term is *En-Sof*, applied to the Deity. These words mean literally 'No End.' The Deity is boundless, endless. The *Zohar* was not the first mystical work to use the words. The underlying idea was probably supplied by the idea underlying the description of the Godhead in the philosophy of Ibn Gabirol, the Spanish-Hebrew poet and mystic philosopher of the eleventh century. He describes the Deity as the '*shĕ-ĕn to tiklah*,' i.e. the one who has no bounds or ends. Ibn Gabirol was a Neoplatonist, and much of his philosophy shows the influence upon him of Plotinus. But he forsakes his master and follows strictly in the line of Jewish tradition in one respect, *viz.* that in order, as he thought, to safeguard the Jewish doctrine of monotheism, the Deity must be freed from the ascription to Him of all attributes. Hence God can only be properly described by a title which emphasises the negation of all attributes. The *En-Sof* of the *Zohar* and its predecessors is probably an echo of this ultra-negative characterisation of the Deity. Let us quote the *Zohar*:

"Before having created any shape in the world, before having produced any form, He was alone, without form, resembling nothing. Who could comprehend Him as He then was, before creation, since He had no form? It is forbidden to picture Him by any form or under any shape whatsoever, not even by His holy name, nor by a letter [of the alphabet] nor by a point [the Yod, which is the smallest letter in the Hebrew alphabet, is usually designated as a point]. Such is the sense of the words, 'For ye saw no manner of similitude on the day when the Lord spake unto you in Horeb, out of the midst of the fire' (*Deut.* iv. 15). This means that you saw no other thing which you might possibly represent by a form or shape. But after He had created the form of the Heavenly Man (*Adam 'Ilā-ā*) He used him as a chariot (Merkābāh) on which to descend. He wished to be called by the form which consists of the holy name of Jahveh. He wished to make Himself known by His attributes, by each attribute separately. So He let Himself be styled as the God of pardon, the God of justice, the God omnipotent, the God of hosts and He who is (Jahveh). His object was to make thus intelligible what are His qualities and how His justice and His compassion extend over the world as well as over the works of men. For, had He not shed His brightness over all His creatures, how would we get to know Him? How would it be true to say that the world is filled with His glory? Woe unto the man who would dare to compare Him to even one of His own attributes! Yet still less ought He to be likened unto the man who came from the earth and who is destined for death! It is necessary to conceive of Him as above all creatures and all attributes. And then when these things have been removed, there is left neither attribute, nor shape, nor form" (ii. fol. 42).

From this characteristic extract, the following deductions are possible:

(*a*) God as the *En-Sof* and as a Being utterly divested of attributes is an idea that can only be postulated negatively. You cannot tell what God is; you can only tell what He is not. But if this be so, and if, as is axiomatic to the *Zohar* and all the Kabbalah, the world is contained in God just as a small vessel is contained in a larger, and nothing exists outside of God, how can creation be explained, whence and how arose the universe? The universe is imperfect and finite, and its creation must have involved, therefore, some change in the character of God who *ex hypothesi* is perfect, free from all attributes, and therefore free from all possibility of change. How could this be? The answer is contained in the *Zohar's* teaching on the Ten Sefirot, which will be considered in our coming chapter.

(*b*) The idea of God using the Heavenly Man (*Adam 'Ilā-ā*) as a chariot on which to descend indicates a noteworthy identity of teaching in the *Zohar* and Plotinus. For both systems imply that there is a sort of double movement in the universe, 'a way down and a way up.' There is a process of Divine emanation, *i.e.* an outgoing of God, a self-descent from His transcendent height towards the lowly abodes of man. And correspondingly there is an ascent, a way up, on the man's part. For, just as to Plotinus, the final stage of the soul's return journey to its home in God, consists in its highest experience (brought about by a withdrawal from desires and from objects of sense) of contact and union with God, so also, according to the *Zohar*, the three elements of which the soul is composed, *viz.* the rational (*neshāmāh*), the moral (*ruaḥ*), and the vital (*nefesh*), are each of them, not only emanations from the Sefirot, but also have the potency of uniting him again with the Sefirot, and, in the case of the pious man, of uniting him with the highest of the Sefirot, the Crown or Supreme Intelligence.

(*c*) The idea of the Heavenly Man, or *Adam Kadmon* ('First' or 'Original' Man), or *Shechinta Tā-tā-ā* ('Lower' or 'Terrestrial' Shechinah), is vital to an understanding of the *Zohar* and of all Kabbalistic literature. It has resemblances to the Philonic exegesis on the distinction between "the heavenly man born in the image of God," and therefore having "no participation in any corruptible or earthlike essence," and "the earthly man," who was made "of loose material, called a lump of clay" (*On the Allegories of the Sacred Laws*, i. 12). One thinks also in this connection of Paul's views on the First Adam who was flesh and blood, a 'living soul,' and the Second Adam whom he describes as a 'quickening spirit' (1 *Cor.* xv. 45-49). There is, too, a Rabbinic *dictum* about a "spirit of Adam" which "moved upon the face of the waters" (as did the *Ruaḥ* in *Genesis*, i. 2)--a pre-existent First Man.

The *Zohar* is possibly indebted for its treatment of the Heavenly Man to some one or, perhaps, all of these sources. It says as follows: "The Heavenly Man after he had manifested himself from out of the midst of the upper-world primitive obscurity, created the earthly man" (ii. 70 fol.). This means that the creation of man was the work, not of God, but of His supreme manifestation, His first emanation. This manifestation or emanation is the first of the Ten Sefirot (the Crown), which, as will be shown later, is the primal will of God which contained within itself the plan of the universe in its entire infinity of time and space. To say that the plan of the world in its entirety is contained in one of the emanations of God, is tantamount to saying that man (who is part of the world) is the product of an immanent Divine activity in the world. This immanent Divine activity is denoted by the term 'Heavenly Man,' as also by the term 'First of the Sefirot,' and, in varying senses, by all the Ten Sefirot.

But why, after all, such a title as 'Heavenly Man'? It is because, according to the *Zohar*, man is a copy of the universe below as well as or the universe above. Hence God in His creative capacity chose also the form of man. The *Zohar* puts it thus: "Believe not that man consists solely of flesh, skin, bones, and veins. The real part of man is his soul, and the things just mentioned, the skin, flesh, bones, and veins, are only an outward covering, a veil, but are not the man. When man departs he divests himself of all the veils which cover him. And these different parts of our body correspond to the secrets of the Divine wisdom. The skin typifies the heavens which extend everywhere and cover everything like a garment. The flesh puts us in mind of the evil side of the universe. The bones and the veins symbolise the Divine chariot, the inner powers of man which are the servants of God. But they are all but an outer covering. For, inside man, there is the secret of the *Heavenly Man*. . . . Everything below takes place in the same manner as everything above. This is the meaning of the remark that God created man in His own image. But just as in the heavens, which cover the whole universe, we behold different shapes brought about by the stars and the planets to teach us concerning hidden things and deep secrets, so upon the skin which covers our body there are shapes and forms which are like planets and stars to our bodies. All these shapes have a hidden meaning, and are observed by the sages who are able to read the face of man" (ii. 76a).

THE TEN SEFIROT

ALL finite creatures are, in divergent senses and varying degrees, part and parcel of the Deity. *Creatio ex nihilo* is unthinkable, seeing that God, in the Neoplatonic view, is the Perfect One, 'an undivided One,' to whom no qualities or characteristics can be ascribed, and to whom, therefore, no such idea as that of intention or purpose, or change or movement, can be applied. All existences are emanations from the Deity. The Deity reveals Himself in all existences because He is immanent in them. But though dwelling in them, He is greater than they. He is apart from them. He transcends them.

The foregoing might be said to be a general *résumé* of the philosophy of the Ten Sefirot. To quote a passage from the section of the *Zohar* called the *Idra Zūtta* ('Small Assembly'):

"The Most Ancient One [1] is at the same time the most Hidden of the hidden. He is separated from all things, and is at the same time not separated from all things. For all things are united in Him, and He unites Himself with all things. There is nothing which is not in Him. He has a shape, and one can say that He has not one. In assuming a shape, He has given existence to all things. He made ten lights spring forth from His midst, lights which shine with the form which they have borrowed from Him, and which shed everywhere the light of a brilliant day. The Ancient One, the most Hidden of the hidden, is a high beacon, and we know Him only by His lights, which illuminate our eyes so abundantly. His Holy Name is no other thing than these lights."

The 'ten lights' are, of course, the Ten Sefirot, the ten successive emanations from the Godhead, the ten powers or qualities which were latent from all eternity in the Godhead. But what is meant by saying that 'His Holy Name is no other thing but these lights'? We turn to another passage in the *Zohar* for the explanation. It reads as follows:

"The name 'I am' [in Hebrew, *ĕhĕyĕh*; see Exodus, iii. 14, 'I am that I am'--in Hebrew, *ĕhĕyĕh ăshĕr ĕhĕyĕh*] signifies the unity of all things. Afterwards He brought out that light which is the celestial mother, and when she bare a child, then He called Himself 'that I am' (*ăshĕr ĕhĕyĕh*). And when all else came into existence, and everything became perfected and in its right place, then He called Himself Jahveh" (iii. 65).

The passage seems hopeless as regards a meaning. But on deeper consideration it becomes quite clear. The Divine Name, 'I am that I am,' is inferior to the Divine Name Jahveh. It typifies an earlier, less-developed stage. The student of Hebrew will readily know why this is. Although translated into English as 'I am that I am' it belongs grammatically to what the Semitic philologists call the 'imperfect tense,' representing an unfinished action. But 'Jahveh' is grammatically the 'present tense' (*i.e.* a noun formed from this tense). Hence 'I am that I am' signifies the Godhead as He was when He existed as the 'Hidden of the hidden,' *i.e.* when He was the 'undivided One,' the Absolute containing in Himself the All, before He had, so to speak, unfolded Himself in His creative acts, before any emanations had radiated out from Him. But 'Jahveh' denotes the crown and summit of the Divine self-manifestation; in other words, it denotes God as immanent in all the numberless parts of the cosmos, which is but a revelation, an embodiment of the Divine thought. The idea of the 'celestial mother' having a child is part of the *Zohar's* doctrine of emanation, where, as will be shown later on, a certain one of the Ten Sefirot is called 'father' (*Abba*) and another is called 'mother' (*Imma*), and from the union of the two, there is born another of the Sefirot, called the 'son' (*Ben*).

Hence to say that 'God's Holy Name is no other thing than these lights' is but to say that the Sefirot which represent the world as the copy of an ever-active, ever-energising God, sum up all that the Divine Name stands for. And that the Divine Name denotes a strongly mystical aspect of the relation between God and the universe is abundantly clear from the Essenic literature, as well as from the Book *Yetsirah*. In fact, it appears occasionally in this sense, in the Talmudic and Midrashic records (see, *e.g.*, T.B. *Pesaḥim*, 55b), and the germ of the idea can be traced back to the Old Testament, to such phrases as: "This is my name for ever, and this is my memorial unto all generations" (*Exodus*, iii. 15); or: "Thy name, O Lord, endureth for ever; and thy memorial, O Lord, throughout all generations" (*Psalm*, cxxxv. 13).

One of the clearest passages in the *Zohar* stating what the Ten Sefirot are, is the following:

"For the waters of the sea are limitless and shapeless. But when they are spread over the earth, then they produce a shape (*dimiōn*), and we can calculate like this: The source of the waters of the sea and the force which it emits to spread itself over the soil, are two things. Then an immense basin is formed by the waters just as is formed when one makes a very deep digging. This basin is filled by the waters which emanate from the source; it is the sea itself, and can be regarded as a third thing. This very large hollow [of waters] is split up into seven canals, which are like so many long tubes, by means of which the waters are conveyed. The source, the current, the sea, and the seven canals form together the number ten. And should the workman who constructed these tubes come to break them up, then the waters return to their source, and there remains naught but the *débris* and the water dried up. It is thus that the *Cause of causes* has created the Ten Sefirot. The *Crown* is the source whence there springs a light without end, from which comes the name *En-Sof*, *i.e.* Infinite, designating the *Supreme Cause*; for while in this state it possesses neither shape nor figure; there are no means of comprehending it; there is no way of knowing it. It is in this sense that it has been said, 'Seek not the things that are too hard for thee' (*Ecclesiasticus*, iii. 21). Then there is formed a vessel contracted to a mere point [the letter *Yod*, the smallest letter in the Hebrew alphabet] into which the Divine light penetrates. It is the source of *Wisdom*, it is Wisdom itself, in virtue of which the *Supreme Cause* is called the God of Wisdom. Afterwards, it [*i.e.* the *Supreme Cause*] constructs a channel, wide as the sea, which is called *Intellect* [or *Intelligence*]. From this, comes the title of 'God who understands' [*i.e.* is intelligent]. We must know, however, that God only understands and is wise by means of His own essential substance; for Wisdom does not merit the title by itself, but only by the instrumentality of Him who is wise and who has produced it from the light which emanates from Him. One cannot conceive what 'knowing' is by itself, but by Him who is the 'knowing One,' and who fills it with His own essential substance.

"Finally, the sea is divided into seven parts, and there result [from this division] the seven precious channels which are called: (*a*) Compassion (or Greatness), (*b*) Justice (or Force), (*c*) Beauty, (*d*) Victory, (*e*) Glory, (*f*) Royalty, and (*g*) Foundation. [2] It is for this reason that God is called the 'Great' or the 'Compassionate,' the 'Strong,' the 'Magnificent,' the 'God of Victories,' the 'Creator to whom all glory belongs,' and the 'Foundation of all things.' It is this latter attribute which sustains all the others, as well as the totality of the worlds. And yet, He is also the King of the universe, for all things are in His power whether He wills to lessen the number of the channels and increase the light which springs from them, or whether He wills the contrary" (foll. 42, 43).

According to this characteristic passage, the Sefirot are the Names of the Deity--but only in the deeply mystical sense of 'Names' as has been referred to above. The Divine Name is, on this understanding, equivalent to the Presence of God, the eternal Source of the power and intelligence enshrined in the constitution of the world and the heart of man. The Ten Sefirot together are thus a picture of how an infinite, undivided, unknowable God takes on the attributes of the finite, the divided, the knowable, and thus becomes the cause of, the power lying at the bottom of, all the multifarious modes of existence in the finite plane--all of which are thus a reflection of the Divine. The Sefirot have no real tangible existence at all. They are but a figure of speech showing the Divine immanence in all cosmic phenomena, in all the grades of man's spiritual and moral achievement.

It should, however, be pointed out here, that the functions and natures of the Sefirot are described by the *Zohar* in the most enigmatic of enigmatic language. Hence different deductions have always been possible, and hence, too, the rise of more than one school of *Zohar* interpretation. The view mostly followed--and it may be said to be the universally-accepted standard--is that of the school of Luria and Cordovero, the two most famous Kabbalists of the sixteenth century.

Let us now consider each of the Sefirot separately. What we shall say will amount in substance, though not in form, to a commentary on the lengthy passage from the *Zohar* previously quoted. Prior to the first of the Sefirot must come, what our extract has termed the *Supreme Cause* (literally the 'Cause of causes') or the *En-Sof*. What is the relation of the *En-Sof* to the Sefirot? According to the theories of Luria and Cordovero, all the Sefirot emanate from the *En-Sof*, who, although eternally present in them all, is not comprehended in them, but transcends them. All modes of existence and thought embody some fragment of the *En-Sof*, but, with all this, the *En-Sof* is divided from them by an impassable gulf. He remains the hidden, unapproachable Being. This is why, while each of the Sefirot has a well-known name, the *En-Sof* has no name. Just as in the Talmudic mysticism of the Shechinah the idea of a universally-diffused, all-penetrating Deity is conveyed by the metaphor of light, so in the case of the mediæval Kabbalah the *En-Sof* is likewise spoken of as Light (*Or En-Sof* = 'The Infinite Light'). The Christian mystics also favoured the same figure. Closely connected with this teaching is the general Kabbalistic doctrine of *Tsimtsūm*, i.e. contraction. It, too, is found in the Talmud and Midrashim, and it is from them that the Kabbalah, most likely, received it. Thus *Genesis Rabba*, iv. 5, dwells on the paradox (mentioned also by Philo) of the world being too small to hold God, but yet the space between the Ark's staves being large enough. The Kabbalistic idea of *Tsimtsūm* is an attempt to explain the contraction or limitation of the *En-Sof* (the Infinite), in order to make possible the emanation of the Sefirot, *i.e.* in order to produce the finite world of phenomena. The universal infiltration of the light of the *En-Sof*, its diffusion throughout all the Sefirot, gave rise to the idea of the existence of a changeable and an unchangeable element in each of the Sefirot. The former represents the material, outward, perishable side of man and the universe. The latter is the changeless, unfading eternal quality embedded in man and the universe. It is just this dual aspect which is referred to in the long extract from the *Zohar* quoted above, in the words: "Should the workman who constructed these tubes come to break them up, then the waters return to their source, and there remains naught but the *débris* and the water dried up." In other words, should the *En-Sof* withdraw its eternal immanent light and life from any one of the Sefirot, or, to speak in untechnical language, should God, who is the Life of the universe, the Power lying beneath and behind all phenomena, by some miraculous intervention withdraw or suspend some fragment of Himself, then the cosmos reverts to chaos.

The first of the Ten Sefirot is the Crown (in Hebrew, *Keter*). It is of importance for the reader to note that whereas Neoplatonism is largely responsible for the basis of the *Zohar's* doctrines of emanation, the names of the Sefirot and the teaching embraced and conveyed by those names are entirely drawn from the field of the Old Testament and Rabbinical theology. All ages of Jewish thought (as well as of Jewish art) employ the word, image, and idea of a 'crown' in a considerable variety of senses. In Biblical Hebrew there are no less than five different words all indiscriminately translated as 'crown,' but denoting really either different forms of the thing or different prominent portions of it. In the Apocryphal and Rabbinical literature men 'crowned' themselves in all sorts of ways, and the crown was symbolic of a host of religious ideas. In the theological realm, 'crown' played many parts.

Only two references--both germane to our subject--can be quoted here. In *T.B. Berachoth*, 17a, it is said: "In the world to come there is neither eating nor drinking, nor marrying, nor bargaining, nor envy, nor hatred, nor quarrel; but the righteous sit, *with crowns upon their heads*, and feed upon the splendour of the Shechinah, as it is said of the nobles of the children of Israel, 'He laid not His hand upon them, but they saw God, and this was equivalent to their eating and their drinking' [so the Targumic paraphrase of *Exodus*, xxiv. 11]." *T.B. Megillah*, 15b, says: "In the time to come, God will be a *crown of glory* upon the head of each saint, as it is written, 'In that day shall the Lord of Hosts be for a crown of glory, and for a diadem of beauty, unto the residue of His people' (*Isaiah*, xxviii. 5)." Hence, it is not hard to discover by what process of reasoning the mediæval Jewish mystics thought it fitting to designate the first of the Sefirot as the Crown.

"It is," says the *Zohar*, "the principle of all principles, the hidden Wisdom, the Crown which the Highest of the high, and by which all crowns and diadems are crowned" (iii. 288). It is the first of the emanations from the *En-Sof*. The latter being, as has been said above, the infinite, hidden, unknowable Being, the Crown represents, as it were, the first stage by which the Infinite Being takes on the properties of the finite and becomes drawn out of His impenetrable isolation. But, nevertheless, the Crown is an absolute indivisible unity, possessing no attributes or qualities, and baffling all analysis and description. It is, to quote the original, a '*nekūdah peshtūah*,' i.e. 'a simple point,' or '*nekūda rishōnah*,' i.e. 'a primordial point.' The idea here is that the first manifestation of the Divine is a point, *i.e.* a unity, unanalysable, indescribable, and yet possessing the All. In other words, it is the Hegelian idea of 'pure being' (*das reine sein*). This 'pure being' or 'existence' is the thought or reason of God. The starting-point of everything is the thought as it existed in God. The universe is this 'thought' of God. It is in this 'thought' of God that everything was originally embraced. The first of the Sefirot denotes, then, the primordial Divine Thought (or Divine Will, as the Hebrew commentators often style it); and to say this is tantamount to saying that the Crown contained within itself the plan of the universe in its infinity of time and space, in its endless varieties of form, colour, and movement. And it is an emanation from the *En-Sof* who, while immanent in the Crown, and hence immanent in all the Sefirot, yet transcends them all.

The Crown, for the reasons just mentioned, is ofttimes styled *Resha Hivra*, *i.e.* the 'White Head'--'head' denoting the idea of source, and 'white' being the blend of all the colours (just as the Crown is the blend of all forms in the cosmos). But the idea may possibly be drawn from *Daniel*, vii. 9, where "One that was ancient of days did sit; his raiment was white as snow, and the hair of his head like pure wool" (cf. 1 *Enoch*, xiv. 18-22; *Revelation*, i. 14). The original Aramaic for 'ancient of days' is '*attik*'; and this, too, is a name for the first of the Sefirot, and is frequently employed in the Kabbalah, generally as a designation of the Deity.

Wisdom and Intelligence are the second and third of the Ten Sefirot. They are parallel emanations from the Crown or first Sefirah. Here we alight upon an interesting feature of this mysticism, *viz.* the application of the idea of the sexual relationship to the solution of the problem of existence. "When the Ancient One, the Holy One, desired to bring all things into being, He created them all as male and female" (iii. 290).

Wisdom is the 'father,' *i.e.* the masculine active principle which engenders all things and imposes on them form and measure (an idea derived from Job, xxviii. 12). Intelligence is the 'mother,' the passive, receptive principle (derived from *Proverbs*, ii. 3, "Yea, if thou cry after discernment," *i.e.* 'Binah' in Hebrew; and the word rendered by 'if' can, by the slightest alteration of a vowel, be rendered by 'mother,' and thus the passage is translated by the *Zohar* as, "Yea, if mother thou tallest discernment"). Out of the union of Wisdom and Intelligence comes a 'son' who is dowered with the characteristics of both parents. This son is Reason (*Da'at*), which is, by the way, not regarded as an independent Sefirah. These three, father, mother, son (*i.e.* the two Sefirot, *viz.* Wisdom and Intelligence, and their offspring Reason), hold and unite in themselves all that which has been, which is, and which will be. But they in their turn are all united to the first Sefirah (the Crown), who is the all-comprehensive One who is, was, and will be.

Here one meets again with a foreshadowing of the Hegelian teaching concerning the identity of thought and being. The universe is an expression of the ideas or the absolute forms of intelligence. Cordovero says:

"The first three Sefirot must be considered as one and the same thing. The first represents 'knowledge,' the second 'the knower,' the third 'that which is known.' The Creator is Himself, at one and the same time, knowledge, the knower, and the known. Indeed, His manner of knowing does not consist in applying His thought to things outside Him; it is by self-knowledge that He knows and perceives everything which is. There exists nothing which is not united to Him and which He does not find in His own essence. He is the type of all being, and all things exist in Him under their most pure and most perfect form. . . . It is thus that all existing things in the universe have their form in the Sefirot, and the Sefirot have theirs in the source from which they emanate."

Thus, the first three Sefirot form a triad constituting the world as a manifestation of the Divine Thought. The remaining seven Sefirot likewise fall into triads. The Divine Thought is the source whence emanate two opposing principles, one active or masculine, the other passive or feminine. The former is Mercy (*Ḥesed*), the latter is Justice (*Dīn*). From the union of these two there results Beauty (*Tifĕrĕth*). The logical connections between these three principles, as they stand in the *Zohar*, are extremely difficult to fathom. But Cordovero and other Hebrew commentators give us the needed solution of the problem. The Sefirot Mercy and Justice represent the universe as being at one and the same time an expansion and contraction of the Divine Will. Mercy, as the active masculine principle, is the life-giving, ever-productive because ever-forgiving power innate in man and the universe. Justice is the necessarily-opposed immanent faculty holding in check what would otherwise prove to be the excesses of Mercy. The theology of the Talmudic Rabbis shows itself unmistakably here. In the beginning, say the Rabbis, God thought to create the universe by the 'attribute of justice' (designated by the word 'Jahveh'). But on considering that the universe could not exist by 'justice' alone, He determined to join the 'attribute of mercy' (designated by the word 'Elohim') with the 'attribute of justice,' and to create the universe--as He finally did--by the dual means. Likewise in the *Zohar* mysticism, the moral order of the universe can only follow on a combination of the Sefirot Mercy and Justice. And the inevitable product of the union is the sixth Sefirah, Beauty. The reasoning is apparent. We have thus far seen how the first triad of Sefirot pictures God as the immanent thinking power of the universe, and how the second triad interprets God as the immanent moral power of the universe.

The third triad are: Victory (*Nezaḥ*), Glory (*Hōd*), and Foundation (*Yesōd*). The first of these is the masculine active principle. The second is the feminine passive principle, while the third is the effect of their combination. What aspect of a God-saturated world do these three Sefirot point to? The *Zohar* tells us, as follows: "Extension, variety [or multiplication], and force are gathered together in them; and all forces that come out, come out from them, and it is for this reason that they are called Hosts [*i.e.* armies or forces]. They are [the two forementioned Sefirot] Victory and Glory" (iii. 296). The allusion is obviously to the physical, dynamic aspect of the universe, the ceaseless, developing world with its multiplicity and variety of forces, changes and movements. From their coalescence comes the ninth Sefirah, Foundation. Rightly so; for it is the endless, changeless ebb and flow of the world's forces that, in the last resort, guarantees the stability of the world and builds up its 'foundation.' It creates the reproductive power of nature, endows it with, as it were, a generative organ from which all things proceed, and upon which all things finally depend.

The last of the Sefirot is Royalty (*Malkūt*). Its function is not very apparent, and its existence may be due to the desire on the part of the Kabbalists to make up the number ten--a number which looms largely in the Old Testament literature, as well as in the theology of the Talmud, Midrashim, and Philo. Generally speaking, this tenth Sefirah indicates the abiding truth of the harmonious co-operation of all the Sefirot, thus making the universe in its orderliness and in its symmetry a true and exact manifestation of the Divine Mind--an *'Olam Azilut, i.e.* a world of emanation, as the Kabbalists themselves style it.

The fact that the Sefirot fall into triads or trinities, and the ascription to them of such sexual titles as 'father,' 'mother,' 'son,' has encouraged many an apologist for Christianity to say that the essential Christian dogma of the Trinity is implicit in the Jewish mystical literature. But it is beyond a doubt that the resemblance is quite a matter of accident. It cannot be too often repeated that there is a substantial admixture of foreign elements in all branches of the Kabbalah. The philosophy of Salomon Ibn Gabirol (which largely echoes Plato), Neoplatonism, Gnosticism, Philonism, and other systems have all left indelible traces. But Christianity, be it remembered, besides being a debtor to Judaism, is a debtor to these sources as well; so that what appears to be Christian may be, in reality, Jewish; a development of the original material by an unbroken succession of Jewish minds. This original material is the old Talmudic and Midrashic exegesis upon which was foisted the alien philosophies just alluded to. That there should be a resultant resemblance to Christianity is quite a normal outcome; but it is beyond dispute that the Christian Trinity and the trinities of the Ten Sefirot lie in quite distinct planes.

The Jewish Prayer Book echoes much of the theological sentiment of the *Zohar*. There is a fine hymn in the Sabbath-morning service which, while giving a noteworthy prominence to the *names* of the Sefirot, reproduces with a charming simplicity of Hebrew diction, the main body of the Zoharic doctrine, its cosmology, angelology, astrology, and psychology. It is as follows: [3] "God, the Lord over all works, blessed is He, and ever to be blessed by the mouth of everything that hath breath. His greatness and goodness fill the world; *knowledge*

(*Da'at*) and *understanding* (*Tebūnah* = *Bīnah*) [*i.e.* intelligence] surround Him. He is exalted above the holy Ḥayot, and is adorned in *glory* (*Kabod* = *Hōd*) above the celestial chariot (*merkabah*); purity and rectitude are before his throne, *loving-kindness* (*Ḥesed*) and tender mercy before his *glory*. The luminaries are good which our God hath created: He formed them with *knowledge*, understanding, and discernment; He gave them might and power to rule in the midst of the world. They are full of lustre, [4] and they radiate brightness; beautiful is their lustre throughout all the world. They rejoice in their going forth, and are glad in their returning; they perform with awe the will of their Master. *Glory* and *honour* they render unto his name, exultation and rejoicing at the remembrance of his *sovereignty* (*Malkūt*). He called unto the sun, and it shone forth in light; He looked and ordained the figure of the moon. All the hosts on high render praise unto Him, the Seraphim, the Ophanim, and the holy Ḥayot ascribing *glory* (lit. beauty, *i.e. Tifĕrĕth*) and *greatness*."[5]

---

1. One of the favourite names for God in the mediæval Kabbalah. It is based on the phrase in *Daniel*, vii. 9, 13, 22, 'ancient of days.'
2. Some authorities invert the order of *f* and *g*.
3. From the Authorised Daily Prayer Book, ed. Singer, p. 129.
4. *Ziv* in Hebrew, a mystical term for the shining of the Shechinah.
5. Another appellation for *Ḥesed*, the fourth Sefirah.

THE SOUL

As in all systems of mysticism, the soul plays a towering part in the theology of the *Zohar*. Mysticism's centre of gravity is the close kinship between the human and the Divine; and the only avenue through which this kinship can become real to us is the soul. The soul, as a spiritual entity playing the highest of high parts in man's relation with the Unseen, is not a conspicuous element of either the Old Testament or the Talmudic-Midrashic writings; and the critics of Judaism have a way of saying harsh things about that religion on the grounds of its deficiency in this respect. But the shortcoming is amply atoned for by the large part assigned to the function of the soul in all branches of the mediæval Kabbalah.

That the *Zohar* is a debtor to a double source--the Talmudic teachings and the teachings of the Neoplatonists--is very apparent from its treatment of the soul. A passage from the former reads as follows: "Just as the soul fills the body, so God fills the world. Just as the soul bears the body, so God endures the world. Just as the soul sees but is not seen, so God sees but is not seen. Just as the soul feeds the body [*i.e.* spiritually, intellectually], so God gives food to the world" (*T.B. Berachoth*, 10a). The predominant influence of the soul over the body, the body as overflown in all its parts by the soul and dependent upon it for the source of its life--these are the implications of the passage just quoted; and they are the substratum of the Zoharic ideas of the soul.

Neoplatonism gave to the *Zohar* the idea of the soul as an emanation from the 'Overmind' of the universe. There was originally one 'Universal Soul,' or 'Over-soul,' which, as it were, broke itself up and encased itself in individual bodies. All individual souls are, hence, fragments of the 'Oversoul,' so that although they are distinct from one another they are, in reality, all *one*. Thus, to quote the *Zohar*:

"At the time when God desired to create the universe, it came up in His will before Him, and He formed all the souls which were destined to be allotted to the children of men. The souls were all before Him in the forms which they were afterwards destined to bear inside the human body. God looked at each one of them, and He saw that many of them would act corruptly in the world. When the time of each arrived, it was summoned before God, who said to it: 'Go to such and such a part of the universe, enclose thyself in such and such a body.' But the soul replied: 'O sovereign of the universe, I am happy in my present world, and I desire not to leave it for some other place where I shall be enslaved and become soiled.' Then the Holy One (blessed be He) replied: 'From the day of thy creation thou hast had no other destiny than to go into the universe whither I send thee.' The soul, seeing that it must obey, sorrowfully took the way to earth and came down to dwell in our midst" (ii. 96).

There is more than one echo of Plotinus--the master-mind of Neoplatonism--in this Zoharic extract. 'The world coming up in His will before Him' is Plotinus' teaching about God thinking out the original patterns of all things, the first manifestation of God being Thought. 'The souls were all before Him in the forms which they were after-wards destined to bear' is clearly an allusion to the splitting-up of the Oversoul, so that its fragments might get embodied in individuals--as Plotinus taught. But although the *Zohar*, like Plotinus, draws a distinction between *lower* souls ('they who would act corruptly in the world') and higher souls, it, unlike Plotinus, makes every soul descend into some body. Plotinus has quite a different teaching.

"The lower soul desires a body and lives in the stage of sense. . . . The higher soul, on the other hand, transcends the body, 'rides upon it,' as the fish is in the sea or as the plant is in the air. This higher soul never absolutely leaves its home, its being is not here but 'yonder,' or, in the language of Plotinus, 'The soul always leaves something of itself above'" (Rufus M. Jones, *Studies in Mystical Religion*, p. 74).

According to the *Zohar*, while there are distinctions there, too, between superior and inferior souls--as is shown by their belonging to a higher or lower Sefirah--they must all descend to earth and unite with the body, returning, all of them, at death to their fountain-head, God.

The *Zohar* is, after all, but a commentary on the Hebrew Bible, and however much it may, at times, forsake the traditional Jewish pathways in favour of alien philosophies, it is always strictly conservative where the fundamental axioms of the Jewish faith are concerned. That every body possesses a soul which in its pristine form is 'pure,' that recompense in an after-life awaits it on a scale commensurate with its deserts, is an impregnable tenet of Judaism. The *Zohar*, wherever it may wander, must come back to this central point.

The soul is a trinity. It comprises three elements, *viz.*: (*a*) *Neshāmāh*, the rational element which is the highest phase of existence; (*b*) *Ruaḥ*, the moral element, the seat of good and evil, the ethical qualities; (*c*) *Nefesh*, the gross side of spirit, the vital element which is *en rapport* with the body, and the mainspring of all the movements, instincts, and cravings of the physical life.

There is a strong reflection of Platonic psychology in these three divisions or powers of the soul. More than one mediæval Jewish theologian was a Platonist, and in all probability the *Zohar* is a debtor to these. The three divisions of the soul are emanations from the Sefirot. The *Neshāmāh*, which, as has been said, is the soul in its most elevated and sublimest sense, emanates from the Sefirah of Wisdom. The *Ruaḥ*, which denotes the soul in its ethical aspect, emanates from the Sefirah of Beauty. The *Nefesh*, which is the animal side of the soul, is an emanation from the Sefirah of Foundation, that element of divinity which comes, most of all, into contact with the material forces of earth.

To sum up the matter in general and untechnical language, the three divisions or aspects of the human soul enable man to fit himself into the plan and framework of the cosmos, give him the power to do his multifarious duties towards the multifarious portions of the world,--the world which is a manifestation of God's thought, a copy of the celestial universe, an emanation of the Divine. The *Zohar* puts it poetically thus:

"In these three [*i.e. Neshāmāh, Ruaḥ, Nefesh*] we find an exact image (*diyūkna*) of what is above in the celestial world. For *all three* form only *one* soul, one being, where all is *one*. The *Nefesh* [*i.e.* the lowest side of soul] does not in itself possess any light. This is why it is so tightly joined to the body, acquiring for it the pleasures and the foods which it needs. It is of it that the sage says, 'She giveth meat to her household and their task to her maidens' (*Proverbs*, xxxi. 15). 'Her household' means the body which is fed. 'Her maidens' are the limbs which obey the dictates of the body. Above the *Nefesh* is the *Ruaḥ* [the ethical soul] which dominates the *Nefesh*, imposes laws upon it and enlightens it as much as its nature requires. And then high above the *Ruaḥ* is the *Neshāmāh*, which in its turn rules the *Ruaḥ* and sheds upon it the light of life. The *Ruaḥ* is lit up by this light, and depends entirely upon it. After death, the *Ruaḥ* has no rest. The gates of Paradise (*Eden*) are not opened to it until the time when *Neshāmāh* has reascended to its source, to the Ancient of the ancients, in order to become filled with Him throughout eternity. For the *Neshāmāh* is always climbing back again towards its source" (ii. 142).

It can be gathered from this passage, as from many similar ones which might have been usefully quoted had space allowed, that *Neshāmāh* is only realised, that man only becomes conscious of *Neshāmāh*, after death. A whole lifetime is necessary (and in some cases more than one lifetime, as we shall see) in order that *Neshāmāh* should be able to mount up again to the Infinite source from which it emanated. And it is the inevitable destiny of *Neshāmāh* to climb back and become one with the 'Ancient of ancients.'

But if *Neshāmāh* is so exalted, so sacrosanct, why should it have emanated from its immaculate source at all, to become tainted with earth? The *Zohar* anticipates our question and gives its answer as follows:

"If thou inquirest why it [*i.e..* the soul] cometh down into the world from so exalted a place and putteth itself at such a distance from its source, I reply thus: It may be likened to an earthly monarch to whom a son is born. The monarch takes the son to the countryside, there to be nourished and trained until such a time as he is old enough to accustom himself to the palace of his father. When the father is told that the education of his son is completed, what does he do out of his love for him? In order to celebrate his home-coming, he sends for the queen, the mother of the lad. He brings her into the palace and rejoices with her the whole day long.

"It is thus with the Holy One (blessed be He). He, too, has a son by the queen. This son is the high and holy soul. He conducts it to the countryside, *i.e.* to the world, in order to grow up there and gain an acquaintance with the customs appertaining to the royal palace. When the Divine King perceives that the soul has completed its growth, and the time is ripe for recalling it to Himself, what does He do out of His love for it? He sends for the queen, brings her into the palace, and brings the soul in too. The soul, forsooth, does not bid adieu to its earthly tenement before the queen has come to unite herself with it, and to lead it into the royal apartment where it is to live for ever.

"And the people of the world are wont to weep when the son [*i.e.* the soul] takes its leave of them. But if there be a wise man amongst them, he says to them, Why weep ye? Is he not the son of the King? Is it not meet that he should take leave of you to live in the palace of his father? It was for this reason that Moses, who knew the Truth, on seeing the inhabitants of earth mourning for the dead, exclaimed, 'Ye are the children of the Lord your God; ye shall not cut yourselves, nor make any baldness between your eyes for the dead' (*Deut.* xiv. 1). If all good men knew this, they would hail with delight the day when it behoves them to bid adieu to the world. Is it not the height of glory for them when the queen [*i.e.* the Shechinah, the Divine Presence] comes down into the midst of them to lead them into the palace of the king to enjoy the delights thereof for ever-more?" (i. 245).

It should be noted, by the way, that there are many instances in Talmudic literature, of men seeing the Shechinah at the hour of death. It is the signal of the return of *Neshāmāh* to its home, the Oversoul, of which it is but a loosened fragment; and the return can only begin after it has completed its education within the life-limits of an earthly body.

It seems to follow, as a necessary corollary from the foregoing doctrine, that the *Zohar* must give countenance to some theory of the transmigration of souls. If it is imperative upon *Neshāmāh* to climb back again to the Oversoul and obtain union with it; and if, in order to effect this end, it must previously have reached the summit of purity and perfection, then it stands to reason that its sojourn within the confines of one body may, on occasions, be inadequate to enable it to reach this high and exacting condition. Hence it must 'experience' other bodies, and it must repeat the 'experience' until such a time as it shall have elevated and refined itself to the pitch at which it will be able to become one again with the fountain from which it emanated. The *Zohar* does contain some such tenet as this, although for the full and systematic treatment of the subject one has to look to the Kabbalistic writers who built upon the *Zohar*. The *Zohar* states as follows:

"All souls must undergo transmigration; and men do not understand the ways of the Holy One (blessed be He). They know not that they are brought before the tribunal both before they enter into this world and after they leave it. They know not the many transmigrations and hidden trials which they have to undergo, nor do they know the number of souls and spirits (*Ruaḥ* and *Nefesh*) which enter into the world, and which do not return to the Palace of the Heavenly King. Men do not know how the souls revolve like a stone which is thrown from a sling. But the time is drawing nigh when these hidden things will be revealed" (ii. 99).

To the minds of the Kabbalists, transmigration is a necessity not alone on the grounds of their particular theology--the soul must reach the highest stage of its evolution before it can be received again into its eternal home--but on moral grounds as well. It is a vindication of Divine justice to mankind. It settles the harassing query which all ages have propounded: Why does God permit the wicked to flourish as the green bay tree, whereas the righteous man is allowed to reap nothing but sorrow and failure? And the only way for reconciling the dismal fact of child-suffering with the belief in a good God, is by saying that the pain is a retribution to the soul for sin committed in some one or more of its previous states. As has been already mentioned, the Jewish literature of this subject of transmigration is an exceedingly rich one. But it lies outside the scope of the present book.

Not only does the *Zohar*, as we have seen, teach the emanation of a threefold soul, but it also propounds a curious theory about the emanation of a pre-existent form or type of body, which, in the case of each one of us, unites the soul with the body. It is one of the strangest pieces of Zoharic psychology extant; and the object is probably that of accounting, on one and the same ground, for the varying physical and psychical characteristics embedded in each of us from birth. The passage runs as follows:

"At the moment when the earthly union [*i.e.* marriage] takes place, the Holy One (blessed be He) sends to earth a form [or image] resembling a man, and bearing upon itself the divine seal. This image is present at the moment just mentioned, and if the eye could see what goes on then, it would detect above the heads [of man and wife] an image like a human face, and this image is the model after which we are fashioned.... It is this image which receives us first on our arrival into this world. It grows in us as we grow, and leaves us when we leave the world. *This image is from above*. When the souls are about to quit their heavenly abode each soul appears before the Holy One (blessed be He) clothed with an exalted pattern [or image or form] on which are engraven the features which it will bear here below" (iii. 107).

But of far greater consequence in the history of Jewish mysticism is the commanding place assigned by the *Zohar* to the idea of Love. Indeed, Jewish mysticism is here but a reflection of the nature of the mysticism inherent in all other creeds. The soul's most visible, most tangible, most perceivable quality is love. The soul is the root of love. Love is the symbol of the soul. "Mystic Love," says Miss Underhill, "is the offspring of the Celestial Venus; the deep-seated desire and tendency of the soul towards its source." The soul, says the mystic of all ages, seeks to enter consciously into the Presence of God. It can do so only under the spur of an overpowering ecstatic emotion called love. Although, according to the *Zohar*, the soul in its most exalted state as *Neshāmāh* can only enjoy the love inherent in its union with its source after it has freed itself from the contamination of earthly bodies, it is nevertheless possible, under certain conditions, to realise this ecstatic love while the soul is in the living body of an individual. One of these conditions is *the act of serving* God, the chief outward concomitant of which is *prayer*.

"Whosoever serves God out of love," says the *Zohar*, "comes into union (*itdaḅak*) with the place of the Highest of the High, and comes into union, too, with the holiness of the world which is to be" (ii. 216).

This is to say that the service of God, when effected with love, leads the soul into union with the place of its origin, and it gives it, as it were, a foretaste of the ineffable felicity which awaits it in its highest condition as *Neshāmāh*.

The verse "Hear, O Israel, the Lord our God the Lord is One" (*Deut.* vi. 4) hints, says the *Zohar*, at this blending of the soul into a Unity. For this branch of its teaching the *Zohar* is certainly not indebted to Neoplatonism or any other alien system. It got it from its Jewish predecessors--the Midrashic homilists who enriched the Jewish literature of the opening centuries of the Christian era with their mystic interpretations of the *Song of Songs*. Verses like "I am my beloved's, and my beloved is mine" (vi. 3) served them as a starting-point for their sermons on the nearness of man and God to one another, brought about by the instrumentality of love.

When the soul has completed the cycle of its earthly career and hurries back to become blended with the Oversoul, it revels in ecstasies of love, which the *Zohar* describes with a wealth of poetic phraseology. The soul is received in what is termed a 'treasury of life,' or sometimes a 'temple of love,' and one of its crowning joys is to contemplate the Divine Presence through a 'shining mirror.' The Rabbis of the Talmud and Midrashim used the same phrase. Thus a passage in *Leviticus Rabba*, i. 14, reads thus: "All the other prophets saw God through nine shining mirrors, but Moses saw Him through only one. All the other prophets saw God through a blurred mirror, but Moses saw Him through a clear one." The meaning is that Moses had a clearer and nearer apprehension of the Deity than all other prophets.

Thus we read: "Come and see! When the souls have reached the treasury of life they enjoy the shining of the brilliant mirror whose focus is in the heavens. And such is the brightness which emanates therefrom that the souls would be unable to withstand it, were they not covered with a coat of light. Even Moses could not approach it until he had stripped off his earthly integument" (i. 66). Again: "In one of the most mysterious and exalted parts of heaven, there is a palace called the Palace of Love. Deep mysteries are enacted there; there are gathered together all the most well-beloved souls of the Heavenly King; it is there that the Heavenly King, the Holy One (blessed be He), lives together with these holy souls and unites Himself to them by kisses of love" (ii. 97).

The Talmudic Rabbis described the way in which death comes to the righteous as 'death by a kiss.' The *Zohar* defines this 'kiss' as 'the union of the soul with its root' (i. 168). There is, in fine, an exceptionally high degree of optimism encircling the *Zohar's* treatment of the soul.

If the theology of the early Rabbinic schools of Palestine and Babylon errs, as its critics say, in the direction of making Judaism too much of a rigid discipline, too much of a law-compelling, outward obedience rather than inward feeling, the balance is redressed by the theology of the *Zohar* which, by making the soul, on the completion of its earthly work, so great a partaker in the Divine love, emphasises the deep spirituality inherent in Judaism, the emotional element which it calls forth in those who rightfully and adequately put its teachings into practice. It thus imports an added brightness into Jewish life. It inspires the Jew with the conviction that a high destiny awaits him in the hereafter. It makes him put a premium upon virtue, and encourages him to raise himself to the sublimest pitch of moral and religious worth. Judaism for the Jew can never be a mere soulless formalism so long as the *Zohar's* doctrine of Divine love is an integral part of Judaism. Such a consummation is well attested by such a passage from the *Zohar* as the following .

"When Adam our first father dwelt in the garden of Eden he was clothed, as men are in heaven, with the Divine light. When he was driven forth from Eden to do the ordinary work of earth, then Holy Writ tells us that 'the Lord God made for Adam and for his wife coats of skin and clothed them.' For, ere this, they wore coats of light, of that light which belongs to Eden. [1] Man's good deeds upon earth bring down on him a portion of the higher light which lights up heaven. It is that light which covers him like a coat when he enters into the future world and appears before his Maker, the Holy One (blessed be He). It is by means of such a covering that he can taste of the enjoyments of the elect and look upon the face of the 'shining mirror.' And thus, the soul, in order to become perfect in all respects, must have a different covering for each of the two worlds which it has to inhabit, one for the terrestrial world and the other for the higher world" (ii. 229).

And this cheerful view of the soul is an incitement to nobler effort, not only for the Jew as an individual, but also for the Jew as a unit of a race which, according to Scriptural prescription, looks forward to its highest evolution in the arrival of a Messiah. The *Zohar*, truly enough, is comparatively silent upon this theme. But the famous Kabbalist and mystic Isaac Luria, who is the chief expounder of the *Zohar*, and who carried many of its undeveloped dogmas to their logical conclusions, has elaborated this point in a strikingly ingenious and original way. Luria held a peculiar theory of the transmigration of the soul; and conjoined with this there went, what might appear to some, an approach to Christian teaching about the truth of original sin. With the *Zohar*, Luria maintained that man, by means of his soul, unites the upper and the lower world. But he maintained further that with the creation of Adam there were created at the same time all the souls of all races of mankind. Just as there are variations in the physical qualities of men, so there are corresponding variations in their souls. Hence there are souls which are good and souls which are bad and souls of all the shades of value which lie between these two extremes. When Adam sinned there was confusion in all these classes of souls. The good souls became tainted with some of the evil inherent in the bad souls, and, on the contrary, the bad souls received many an admixture of goodness from the superior souls.

But who emanated from the inferior sets of soul? According to Luria, the pagan world. Israel, however, issued from the superior souls. But, again, seeing that the good souls are not wholly good nor the bad souls wholly bad by reason of the confusion ensuing upon Adam's fall, it follows that there can be no real unalloyed good in the world. Evil infests some spot or other everywhere. A perfect condition of things will only come with the coming of the Messiah. Until that time, therefore, all souls, tainted as they all inevitably are with sin, must, by means of a chain of transmigrations from one body to another, shake off more and more of the dross clinging to them, until they reach that summit of purity and perfection when, as *Neshāmāh*, they can find their way back to unite with the Infinite Source, the Oversoul. Hence the individual Jew in promoting the growth of his own soul is really promoting the collective welfare of his race. Upon the weal or woe of his own soul hangs the weal or woe of his people.

Luria's arguments, when fully stated, have a decided air of the fantastic about them. But that his conclusion is sound and valuable, no one will doubt. He encourages the Jew to the pursuit of a lofty communal or national ideal. He reminds him, too, of the imperative necessity of Israel's solidarity. For the Jew, taking his stand upon many a text in the Old Testament, has always felt that his thought and his work must not be for himself alone. His prayer has ever been for the well-being of Israel rather than for the well-being of individual Israelites. What he counts, in God's sight, as a separate entity is small in comparison with what he counts as an inseparable unit in the compact body of Israel. In this voluntary, self-forgetful merging of the smaller interests of the part in the greater interests of the whole lies much of the secret of the long roll of Israel's saints and heroes, his martyrs and his mystics.

---

1. In Hebrew there is a great similarity in sound between the word for 'skin' and the word for 'light.'

CONCLUDING NOTE

THE course of Jewish mysticism subsequent to the *Zohar* consists, in the main, of developments and elaborations, by Jews in many lands, of the doctrines taught in that unique work. There is an enormous fund of originality in many of these elaborations. Their writers were men engrained with the deepest of mystical sentiments, men whose lives accorded with the high strain of their teachings, and whose writings constitute a material addition, for all time, to the body of Jewish spiritual literature. But limits of space prevent the consideration of this subject. At the beginning of the eighteenth century there arose, among the Jews of Poland, a great religious movement known as 'Ḥasidism' (from Hebrew *ḥasid* = pious). Its aim was to revive the spiritual element in Judaism which had been largely crushed out of existence by the dead-weight of Rabbinical formalism. Ḥasidism was invented in order to show that Judaism meant not merely law and commandment, ritual and dogma, but denoted also the emotions of love and aspiration and faith felt towards a Father who was eternally near, and whose heart overflowed with a father's compassion for his children. Ḥasidism strove to effect for Judaism the supremacy of inward 'first-hand' religion over the dogmatism of outward traditionalism. Judaism needed this corrective. And although Ḥasidism is often flouted as a failure, and its adherents depreciated as the devotees of excess and extravagance in religious exercise, it nevertheless was a force, and deserves an abiding place in the history of Jewish theology, if only on the ground that it tried to do for Judaism what the general mystical tendencies of our own day are more and more doing for it, *viz.* to make it conscious of how dominating a part is played in it by the inner impulse urging us to seek and to find a pathway to the realised Presence of God.

Copyright © 2021 by FV Éditions
Cover Design: Canva.com
All rights reserved.

www.ingramcontent.com/pod-product-compliance
Lightning Source LLC
LaVergne TN
LVHW091636070526
838199LV00044B/1090